MIDLAND RED
Evolution or Revolution?

Introduction

Many readers will remember the Midland Red with affection. I have written about many of the salient parts of the vast Midland Red history in my earlier books, and here I will offer some more interesting facts and stories, and hopefully bring them to life as much as possible. 'Evolution or Revolution', the title of this book, is presented as a *question*. I surmise that each individual reader will have their own opinion on what is evolutionary and what is revolutionary. What is certain is that the Birmingham and Midland Motor Omnibus Company was an individual and unique entity in the passenger transport industry. Each type of bus that was produced would be an improvement on the last. Then each decade or so, the company would create a real show-stopper that embraced new designs and technical advancements – the D9 comes to mind. My time with Midland Red spanned a period when buses from the 1950s were still in regular service. I experienced the delights of working in the cab and at the back of the wonderful D9s, and there were still CM6Ts doing what they did so well! You'll see me at the top of this page in the cab of another favourite type, the S22. Oh for a return to those days for a shift or two!

Midland Red ran their familiar red buses in almost every city, town, village and hamlet throughout 12,000 square miles of the Midlands. After all, it was the biggest UK bus company outside of the capital and made a big impression on folk living, working or just passing through the Midlands area.

It was an empire-like operation – confident and self-contained, and a force to be reckoned with for the greater part of its life. With its official name of the Birmingham and Midland Motor Omnibus Company (BMMO), it began life in 1904 with horse buses and early unreliable motorbuses; the latter were sold off in 1907 and the horse buses plodded on until 1912 when the motorbus had developed into something more reliable. In 1914, Birmingham Corporation decided they were going to operate services wholly within the city of Birmingham, which forced BMMO to look further afield where they could run local services and operate journeys into Birmingham. Although they were not allowed to pick up within the city boundary, it made their journeys much quicker into the city.

The company then grew rapidly and not only ran bus and coach services, but designed and built their own buses and coaches from the floor up in their own factory and well appointed workshops in Bearwood garage and later at Central Works in Edgbaston, Birmingham. They even produced their own highly successful engines from 1923 until 1970.

They had 35 depots and even more bus stations, and operated up to 2,000 vehicles. They showed consideration for their passengers, and were first to provide folding platform doors on buses, making travel safer and warmer. They made their own bus stops (even the concrete poles), bus shelters and timetables. They had their own considerable inter-garage fleet of delivery trucks and vans, company cars, breakdown recovery vehicles, mobile workshops, tree loppers, publicity vehicles and recruitment vehicles. There was a fully equipped training school for drivers at Bearwood, conductor schools at selected local main garages, and teams of engineers, inspectors and enquiry office staff and cleaners. For some years, they even had hostels for drivers and conductors who came to the Midlands for work and needed somewhere to live, and these were looked after by the company's own welfare department. There was an active sports and social club with inter-garage games days and annual sports days held on Midland Red's own sports ground in Quinton, Birmingham.

In total the workforce comprised around 8,000 men and women. From the late 1920s a staff magazine circulated to all departments on a monthly basis, except during wartime. All in all, it was a self-assured operation owning everything it needed, and had that big family feel.

However, just as other empires fall, the fortunes of the company changed. Midland Red, like a lot of the British bus scene, was nationalised from the late 1960s and throughout the 1970s. The grand Midland Red had its heart stolen when its moneymaking Birmingham and Black Country routes were taken by government restructuring and the formation of the West Midlands Passenger Transport Authority. Then in the 1980s came privatisation. Midland Red was too big to sell as one company, so it was carved up into six divisions: four bus companies (North, South, East/Fox and West), a coach company called Midland Red Coaches and an engineering business called Midland Red Engineering (later Carlyle Engineering). Carlyle Works was the alternative name that Central Works was known by, as it was situated at the end of Carlyle Road in Edgbaston, Birmingham. They all subsequently had management buyouts in the 1980s and were sold again into the big emerging bus groups in the 1990s. Today, they are no longer recognised as Midland Red, except when things go wrong, and the legal names (still containing the words 'Midland Red') emerge from the past, perhaps to protect the reputation of their new owners. The engineering company closed, and was later reformed at a different site and on a much smaller scale by a team including ex-Midland Red employees, but it too eventually closed. The once large company-wide coaching activities were scooped up into a Birmingham-based Midland Red Coaches, which could never work in an operational area of 12,000 square miles of the Midlands; for a time, it concentrated on the western side of the old company territory, mainly Birmingham and Worcestershire, yet despite the efforts of Ken Mills, leader of Midland Red West at the time, it sadly disappeared. The services that were previously operated by Midland Red are now mainly operated by three of the UK's major bus giants (Arriva, Stagecoach, and First Bus).

However, in an effort to keep the nostalgia of the old Midland Red alive, I had a fleet of vintage buses and coaches, where for 25 years the flag was kept flying for Midland Red Coaches, operated by Wheels. The Midland Red Coaches Limited company had been owned by a south west coast hotelier who sold it to me. Some Midland Red-built vehicles, including S23s and a wonderful D9, were part of our entirely British-built heritage fleet, and they were operated in the same tradition as Midland Red had done over 50 years before; they provided good service in the spirit of a bygone age until my chosen early retirement from buses in 2014, as I didn't like the way our industry was headed. Over the lifetime of my interest in buses, over 60 buses and coaches passed through my hands, some moving on after a time to other preservationists, others kept for enjoyment, and some for business, and I'm pleased to say that this included a number of vehicles from the BMMO stable. I was instrumental in buying an S16 and a CM6T for preservation on behalf of The Midland Red (Leamington) Preservation Society whilst I was still a Midland Red employee, then later in life came along examples of the S21, S22, D9, and two S23s. I have many happy memories of being behind the steering wheel of hundreds of BMMO buses and just a few coaches, and I cherish those days immensely.

I consider myself extremely fortunate in having a lifetime of work in an area of transport that was also my principal hobby. The opportunity to continue the traditions and operating style set years before by Midland Red, which in more modern times had become captivating and nostalgic, created 25 years of pure Omnibus Theatre. We provided special occasions for passengers, whilst never forgetting our deep and established Midland Red roots.

Today, the biggest Midland Red collection of buses, coaches, ephemera, memorabilia, historic records and models can be seen at Transport Museum Wythall, nowadays the only place where you can take in the company's breadth of history and take a ride on some very rare Midland Red vehicles, especially during their event days.

What has been very evident while speaking with retired Midland Red colleagues about their working life at BMMO is that most are now sadly approaching their later years and, indeed, many are no longer with us nor able to tell us their tales. Contributions to Midland Red life and our industry and heritage are very important to document, but these veterans of BMMO service often seem to think that they don't have anything useful or interesting to offer that would be good enough to appear in print. Yet when they are engaged in conversation with their old colleagues and their old memories, they start to remember other, much more interesting stories that have not been previously recorded; as part of everyday life back then, they may still seem mundane to the teller, but it is so important to capture these unique stories and memories to ensure that the magical Midland Red spirit is remembered long into the future. I do hope that the stories and images contained in this book help you to gain a closer appreciation of the real Midland Red.

Ashley

Author Ashley stands in front of D9 5355 in Tamworth bus station, prior to operating an enthusiasts' excursion to Worcester in the late 1970s. The D9 had recently been painted in National Bus Company poppy red livery which involved the overpainting of the previously illuminated 'MIDLAND' sign just above the destination blinds

The rights of Ashley Wakelin to be identified as the author of this work have been asserted by him in accordance with the Copyrights, Designs and Patents Act, 1988.

All rights reserved. No part of this publication may be copied, stored or reproduced, or placed in a retrieval system, or transmitted in any form, or by any means without the prior and written permission of the publisher. Any person who does any unauthorised act in relation to this publication may be liable to prosecution and or civil claims for damages.

This book is sold subject to the condition that it will not, by way of trade or otherwise, be lent, hired out, re-sold or otherwise circulated without the author's prior written consent and agreement.

Typeset by: Stephen Duxbury, Prestset Ltd

Printed by: Flexpress, Leicester.

ISBN: 978-1-7391593-5-1

First published 2025.

Copyright © Ashley Wakelin 2025

CONTENTS

Introduction 1
Foreword by Colin Webster 5
The Early Years 6
The Coming of Associated Motorways . . 16
Digbeth Coach Station Refreshed 19
Cycles of Progress 20
Wartime and the Troubled Forties 25
Renewing the Fleet 30
The Prosperous 1950s 33
A 'National' Identity Crisis 62
The Revolutionary Motorway Express . . . 65
Casualties 84
The Human Side 91
Respect Over a Lifetime 108
How Did It All Happen 113
Where the Magic Happened 116
Where the Money Came From 124
Far and Wide 128
Enthusiasts 131
Talking About Bus Fires 135
Electrobus: An Opportunity Missed? . . . 144
Reflections 149
Looking Beyond the Grave 155
Acknowledgements 160

Left: The prototype of the C5 family which developed into the famous Motorway Expresses of the late 1950s.

FOREWORD

By Midland Red's Colin J. Webster.

Several years ago I was given the opportunity to write the foreword of a book that was being prepared for publication by Ashley Wakelin.

I had known Ashley for a long period of years, as I made clear in that foreword, and he was then about to relate his desire to work for, and his working experience over many years with, the much loved Midland Red in his first book entitled *Inside Midland Red*.

It was my own personal view that this would be a task of considerable magnitude. Would there be sufficient people with such a great interest to be prospective purchasers? Then there's the likely costs involved in producing such a quality book, and the very substantial research of the content which needed to be wide enough to appeal to more ordinary readers and yet be intimate enough to relate the stories from the inside. This was so daunting that Ashley could only be wished well.

But now we are at book number four – how could I have had any such doubts! His books not only recall his own career in the bus industry, but others at Midland Red, at all levels, who directed the company to become the biggest of Great Britain's provincial bus and coach operators. He tells stories of the long careers of superb tradesmen who designed and built Midland Red's unique fleet of buses. The men who managed the company from top and middle management, superintendents and inspectors, to the characters who drove the buses and coaches, the conductors and conductresses who collected the fares, and the engineers who maintained the fleet – and even remembering the humble cleaners!

Of course, his books talk about the buses and coaches, but they are about much more. Midland Red was an enterprising and entrepreneurial company that was always ahead of its game. Ashley's books, with their entertaining content, are not just suitable for enthusiasts with similar interests to his own, but equally for those interested in transport development and social history, because Midland Red led the way in innovative bus and coach designs for most of its existence. The company was such a big part of the community of folk in the Midlands, being their major provider of school, shopping and work services, and most folk relied on them, in the years when motorcars were scarce, for their days out and holidays!

Ashley has not just grown and retained his passion for Midland Red (and one or two of its associated companies in that era) but is now sharing a history which he has gathered together from all sorts of interesting people he has worked with over the years. Having such personal stories is both rare and special, and the stories are from ex-employees, many who sadly are not able to tell the tale again. Ashley ensures that the greatness of Midland Red can be remembered long into the future through his books.

On a recent visit with Ashley to see the wonderful collection of Midland Red buses at Wythall I met up with Paul Addenbrooke, a colleague I had worked with. It was the first time we had met in 30 years, and as I looked up into the cab of one of the types I used to drive I found myself saying out loud, "How the hell did I used to jump up into these, up to a dozen times a day?" Back then it was just in a day's work. Good colleagues, pleasant passengers and a good job – I'd go back tomorrow!

Colin J. Webster
Former career employee BMMO, Midland Red Omnibus Co., Midland Red South Ltd.

THE EARLY YEARS

Birmingham and Midland Motor Omnibus Co Ltd (BMMO) began life in 1904 as a company created by the directors of Birmingham Motor Express (BME) to raise more capital. The following year, the directors sold BME and BMMO to the giant British Electric Traction Company (BET) who consolidated its Birmingham bus operations into BMMO. Thus began the story of BMMO.

Its growth since WW1, when BMMO painted the Midlands 'RED' with so many of their buses, brought about the familiar 'Midland Red' brand name that we knew so well for much of the 20th century.

Those vehicles that spread across the growing 12,000 square miles of operating area in the centre of England and all over the United Kingdom on express services, tours, inclusive coach cruises and private hire duties were brought into being by the skill, tenacity and persistence of that 'awkward' but genius Chief Engineer Loftus George Wyndham Shire.

He started his career in transport with Croydon Tramways, and so became known to members of staff of the growing empire of British Electric Traction Co (BET). His next appointment was at a smallish BMMO/BET subsidiary in Kent known as Deal and District, which was later incorporated into the better-known East Kent Roadcar Company. Deal and District was the concern that inherited BMMO's unreliable early motorbuses at the time they reverted to horse bus operation, probably the company's only seemingly backward step.

One of the early, unreliable BMMO buses after its transfer to Deal and District Motor Services. Two people in this image are of particular interest. In the driving seat is L. G. Wyndham Shire and on the starting handle is Master Collyer, a young apprentice (fitters boy) of Wyndham Shire who later accompanied him to Birmingham for a career with BMMO.

Early motorbuses were not a refined product and needed some years of development to see them fit for purpose. In fact there were many complaints from residents along the routes protesting about petrol fumes, oil spills and noise, not to mention the large number of breakdowns on the roads. It had just been the clippety-clop of the horse buses before then, but even they had the substantial problem of incidental dropping of manure which caused all sorts of problems: on hot days drying, crumbling and blowing like dust in the wind, or on wet days forming a slippery slime all over the road and getting into drains and watercourses.

Although these old BMMO buses were refurbished and some rebodied whilst on their way to their new Kent operator, they were still found to have shortcomings. L. G. Wyndham Shire proved his worth by overcoming many of the issues, personally spending hours in inspection pits and at workbenches, manufacturing new parts to make the vehicles more reliable. His progress at Deal and District was being carefully watched – the son of the head of BET regularly visited, as his girlfriend's home was nearby.

At the time of the re-introduction of motorbuses by BMMO in Birmingham in 1912, they were much improved technically, and at the time of their resurgence Wyndham Shire was offered the job of chief engineer in Birmingham with BMMO. He accepted the post and brought with him from Deal a young lad named Master Charles Collyer, who was probably a fitter's boy that Wyndham Shire had mentored.

As explained in my previous book, *Midland Red and its People*, Mr Collyer went on to save the life of one of his colleagues while working at Bearwood garage, when a spot of petrol from a carburettor being repaired or adjusted in situ spilt onto the hot exhaust of the bus and burst into flames. The bus was parked just inside the garage; he threw his colleague out of the building and then smothered the flames with his coat on the pavement while others attended to the bus engine fire, which was successfully doused. Mr Collyer married his fiance, who also worked for the company, and they both enjoyed a lifelong career with Midland Red. It is presumed that Master Collyer was perhaps a young apprentice, or 'fitters boy' as they were known back in the days before indentured apprentices were common in the industry. Whatever his actual status, it is apparent that he was 'under-age', and at Deal was often pushed out through the small toilet window when the factory inspectors came to call.

The company's growth was rapid after 1914, when BMMO gave up their local services to the Corporation of Birmingham, and they spread their wings to the surrounding towns and villages.

Motorbuses were still not reliable, but much improved from their pre-1907 examples. Gangs of engineers with tool chests mounted on early motorcycles attended breakdowns to avoid expensive recovery costs. It should be noted that the practice of repairing breakdowns at the roadside where possible remained company policy into the 1960s.

In Coventry the Tilling Stevens bus with solid tyres, adorned with advertising and front and side destination boards. After the 1927 route numbering revisions this service became known as service 159 and was also later served by the X68 Birmingham Coventry Leicester service.

Mr and Mrs Collyer in their later years, photographed at a Midland Red long service awards dinner. Both are proudly wearing their long service medals. You will notice that both are wearing a 25 years circular brooch but Mr Collyer has a bar attached to the bottom of his, indicating his 40 years of service.

One of the first buses to operate from Birmingham to Coventry. It is hard to believe that this is the A45 between Elmdon and Stonebridge, with hardy passengers up top.

Mr Wyndham Shire was a dedicated problem solver. He continued to improve the designs of proprietary manufactured buses by proving his designs at Bearwood and then requesting Tilling Stevens (the Maidstone-based manufacturer of buses) to include his improvements in their designs for future deliveries to his company. His speciality was in keeping with his beliefs that lasted over the life of Midland Red-built buses – that buses should be fast, economical, light and reliable.

Tilling Stevens became intolerant of his persistent requests and eventually refused to incorporate them, but with characteristic stubbornness he persuaded his directors to allow him to both design *and* build a new type of vehicle, complete with all of his

This is the Tilling Stevens TS3 omnibus with what became known as the No1 style of bodywork. Deliveries to BMMO began in 1914 and it became the standard single-decker for the duration of wartime. Registration number OA 4572 was one of the first buses to work at Tamworth as BMMO spread its wings 'all over the Midlands,' as the slogan says. They painted the Midlands red with so many buses and became known as 'Midland Red'. This bus was operating to Polesworth just a few miles away.

modifications, that was totally suited to the needs of its user, rather than just being a manufacturer-led product. It is likely that within British Electric Traction Co. (BET) word had spread rapidly that this up-and-coming dedicated engineer would not let them down. Indeed there were BET people on the board of directors who appointed him. This is perhaps where the stubborn Midland Red spirit came from.

Wyndham Shire's commitment and determination won the day. His product was better than that offered by one of the biggest bus and commercial vehicle makers at that time. Of course, his new vehicles did prove themselves very quickly and were noticed throughout the country.

The vehicle type was known as SOS - and knowing of its creator's arrogance and self-importance, this probably stood for Shire's Own Specification. There is however an alternative theory that SOS could have meant Superior Omnibus Specification, as this has been seen on a work's design drawing, but the former is, in my opinion, the most likely derivation.

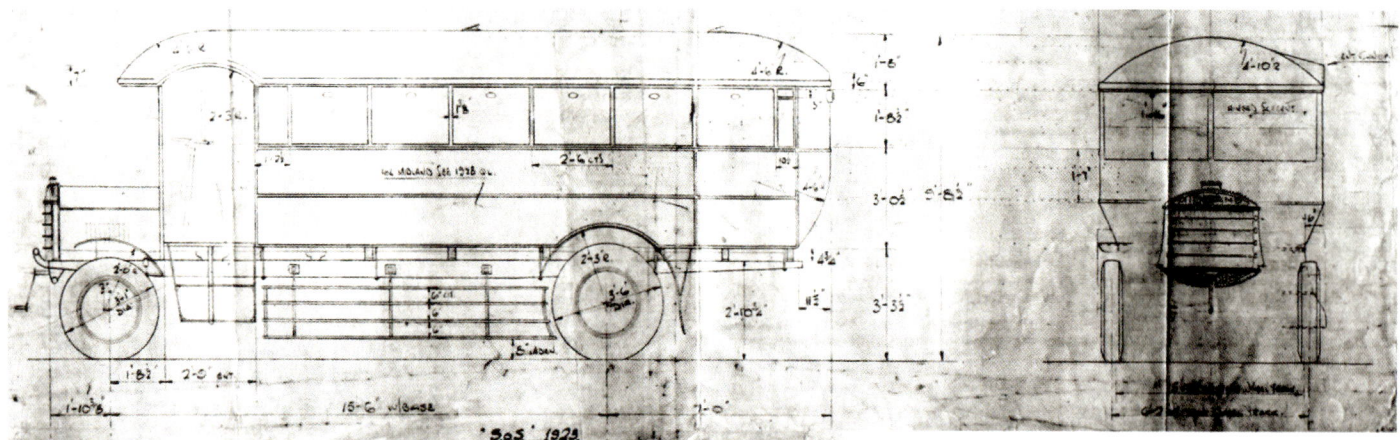

Shire lived for his work and enjoyed engineering matters. He had undertaken rebuilds and modifications to existing Tilling Stevens vehicles. He converted some from petrol-electric powered, to petrol-engine powered with more conventional gearbox transmissions. He also bought-in small Model T charabancs and American-built Garford buses, taking from them the best design parts and styles to help create his dream of 'the perfect omnibus'.

Among these experiments, some early 'HA' registered buses, using Tilling Sevens TS3 chassis, were constructed as double-deckers. These were interesting in that they had front entrances like Tilling Stevens single-deckers of the time. Upper deck seating was outward facing, running along the centreline of the vehicle.

This was at a time when BMMO were almost ready to launch into full vehicle production. The engines for these own-built vehicles were Tilling Stevens, but they had BMMO-designed cylinder heads and became known as the BMMO 'wonder engine', first built in 1922. These open-topped double-deckers were given the classification of Tilling Stevens FS type – not be confused with the SOS FS type (FS meaning Forward Steer, where the driver sat alongside the engine). Fifty-six of this type were built and many were allocated to Leicester. Wooden slatted seats and solid tyres would result in an uncomfortable ride – but the pneumatic tyre was about to be launched.

In this publicity picture of 1923, HA2254 is seen sitting on the crown of the original Wharf Bridge above the Coventry Canal at Chilvers Coton.

Buses at that time were usually heavy and slow, and so Shire involved Ricardo to assist in the design of his own engine, which, although being a bus engine, had, he insisted, to have the characteristics of a racing car, to be reliable, and capable of out-running the competition. The resulting four-cylinder engine of 4.3 litres was precisely what was required, and castings were made at Beans Industries in Tipton. Beans had been an early car maker but they had just ceased that business, and welcomed the new work. They provided Midland Red with castings over many years. The parts were machined and assembled in the workshops at Bearwood garage, which became the head office of the company until 1952, when the head office function was moved to Midland House, 1 Vernon Road, Edgbaston.

From the mid-1920s, bus manufacturing in Bearwood was gradually moved to Central Works in Edgbaston, although this took many years. In fact the move was not complete until the makeover of Central Works was finished, and it was fully operational.

One of the few people close to Wyndham Shire was Norman Parkes who worked more or less as his personal engineer, and there sometimes had to be some 'straight talking' when he knew alterations had to be made to Wyndham Shire's designs. Equipped with his own private workshop, he had just one assistant, yet he created and perfected the many prototypes from Wyndham Shire's designs and ideas. More on Mr Parkes can be found in my previous books.

The first type of production SOS bus was the S (Standard) type shown on the left. The next version, the FS (Forward Steer), is shown on the right. The 'porch' type entrance was common in the 1920s.

The bus had gradually progressed from the crude commercial products available to all bus companies into something of a BMMO speciality, evolving from the SOS S (Standard) to many, slightly better, slightly bigger versions. That original four-cylinder engine design (4.34 litres) accompanied the development of buses for a further six years, and was then joined by a six-cylinder version. By 1925, nearly half of the 200+ new vehicles produced by BMMO over the previous 18 months were supplied to associated BET operators around the UK, thereby proving their worth.

The original S type had seating for 32 passengers in a 'normal control' layout where the driver sat behind the engine, rather like a car. But later advances pushed the driver to the side of the engine in a narrow cab which allowed for two more seats – and more revenue! This type was known as FS or Forward Steer. The next development was the Q and later the QL (Queen and Queen Low). Before the QL, SOS buses had front wheels smaller than the rear, and only single rear wheels, but more alarmingly they only had brakes on the rear axle. But with the launch of the QL, the front wheel size was adopted all round, rear wheels were twinned and brakes were fitted to *all* wheels.

The QL (Queen Low) was a very popular and long-lived type. Many of my earlier working colleagues spoke affectionately about it, particularly vehicles 860 and 949 which were based at Nuneaton and Leamington garages until the early 1950s and used on light duties and for towing work. Quite an achievement for an over twenty-year-old bus with a plywood body!

It was a fast-growing business for Midland Red and their empire was expanding rapidly. They provided mobility for people not just to get to and from their place of work, but also to meet the growing desire for leisure journeys and weekend visits to the countryside – something that had previously been very difficult for city folk as trams were not able to stray from their fixed tracks. It was only now that a growing network of regular, reliable and well publicised bus routes was emerging.

Publicity, marketing and promotion were things Midland Red did well and profusely, from the early days of hand-coloured glass plate images of their vehicles to colourful artwork posters. This was all orchestrated through the Midland Red publicity department with its own superintendent and team of staff, all overseen by James Savage, who was instrumental in growing much of Midland Red's early leisure business.

There is no doubt that Mr Savage worked some magic to give working people the opportunity to take hard-earned days out, simply by using the company's normal everyday bus services. He even published itineraries for a complete day out that included a walk to link up with other bus services – for example, taking a Coventry-bound bus from Birmingham, alighting at Stonebridge, then walking to Coleshill to catch a bus on a different route back into Birmingham. The company had hired out vehicles for any purpose since horse bus days, but the desire to travel was further satisfied by the introduction in 1925 of charabancs – literally translated as 'wagon with benches'. These were based on the new SOS own-make of bus chassis, featuring newly developed pneumatic tyres and soft-top bodywork.

James Savage.

Savage was a keen cyclist and was always out and about, discovering new places that would be suitable for outings by bus. He produced booklets with suggested journeys by ordinary service bus, giving an itinerary of things to look out for along the route. The success of these led to his introduction of Mascot Tours, where the map of each route was shaped like the outline of an animal. Private hires were promoted at every opportunity, with publicity material available at every office and garage.

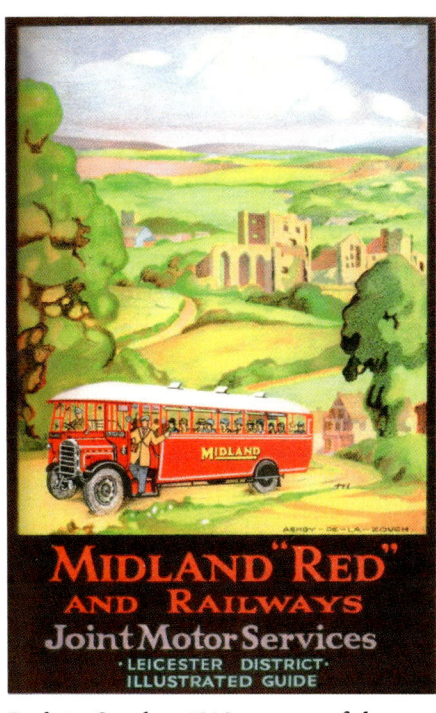  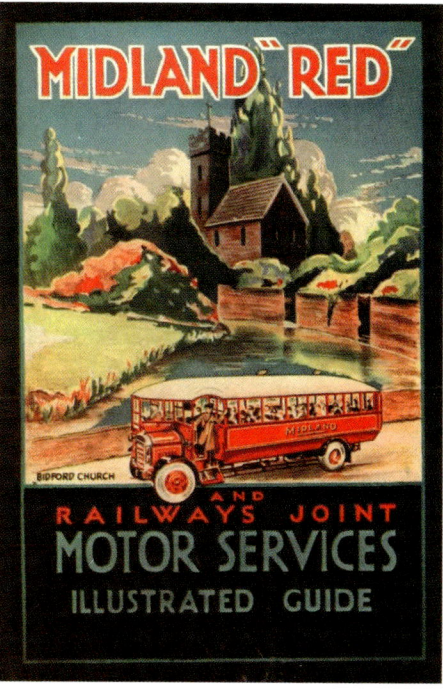

Back in October 1919, as part of the company's natural expansion plans, the company had established a temporary depot in the town of Banbury and rented part of Cherwell Works, not far from its later established garage in Canal Street, which was built just a year later. Just a month after starting their operation, the board of directors of BMMO came to Banbury to entertain the mayor and corporation officials at a fine hotel, where they were wined and dined in style. The chairman of the BMMO board, Mr Howley, addressed the great and the good of the town and claimed that business in and around Banbury would "grow and develop to an extent so far as none of you can at present anticipate." Within a few short years, the town benefited from brand new buses of a type not seen before, and services in the area were promoted by attractive booklets and fold out maps, showing fares charged and discounts offered for regular users.

 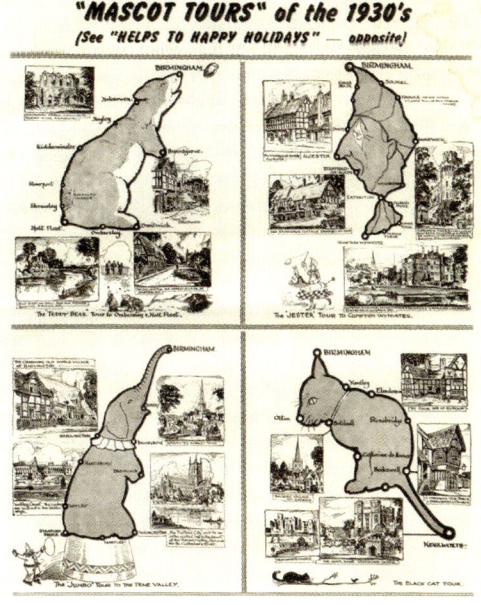

Local charabanc services were introduced during the summer and on Sundays out to the local attraction of Edge Hill, and evening services were extended so that locals could go for a drink out in Chipping Norton and Bloxham. The famous Banbury Fair benefited from special services that brought people from far outlying villages into town. To enable more people to travel further to work, Midland Red set up special works services to sites like Alcan and Northern Aluminium Company and covered all their shift patterns, even those starting at 5am.

Banbury Town Council had over the years been grateful for the service of Midland Red, even acknowledging in the 1970s the long service of one of the Midland Red family who had accrued 46 years of service; the mayor presented him with a special award and remarked that Banbury was exceedingly pleased and proud to have bus crews with such fine records as his. Banbury was just one of six towns to become Midland Red outposts in 1919 alone, as the company "painted the Midlands red" with so many buses.

A printed story in the 1950s that publicised improvements made to Digbeth coach station (reproduced on page 19) was noticed by a family who were regular travellers with Midland Red over the years, and it prompted them to write in to Bearwood with their own interesting account.

"My family and I are delighted to read about the wonderful development of our own Midland Red. I say 'our own' Midland Red because I think that we must have been some of the earliest passengers to travel with the company on its 'express' services. Those very far-off days are not mentioned in the account, but we remember the point of departure for long-distance services was 1926, and then, the status of coach had not been reached, they were just buses. For the Llandudno service, there was a small booking office in Lionel Street. The next year (1927), we departed for North Wales from Seymour Street. The vehicles were then just buses or open-top charabancs, the type with a hood usually folded at the back, and would be drawn over the passengers should the weather be wet. The next year (1928) saw a great improvement all round, there was a comfortable furnished waiting room in the Bull Ring at the corner of Moor Street. We could reserve our seats anytime from 8am in the morning until 10pm at night, and the buses by then were half-way to being to the comfort of coaches.

In the days before the vehicle known as the coach appeared, ordinary buses operated early long-distance services. The driver in his brown smock and the conductor stand at the front of OH 1233, one of the Tilling Stevens buses that were modernised by Midland Red. The passenger is the daughter of the writer of the letter.

"I enclose a small photograph taken at the Llangollen rest stop on our way home from Llandudno. The girl is my daughter, and the driver and conductor (regulars on this route) were Jack Price and Joe Birch. Throughout all of the years since 1926, with the exception of 1942 to 1945 – some of the war years – we have travelled by Midland Red. Indeed we are only just home again from Seaton and are booked again for Teignmouth in September. I am now 81 and still look forward to my next Midland Red holiday. 'Good Luck', and thank you for our delightful journeys!" - from Mrs Lillian Wakeman.

Of major importance in the growth of the company was that since 1923 new Midland Red buses had pneumatic tyres, which provided a marked change in comfort levels from the solid tyres of many of their competitors.

Charabancs became more passenger friendly and comfortable. HA 3669 is a QC, the coach version of the QL bus. The QC had a centrally placed radiator and side window protection, 2+2 seats with a central gangway, and a folding hood which was stored at the rear folded position. The top edge of the side windows had a runner for the sides of the folding hood to slide, and the driver could operate the folding roof by standing in the central gangway, which was much quicker than in previous charabancs. You will notice that the driver and the conductor wore different coloured uniforms in true company style!

Each year, Midland Red provided up to 30 vehicles for underprivileged children in the Nuneaton area to enjoy a day trip out. The event was paid for by the drivers and conductors from the garage. HA 5036 is seen here in 1932, just pulling away from Nuneaton, on its way to Wicksteed Park in Northamptonshire for an event-packed day out.

Below: Another QLC coach with ladies boarding at Fillongley, Warwickshire in what seems to be a Women's Institute outing in May 1938. Later the following month, this coach was transferred from Nuneaton to Leicester garage.

It was *buses* that people used for all of their journeys; proper coaches did not really emerge until the later 1920s when the charabanc gave way to more stylish coaches. The six-cylinder version of the SOS engine that came out in 1929 (5.98 litres) was used firstly in coaches, and then developments came for buses. This was a welcome introduction, especially as services were growing with the emergence of longer-distance bus services, which benefited from the larger engine size.

A luxurious coach appeared in 1929 called the XL, probably meaning simply 'excel'. This really looked the business, as Midland Red entered the 1930s period of decadent styling. It had a very attractive body; 40 were built by Brush at Loughborough, and 10 were built in-house by Carlyle, the bodymaker name used by BMMO. They featured full leather upholstery and a front dome with stencil route indicator. They were presented in a livery of red and maroon, the latter of which had been a traditional BET colour.

It was the first purpose-built coach intended to be the mainstay of the growing express route network, and the first type that gave passengers a permanent roof over their heads. However, it was built on a modified bus chassis, and its handling characteristics were unstable, as the coachwork was heavier than previously used, in part due to its luxurious appointment. According to a driver of the day, and retold by his son, an elderly Leamington garage-based coach driver, the coach 'wallowed' on cornering and was quite unpredictable and underpowered.

The early vehicles that were delivered were operated, as would be expected, from the brand-new Digbeth garage and coach station, but were withdrawn after being in service for only a few months; some were new and had not even entered service. Their existing bodies were removed and bus bodies built by Ransomes were fitted to the old XL chassis. They were then re-registered.

The luxury XL coach bodies retained their original registration numbers and were fitted with a brand-new chassis specifically designed for these heavier coach bodies. They were more powerful, being fitted with the brand new RR2LB (Large Bore) engine, rather than their earlier RR2SB engine, and a new radiator design which would become the standard fitting on buses for the next eight years. These coach bodies had their stencil indicator in the front roof dome widened out and fitted with a single-track destination blind. They were now fit for purpose and were used on coach duties as planned. These were special vehicles, yet somehow, I think that the original radiator style suited the overall design better; but with the larger engine now fitted, it needed a larger radiator to assist cooling.

Upon the outbreak of WW2, many coach services were reduced, and from 1941 most were suspended. Some of the coaches were commandeered by the War Department and sent to other users, and many of this type were transferred, loaned or sold to Potteries Motor Traction where some operated in the Staffordshire area until the 1950s, whilst a few were returned earlier to BMMO.

THE COMING OF ASSOCIATED MOTORWAYS

Since their first group of routes in the very early 1920s, Midland Red had built up a network of long-distance services using solid-tyred buses. Then came the humble charabanc that was gradually fitted with pneumatic tyres. Although Midland Red was a dominant operator in the Midlands, other companies that were also members of the British Electric Traction Co (BET) were doing similar things, albeit on a smaller scale. The industry was somewhat disorganised; for example, drivers and conductors of the day were licenced by the local authority. But the wind of change was coming which would regulate the industry, so the industry had to respond to protect its future.

The passing of the 1930 Road Traffic Act brought the first major change to road traffic rules since the Motor Car Act of 1903. There were four amendments to the 1903 Act between 1905 and 1914. Then in 1926, statistics began to be collected, and it was discovered that there were almost 5,000 deaths in nearly 125,000 road incidents.

In 1929, the government discussed the control of traffic on the country's roads, which brought about the Road Traffic Act a year later; this was all-encompassing and included the need for third-party insurance. Incidentally, much of the early discussions were about road speed, yet a speedometer was not an official requirement on motor vehicles until 1932.

The Act particularly involved the road passenger transport sector, and 'traffic areas' were set up covering the whole country. Traffic commissioners and traffic courts were appointed to each area, which controlled the type approval and operation of Heavy Goods Vehicles (HGVs) as well as Public Service Vehicles (PSVs). Administration of licencing applications and the strict checking for suitability of bus drivers and bus conductors also came under their control, which had previously been the responsibility of the local councils. The minimum age of 25 for a driver and 21 for collecting fares soon settled at 21 for drivers and 18 for conductors.

This was also when Construction and Use Regulations first appeared. These controlled the size of vehicles, along with such considerations as their weight, seating capacity, seat spacing, gangway heights, methods of signalling to the driver (e.g. bells) and emergency exit provision. They also required vehicles to be 'type approved', and they would have to be tilt tested to check balance and stability. The Act also introduced a 30mph speed limit for buses and coaches, along with heavy goods vehicles, and introduced the Conduct of Passengers Regulations, which covered passenger behaviour and described the items prohibited from being carried on an omnibus. Periodic vehicle checks were also introduced to maintain safety, where Ministry of Transport vehicle examiners would each have an area of responsibility and visit bus and coach operators with sufficient frequency to enable them to check each vehicle once every year.

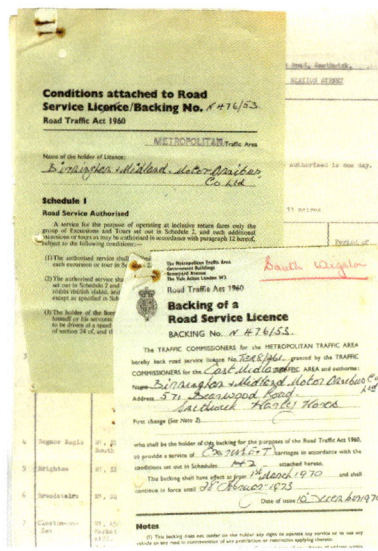

An example of Road Service Licencing. The topmost sheet shows the licence to 'back' the service, issued by Traffic Commissioners. The second sheet shows the Schedule for the actual authorisation to operate the route. The backing sheet shows one of nearly 30 pages of specific route details.

The Act also controlled the routes operated: an operator would propose a new route and have to supply evidence of demand, a proposed timetable, detailed maps of roads covered by the planned service, numbers and types of vehicles involved in providing the service, etc. The application would have to be put to the Traffic Commissioner 56 days before its commencement – the notice period. The application would then be publicised in a document known as 'Notices and Proceedings', which would be seen by anyone subscribing to that document, such as other operators. During the notice period the application would be heard in a traffic court where other operators had the opportunity to object, which could delay the determination of the application. Any ensuing licence to operate that service would be precious indeed. If the operator required any alteration or deviation from the exacting licenced conditions, then application for amendment to the court would be required – all costly, in both time and administration.

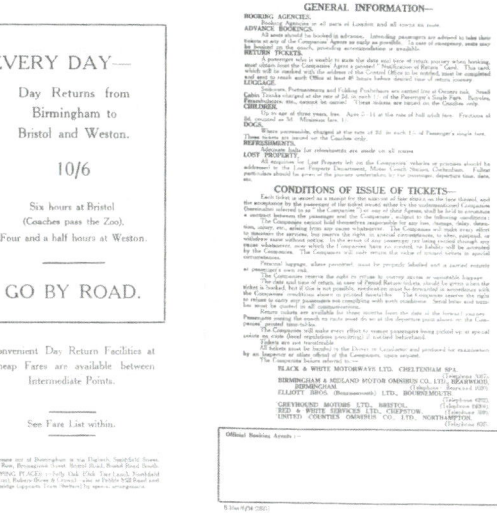

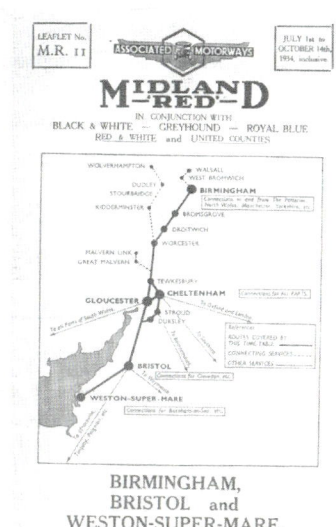

Road service licences were also required for day trips and excursions, and companies changed hands often, depending on which licences they held and if they were of interest to potential buyers. Midland Red kept careful records of both their own and their competitors' excursions and day trips. Advertisements were cut out from the local press, pasted into a report and sent to head office for scrutiny.

To ensure the security and stability of coach services, to avoid unnecessary conflict among operators that had the same aims, and especially to minimise the palaver of the route licencing application system, a group of companies decided to get together in 1934 to protect their existing valuable route licences and market a growing network of coach services over the country to everyone's benefit. Midland Red, Black and White Motorways, Red and White, Bristol Greyhound, Royal Blue and United Counties

A 1928 advert which was filed away, perhaps forgotten, and found in 1971 in a drawer in an office at Leamington garage. Wages at the time were around £4-6 per six-day week, and leisure travel was particularly valued as an escape from day-to-day work.

The logo of Black and White Motorways of Cheltenham, a company owned by BMMO, who were at the centre of Associated Motorways' operations at their base in Cheltenham, at St. Margaret's Road coach station.

were the founding member companies of the group known as Associated Motorways. It was probably the first attempt at the branding of transport services, before the word 'branding' got out of control!

Midland Red's original and longstanding coach services were included in this new consortium. With services to Llandudno, London and Weston-super-Mare, and the services from the other operators, Associated Motorways suddenly had a very fast-growing brand, with booking agents on almost every high street in the vast areas they served. The consortium did not seek to make a profit, but was mutually beneficial to its member companies and did not prevent them from operating their own services as well as providing services to the pool. There was one company that only operated Associated Motorways services: Black and White Motorways of Cheltenham. Their coach station became one of the main hubs for changing coaches, and the mass coach departures at 1430hrs each day was notorious for clogging up the streets of Cheltenham.

Wartime brought about a stop to services from 1941, but when they were reintroduced five years later the Associated Motorways group were joined by other companies, including Eastern Counties and Lincolnshire in the fifties, Crosville in the mid-sixties, and a very late joiner Southdown Motor Services in the early seventies.

The operating companies were affected in 1968/9 by the formation of the National Bus Company which went on to form National Express in 1973. It was, of course, the services of Associated Motorways that provided the backbone for National Express to operate on, and in later times, more emphasis was placed on the use of Birmingham's Digbeth Coach Station as an important hub along with Victoria Coach Station in London. This was due to the growing motorway network, where faster coach services could be provided on traditional Associated Motorways routes that had originally begun when they only had 'A' roads on which to operate. Sadly, this change resulted in the once very important coach station at St Margaret's Road, Cheltenham, becoming less used; in 1984, it was closed and lost almost without trace. Today we hear very little about Associated Motorways, but Britain would not have had such a good coach network without them.

C5 coach fleet number 4827 departing Digbeth Coach Station in 1967 bound for Cheltenham, where passengers travelling onward to the South West of England or South Wales would change coaches. All incoming coaches from far and wide converged at St. Margaret's Coach Station in Cheltenham. There was time to change vehicles, followed by the 1430hrs mass departure – its busiest time.

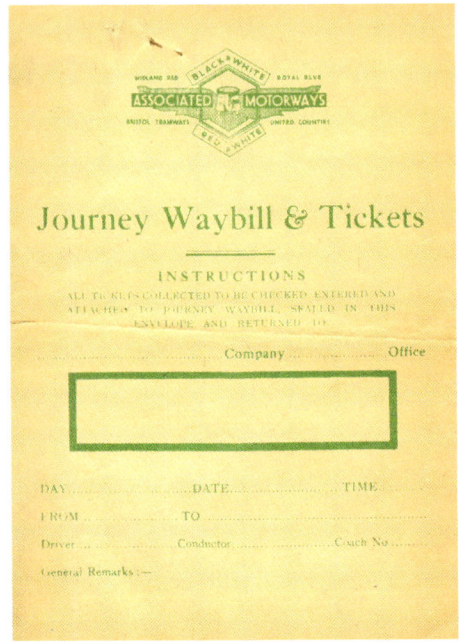

The Associated Motorways journey waybill and journey envelope. This had details of the service operated, the date operated, the journey details, the company operating the route, etc. When a passenger bought a ticket from one of the member companies, an audit copy of the ticket was sent to Associated Motorways at Cheltenham who would bank the payment minus commission for the issuing company. The service itself could be operated by any of the member companies, so the driver collected the passengers' tickets and put them into the journey envelope. The waybill and envelope were then returned to the driver's garage and forwarded to Associated Motorways who would issue payment on a monthly basis to the operating company for the journeys undertaken by the passengers.

DIGBETH COACH STATION REFRESHED

As Midland Red saw increases in coach business based at Digbeth, it was decided to provide a major upgrade to the facilities offered. A large patch of land at the front of the coach station which was once used for parking buses was acquired by the council to widen Deritend into a dual carriageway. Proceeds of the sale were used to build a new commercial and office frontage adjacent to the dual carriageway, to improve the look of the garage and coach station. When the building was completed in the late 1950s, great efforts were made to publicise the opening of the new Digbeth coach station, its offices and its large frontage of shops.

The offices were named Spencer House after Sir John Spencer Wills, the chairman of BMMO and a member of the famous tobacco family. Mr Wills had seen BMMO through both its Silver and Diamond Jubilee years. Midland Red wasn't the only company to benefit from his involvement; he worked for BET (British Electric Traction Co) for 47 years, 22 of those concurrently for Midland Red. He had previously worked for many BET subsidiaries including, in 1926, East Yorkshire Motor Services, a sister Midland Red company which was then in its fledgling years. Sir John Spencer Wills resigned from the board of BMMO just a few months prior to Nationalisation, when the shares of BET were sold to the Government.

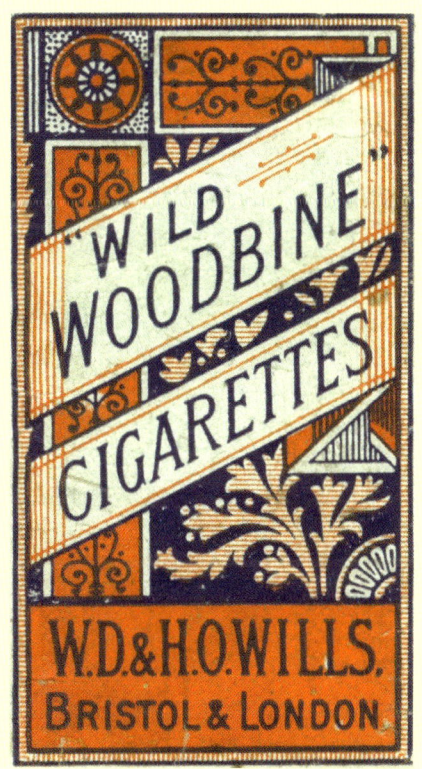

Sir John Spencer Wills (1904-1991).

Spencer House was built adjoining the 1929 coach station. The new building had many new features to improve coach travel for long-distance coach passengers, including a booking hall, waiting room, left luggage department, shops, booking office, and an area equipped with new vending machines. The most publicised feature was the new large cafeteria for 100+ passengers to enjoy meals, drinks and refreshments – even the cups, saucers and plates featured the company name or logo and were British-made in the Potteries. The drivers enjoyed separate canteen facilities at the other side of the kitchen. On the upper floors there were administration offices, including the Midland Red chartroom from whence all of its long-distance services were controlled. Digbeth coach station was a very busy place for bus and coach services, especially at major coach changeover and departure times. It was a hive of activity, confusion and sometimes frustration, with the added delight of diesel fumes as masses of vehicles often departed together. But whatever its downsides, the original Digbeth coach station will be remembered as a significant place in Midland Red history.

CYCLES OF PROGRESS

1932 saw development work start on the first Midland Red-designed diesel engine. It was used only for buses, initially double-deckers from 1934, but then when production levels were achieved, versions for a new range of single-deckers were welcomed that had the luxury of an electric starter motor, so the driver didn't have to 'swing' (i.e. start) the engine from the starting handle at the front of the engine.

The petrol engines needed two well-experienced people to start them, sometimes three. If you were on the starting handle you needed to have your thumb out of the way in case the handle kicked back, as it could easily dislocate your thumb or worse, but that was the same for all petrol manual-start vehicles of that era. In the garage in the morning there would be the starting gang, consisting of four or five people. The starting rope had a steel loop in the end that went over the starter handle at the bottom of the radiator. At the other end of the rope was a handle and just half way was a loop that could be used by another helper. One man held a piece of card with a small hole in it which he placed over the carburettor (as a rudimentary choke), and another man in the cab controlled the advance and retard lever on the steering column. If the driver parked the bus during the day and stopped the petrol engine, he would more than likely have parked on a slope so he could get it running again by putting the bus into second gear and letting the clutch out when the bus was moving, so that the engine would spring into action. The coming of the diesel engine was a blessing for improving the bus drivers' day at work.

Buses fitted with these new diesel engines can probably be described as 'second generation' single-deckers. Known as the ON (ONward) type, they were originally built as petrol-engined vehicles, but later versions were diesel-powered, initially by AEC 7.6 litre engines until sufficient BMMO K type engines could be built. The 'K' referred to the kidney shape designed into the combustion chamber that gave the BMMO engines great economy and efficiency. Some of the petrol-engined ONs were converted to diesel power and designated the CON (Converted ON) type and the later SON (Standard ON) type.

Coaches were still fitted with petrol engines until after WW2, as the quiet running of petrol engines was deemed important for passenger comfort levels.

The SOS S type had clearly been a revolution, and for a few years until around 1932 developments of the S type became more *evolutionary*, with the exception of the luxurious XL type coach and its redesigned RR version. Then in the very early 1930s there were many further developments, with various types, including those known as Madams and Improved Madams.

Then a new generation of single-decker types came along, known as the ON (ONward) family, and these new vehicles provided the mainstay of the single-deck fleet until the end of the war years and beyond. These ONs came about due to new government legislation allowing vehicles to be 27′ 6″ long; the company was always quick to take advantage of the additional capacity that new length regulations brought.

The design of these single-deck vehicles was easily recognisable, even if non-standard. The engine was very short, allowing the front bulkhead to be very close to the back of the front wheels. The driver sat on the petrol tank, the radiator was offset and the cab was very narrow. This allowed for up to 39 seats in a single-decker, and clever design meant that they only weighed around 5 tons – little different to the 32-seat buses ten years earlier! More 'bums on seats' equals more revenue from passengers – this was efficiency and economy at its best.

An example of a later production REDD. The SOS radiator badge is in its more usual position under the Midland Red radiator nameplate.

The REDD prototype. The SOS letters were placed at the bottom of the radiator, with the 'S' sitting above the 'OS'.

At the turn of the 1920s to 1930s it was industrial growth in particular that brought the need for new double-deckers. After almost a decade with no new double-deckers in the fleet, a new type was built using a modified chassis previously designed for the RR coaches, and still with a petrol engine (the larger RR2LB unit). It was first classified as DD (RE), but within a few years it was universally known as the REDD (Rear Entrance Double-Decker).

The prototype was expensive to build; the chassis at some £17k no doubt included development costs. It was bodied by Short Brothers and the upper deck did not continue over the drivers cab and had a slightly pointed appearance at the front. Production REDDs had a revised upper deck arrangement, over the drivers cab, and this increased seating capacity.

Following the REDD type, designers reverted to front-loading double-deckers, similar to the FS double deckers of 1923, a decade before. Like the REDD, the FEDD (Front Entrance Double-Decker) had an initial classification of DD (FE), but within five years or so became known as the FEDD. The first batch was originally built with petrol engines and later vehicles were fitted with diesel engines as they became available; the earlier petrol-engined FEDDs were converted from 1942. They were all were very popular with passengers, crews and engineers.

The FEDD was built in batches right up until the outbreak of war in 1939, and into 1940. Bodywork for these pre-WW2 vehicles was supplied by various manufacturers including Metro Cammell, Short Brothers, Brush, English Electric and Eastern Counties. But, as you might expect, Midland Red built the odd one or two examples, and they certainly altered/improved others throughout their long lives.

Above: The final version of the FEDD in its final, very plain paint job. FHA 248 was one of three FEDDs retained for the special service that the company operated for its staff to travel to and from work, from Bearwood to Central Works. This was when the refurbished Central Works was completed and nearly all manufacturing/overhaul staff were transferred from Bearwood. These missed the preservation era by only a couple of years, with the last ones being driven to Lichfield garage parking area for scrapping in 1961, and sadly, no FEDD was saved.

Above: The first version of the FEDD had an outside sliding entrance door, and a rather attractive appearance. Although the example shown here is HA 9429, they were familiarly known by both staff and enthusiasts as BHAs, as most had BHA prefix registrations.

Too advanced for its time

In the mid-1930s, Wyndham Shire produced designs for rear-engined vehicles that were revolutionary in the UK. Four prototypes were built, and the type was known as REC (Rear-Engined Coach), though only one of the four was actually a coach. These were the height of 1930s modern styling, and some of the very first buses to have a set-back front axle, which allowed for an entrance at the front, beside the driver.

As prototypes, each vehicle incorporated several mechanical and bodywork differences for evaluation: there were two engine sizes, manual and semi-automatic gearboxes, different axle ratios, twin and single radiators, a bus version and a coach version. The basic concept, although totally new to the British bus scene, worked and was successful in the USA. However, in Birmingham and the Black Country the roads were contaminated with debris from engineering industries, so the designs did need further adjustments to improve reliability in their industrial operating area. However, with war looming, efforts were prioritised to build up a working fleet of existing models.

Consequently, these ultra-modern prototypes did not receive the necessary time and expenditure to address their shortcomings. Much to Wyndham Shire's annoyance, they

were deemed a costly distraction at this difficult time. As with most new designs, a careful eye was kept on them in service. Running new designs of buses from a garage near to Central Works was normal practice, and Wyndham Shire kept them running locally, mainly operating from Bearwood garage for most of their lives of up to five years. They went into storage at Bearwood and Central Works soon after war was declared. These prototypes were very well known, mainly due to their simple registration numbers: BHA 1, and CHA 1 to CHA 3. The former was referred to simply as BHA 1, but the others were known affectionately as Charlie 1 to Charlie 3.

In 1971, an old Leamington driver called John Henry told me that he was training at Bearwood in summer 1938, and he saw Charlie 1 with its engine running and with maroon wheel arch valances and trim. He also saw others of the class with their normal black wheel arch valances, on their occasional trips to Leamington. John even drove Charlie 2 – but in its post-war rebuilt style.

These vehicles really were two decades ahead of their time. When they were being live-tested on the usual Midland Red test routes (over some 25,000 miles), they were running to full capacity. Word was quick to get out among the great and the good, even in those days, and almost every vehicle designer, engine maker and bus manufacturer made an excuse to travel to Birmingham to see and ride aboard this latest head-turner, made in Midland Red's own factory. I recall, from discussions I had in the late 1960s, it seemed that these vehicles, being revolutionary in design, must have been a drain on the finite development resources that the company would have had leading up to the outbreak of WW2. Although Wyndham Shire was committed to his designs, he wasn't allowed the freedom to provide the time, money and resources for them to be fine-tuned for successful running.

Birmingham and the Black Country in the 1930s were heavy on engineering and manufacturing, and many roads around

foundries and factories were fouled with swarf from lathes, and other litter and impurities, including oil and sawdust. As the RECs were petrol rear-engined, it was difficult for their design at that time to keep the air intakes free from dirt ingress, so they became prone to engine breakdowns. Also, the drivers blamed the quiet-running petrol engines for not being able to hear what was going on 'at the back', despite the plethora of dashboard gauges and lights giving warnings of fluid levels, and fluid and component temperatures. In this regard, it should be remembered that drivers completely new to this revolutionary layout would have previously been accustomed to sitting next to the bonnet and the throbbing engine of the earlier models.

In hindsight, Wyndham Shire's original thoughts on "keeping everything 'dirty' behind the rear wheels" was the way forward: nearly all passenger vehicles built today are rear-engined. His outstanding designs of 1935 may have been just a glimpse of what the future might have been for the company. Nevertheless, these REC designs did play their part in all future Midland Red designs, and, after later modifications, led to BMMO being at the cutting edge of vehicle advancement in the years after WW2, when almost all mainstream and other manufacturers were still in recovery mode.

By 1940 the vehicles were in storage due to the war, but it is understood that Wyndham Shire was stubbornly still spending time and effort on them, some being stripped of components, perhaps for modification work. But in the same year, he abruptly early-retired, to be replaced the very next day by a new chief engineer. Wyndham Shire had travelled to the USA on numerous occasions, and drew inspiration from visits to bus manufacturing plants and operators there, where rear-engined vehicles were by then becoming commonplace. Had wartime circumstances and his own temperament been more accommodating, the design story of post-war Midland Red vehicles may have been very different.

WARTIME AND THE TROUBLED FORTIES

A new man at the helm

Donald McIntyre Sinclair was appointed in 1940 as BMMO's new chief engineer. He was a trained engineer with wide experience. From school he attended Bearsden Academy of Mechanical Engineering in Glasgow, then started a full engineering apprenticeship with Albion Motors before joining BP as district engineer in Bedford, Croydon and Bristol. His next move was to become assistant chief engineer with Northern General Transport, based in Gateshead. Northern General was a BET company and one of the associated companies who bought SOS buses in the inter-war years, so it would have been familiar with the SOS brand.

He was appointed chief engineer of BMMO and took up office the day after his predecessor, L. G. Wyndham Shire, suddenly left the company. I suspect that there was some behind-the-scenes planning involving the directors and BET officials to enable this rapid transition of power to be smoothly accomplished. Wyndham Shire's engineering plans had been severely restricted and his engineering budgets under very tight control by others. His plans for his rear-engined prototypes could not be further developed which must have been immensely frustrating. Since before 1920, he had more or less been his own man regarding engineering direction and project development, so he must have felt uncomfortable with the new situation he found himself in. But whether he jumped or was pushed is debatable.

BET management had been following Mr Sinclair's career, and had persuaded him to turn down an offer for the post of chief engineer at Glasgow that he had been offered some months earlier. There may have had to be some considerable financial or other persuasion involved.

Other changes happened during wartime, too. In 1943, Mr O. C. Power, the traffic manager, died suddenly while attending a transport conference in London. This was a great shock to the company as he was the power behind much of that unique Midland Red spirit.

The board of directors asked Sinclair to take over the traffic department, too, and in doing so he became widely recognised as Midland Red's first-ever general manager. Now engaged in the biggest job in the organisation, in 1946 he officially handed his chief engineer role to Mr S. C. Vince. But he was never far from the cutting edge, and was just as at home with brave new engineering projects as he was at the boardroom table.

The Midland Red-built SOS QL, one of many sold to Northern General. UP551 is now beautifully preserved at Beamish open-air museum.

Mr S. C. Vince, the chief engineer, appointed in 1946 by Donald Sinclair.

Mr Vince was left a long legacy of pre-war SOS vehicles that were coming to the end of their lives or needing attention after working hard throughout the wartime. Many early models were still working as service buses, and others, more elderly, were converted to driver training vehicles or other service vehicle uses.

Wartime

The SOS brand introduced by Wyndham Shire did not sit comfortably with Donald Sinclair, so he instructed the company to use the initials taken from the official company name, 'BMMO'. He directed that the 'SoS' badges be removed from the buses, but many were left with just the 'o' remaining, as it was part of the centre strip of trim on the bus radiators.

Mr Sinclair's early years in charge during wartime would have seen the handsome LRR (Low Rolls-Royce) class of single-deck coaches and the older-looking tourer OLR (Open Low Rolls-Royce) coaches being converted in 1941 to ordinary service buses. (The Rolls-Royce company had no connection, apart from the name being synonymous with quality.) This was done mainly at Bearwood and Central Works and involved considerable rebuilding and conversion work, especially as the OLRs were originally open-top tourers!

From September 1939 most bus services were rationed, curtailed or suspended. Then, from 1941, almost all *coach* services were suspended, and the coaches were stored at any garage that had sufficient space. BMMO was no longer able to manufacture vehicles by order of the Government, so some of the coaches were converted into buses to help with the supply of vehicles.

The LRR was a well-liked vehicle. Many of these were allocated to Leamington garage until their withdrawal, and older driver colleagues often spoke fondly of the LRR. The company often featured their vehicles proudly on publicity material. This image is taken from a Bridge trump selector that was given away to clients.

The OLR open tourers that were used on coach tours, excursions and private hires were converted to service buses with a half-cab layout, rather than their original normal control design. The passenger entrance was a sliding door, behind the engine at the second passenger window space. Provision of new or replacement vehicles during wartime, when manufacturing had almost ceased and was in control of the Ministry of Supply, made things difficult, but Midland Red had the facilities to use converted coaches to help with vehicle shortages. These continued in service until the early 1950s, allowing the company to build up post-war manufacturing. These images show the OLR in original condition (AHA 612) outside a Devon hotel, and the rebuilt bus version (AHA 631) sitting in Shrewsbury on a hot summer's day, with bonnet and windscreen open to allow additional ventilation. The crew had gone for a cuppa before operating a local service S12 to Castlefields. Notice the difference in lettering on the radiator: the original version (top) had 'SoS', but after wartime conversion from tourer to bus (above) just the 'o' remained, when Mr Sinclair insisted that the S's were removed.

War Time Services
Petrol Rationing
REVISED SERVICES

Revised services and petrol rationing meant conserving reserves. Some emergency provision was needed for troop movements, sometimes at very little notice. Drivers were often expected to drive at night in unfamiliar areas without lights — apart from the glimmer of the shrouded vehicle lights. It was during this time of fuel rationing that drivers' bonuses changed and a fuel-saving bonus was given for saving fuel beyond the pre-war miles per gallon allocations. This encouraged drivers to coast along in neutral, a practice later frowned upon.

There were many other experiments and modifications carried out, even during the wartime years. Tests involving fuel and oil types and consumptions, new diesel engines (both AEC and BMMO's new K type engine being fitted into older petrol-engined buses) and body swaps all kept Bearwood and Central Works busy. In an effort to save fuel, some vehicles were converted to accept producer gas units, which were trailers towed behind that burned anthracite and produced a fuel gas that powered the vehicle. Producer gas units were only used at a few garages, and had to be disconnected to revert to conventional fuel operation once darkness fell to avoid being seen during blackout conditions, as the burner would glow red!

Although conditions varied over Midland Red's vast operating territory, in areas of high risk, buses were often parked outside overnight, perhaps in woods or places where they were difficult to see from enemy aircraft above. A garage full of petrol-engined buses, often in a built-up area, would have been at very high risk during air raids.

Some garages lost normal vehicle capacity when wartime diktat meant that garage floor space was required for production of items for the war effort. This included firms such as Alvis. Even Spitfire wings were being produced in bus garage micro-factories.

Donald Sinclair, the chosen replacement for Wyndham Shire, had previously been assistant chief engineer at Northern General Motors in Gateshead and had gained experience working with their side-engined Sentinel vehicles. He therefore felt that the future lay with a similar underfloor-engined layout that provided a flat bus floor, clear of obstructions. At least one of the pre-war REC rear-engined prototypes was partly dismantled at the workshops, and they were seen by Mr Sinclair as ideal candidates for conversion, especially as during wartime they were prevented from building brand new vehicles. The RECs were donor vehicles and were classed as rebuilds, but these were *extensive* rebuilds; some new parts were required including a full body for the REC that had originally been built as a coach. In the wartime, rebuilding coaches did not figure in plans, so the original very stylish body was removed and sold on to a Black Country coach operator who had it fitted to a second-hand ex-Ribble Leyland coach that they had bought.

The prototypes were converted at a pace of almost one per year and a new classification was given; hence the S1 of 1941, the S2 of 1942, and so on. Then, in 1945, a fifth prototype appeared which was another major development, even though its bodywork looked much the same as the S1 to S4 series.

BHA 1 has the frontal design makings of the future post-war design, and still retains its pre-war style of sides with wind-down windows.

This was the completely new body built on the chassis of the coach-built REC. It is seen here when brand new, complete with wartime headlight masks and white painted side markings so as to be visible during blackout conditions.

The last of the rebuilds, again seen during wartime, but rapidly evolving into the mass-produced Midland Red buses of the early post-war period.

A further rebuild of BHA 1 occurred, following a front-end accident in 1951. An odd combination of a modern frontal design yet still with its pre-war side panels and wind-down windows. This shows its post-war style gold MIDLAND fleet name, whereas the previous three images show the black shadowed pre-war style fleet name

This new S5 was revolutionary in that it was built without a conventional chassis. The experience gained from its development, especially in the stresses to bodywork and subframes and on-road behaviour, was used to produce all future vehicles to a monocoque design, allowing the themes of light, fast, reliable and economical to continue in BMMO designs. More information on the rebuilds is given in my earlier book *Midland Red and its People*.

The revolutionary and highly advanced S5 carried the final pre-war fleet number 2579.

Wartime put the company, its staff and its vehicles under tremendous pressure. Service cuts were implemented to save fuel, but were also due to staff shortages, as men received their call-up papers and left the company's service to fight for their country.

There was an influx of lady drivers from existing conducting staff, office staff and outsiders, which kept the training school busy.

'Charlie 3', one of the pioneering underfloor-engined prototypes sitting new at Central Works with a group of newly-employed lady drivers. The headlight masks and white painted wheel arches dates the image to 1942/3.

The lady drivers were generally very successful in their new roles and all passed their tests first time. Although their new employment was primarily for wartime, a few did continue employment after the war with Midland Red in driving and office-based roles. The accident rate of the wartime lady drivers was extremely low, despite conditions being far from normal on occasion. Headlight covers were mandatory; these allowed only small slits of light through which was virtually useless. Drivers were most comfortable on routes they were familiar with, but during wartime there were many additional routes operated, such as those to munition factories and the many hires by the military for the movement of troops, often at very short notice, to wherever they were required and in blackout conditions.

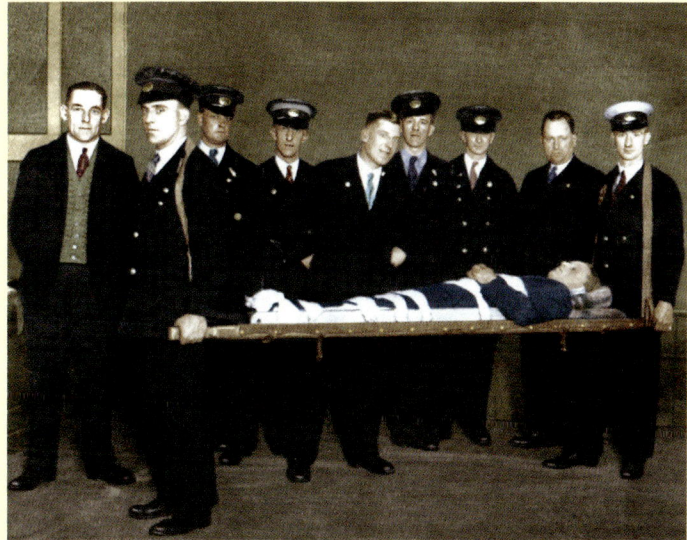

Training during wartime included first aid and stretcher work. Some buses were converted into ambulances, where multiple stretchers could be transported. This training scene is at Southgate Street garage, Leicester.

Vehicles suffered during wartime. They only received bare essential maintenance, and the company's suppliers were also short of raw materials. The fleet normally received attention on a strict mileage basis where units were exchanged upon mileage limits being attained. During wartime this was relaxed and the miles were clocked up, largely without incident, but when the war was over, it left a glut of overdue overhauls. Mechanical attention was given at Central Works, and many pre-war single- and double-deckers were sent out for body overhauls and refurbishments to keep them going until new vehicles could be manufactured.

Early in the company's existence, the life expectancy of a bus was as low as seven or eight years, but by the 1930s, vehicles would have much longer lives. Some examples of the ON family of vehicles gave 18 to 21 years service, and another 5 to 8 more years if converted for use by the training school as driver training vehicles. FEDD double-deckers often gave well over 15 years service, with the longest-lived examples from 1938/9 continuing until 1960/1. They spent their last years on ancillary duties, as tree cutters and driver trainers. Some were used as staff buses for workers, who were given a free service to transport them from Bearwood to Central Works which was their new place of work when its rebuilding was complete in 1954.

The mid-1930s prototype REC class which, after conversion, became the post-war prototypes S1 to S4 had amazingly long lives and only missed the preservation era by just a few years. S1 had a twenty-one year life, S2 twenty-three years, S3 twenty-two years, and S4 twenty-one years. They saw extensive use over a wide area of the company's operations.

RENEWING THE FLEET

After the war, bus production continued apace as soon as wartime regulations allowed. It was decided to recommence post-war fleet numbers at 3000. The company had amassed parts ready to launch the S6 model, a 40-seater service bus that appeared in 1946. They were built to the then maximum dimensions of 27′ 6″ long and 7′ 6″ wide. Central Works was already working at capacity on chassis and the backlog of overhauls that were unable to be done due to the stresses of war, so the Midland Red-designed bodywork was built equally by Brush at Loughborough and Metro-Cammell in Washwood Heath, Birmingham. Both of these companies had been heavily involved in producing items for the war effort for the Ministry of Supply, and so needed more new work once peace was declared. The bodywork design closely followed the converted wartime prototypes, with an updating of the body side and rear design.

It was quite an event when new buses were delivered to garages after the austerity of wartime. A dozen new S6s were delivered new to Leamington. They were lined up in Leam Terrace and photographed with their drivers.

Hundreds more outwardly similar vehicles to the S6 appeared over the next five years. Some, as soon as permissions allowed (from 1 June 1950), were increased to the new maximum dimensions of 30′ long and 8′ wide, which allowed an additional four seats. The S12 type was built to the new larger size.

These types included the S6, S8, S9, S10, and S12, and all had open steps and a hinged door at the entrance to the saloon that was operated by the conductor. The driver gained access to his cab via a separate hinged door on the offside which had a stylish curved sliding window, for the driver to give hand signals.

There was a solitary experimental S11 (fleet number 3703), which was essentially an S10 fitted with independent front suspension when new in 1950. Like many others it was lengthened from its original 27′ 6″ to 29′ 3″ at Charles H. Roe in Leeds, when two years old, which added four additional passenger seats. In 1957, after almost eight years of test and assessment work, the very modern independent front suspension was replaced with a conventional beam front axle and leaf springs, bringing it into line with other vehicles of the time. After being under the initial care of the development department when it was allocated to Bearwood garage, the S11 worked at Banbury, Bromsgrove, Malvern and Worcester garages, and was withdrawn in summer 1965 after 15 years of service.

S6 fleet number 3029, once allocated to Nuneaton garage. By the time this photo was taken it was being used by the development department at Central Works. Here, it was undertaking exhaust emissions trials.

The S8 was the first type to be built to the new width of 8' 0", providing more generous seats. 3863 is seen resting at the rear of the old Coton Road garage in Nuneaton. It was the very last bus to leave when this garage finally closed and vehicles were transferred to the new Newtown Road garage.

The S12, number 3737, spent its entire life allocated to Digbeth garage.

S9 fleet number 3419 seen in Pool Meadow, Coventry when allocated to Rugby garage for its last few days in service, prior to withdrawal.

The interior and seats of the early S types were all similar in design and appearance, and comfortable for the time. In the holiday season, or if there were vehicle shortages, it was not uncommon to see the S types allocated to duplicate London services and occasionally on excursions, especially the shorter afternoon or evening tours.

The S10 seen on service 500, a rural service from Banbury.

To supply the need for post-war double-deckers, the company made good use of its pre-war experiments and modifications to the FEDD double-decker bodywork styling and the post-war prototype, the D1, which evolved to combine many of the earlier ideas. This certainly set the trend for the first few hundred buses after the war, starting with the D5 and the later D5B that was fitted with electrically-controlled folding platform doors. These were fine vehicles, smooth and quiet, seating 56 passengers and 8 standing. A similar body was used for 100 AEC Regent buses that were supplied to some garages, as demand grew in the gradual return to normality after the war. The first batch had Metro Cammell bodywork and looked slightly more dated and romantic than later batches. They had a sliding entrance door.

This FEDD is from the intermediate batches (1937/8), and had a radiator with a wide Midland Red badge across the top of the tank. The last versions from 1939 and 1940 had the tall radiator with an SOS badge, and later a BMMO badge, although it should be said that, like anything Midland Red, there were many individual updates and modifications where radiator types were exchanged.

Right: EHA 299 had an experimental enclosed radiator and full width front, which was the next step towards what would become the new standard for post-war production double-deckers. Seen with its headlight masks and wartime roof colour.

Below: HHA 1 of 1945, the prototype for the future design and known as the D1. Similarities can be seen to the modified FEDD on the right. The D1 is very close to the design of the next few hundred production vehicles. No headlight masks here, but the white painted mudguards and side liferail were still fitted.

To bring designs up to date, the full front design was tried out on three FEDDs. EHA 290 is shown when first converted and looking stylish.

THE PROSPEROUS 1950s

The 1950s really were the years of major advancements for Midland Red. Mr Sinclair now had 10 years at the helm.

Although wartime rationing was still in place until 1954, some restrictions were lifted earlier. The resurgence of coach travel started in 1948 when new vehicles arrived to help relieve the tired pre-war coaches on the recently re-introduced long-distance coach routes across the country. The classification C1 and C2 (first and second coach type, post-war) was given to forty-five C1s and twelve C2s.

The C1 type was designed with 30 seats, for use on long-distance coach services, tours, excursions and private hire duties. The driver had a separate cab door to gain access to a partitioned cab area. A central sliding entrance door was fitted and the driver's side windscreen was recessed in an effort to avoid reflections.

The C2 type was used to launch the post-war Midland Red Coach Cruise holiday tours and had only 26 seats with more generous leg room. It had an outward opening door and a more balanced frontal appearance, with both windscreens recessed. The driver had access to his cab from the inside gangway. Both types of coach had wind-down passenger windows (a throw back from pre-war designs) and a similar chassis to the S6 bus, but had five-speed overdrive gearboxes fitted. Their bodies were 7′ 6″ wide and were built to the company's design by Duple of Hendon.

After the austerity of wartime, people were eager to partake in leisure travel once again and the Midland Red inclusive coach holiday market benefitted immediately, with strong bookings for almost all of their tours. The Scottish tour programme had always been popular, but post-war, the number of tours and destinations rose to meet ever increasing demands.

Above: C1 coaches were normally used on ordinary scheduled coach services, private hires and excursions, but occasionally they were used on extended tours. Here, a Bearwood-based C1 with its contented holiday passengers pauses for a group photograph outside a Scottish hotel. The driver is sitting in the front row whilst the coach courier is standing extreme right. The lady on the right of the front row was from Allesley, Coventry and this was the second of 20 Midland Red holiday tours she enjoyed into the 1970s. I met this lady at the launch event for my coach holiday programme in the 1990s where she cut the cake (the story is featured in my earlier book Midland Red Influence), and she enjoyed two further Midland Red branded holidays when she was well into her 90s.

The 26-seater C2 touring coach.

S13 fleet number 3899 in its black top dual-purpose livery sits in Coventry Pool Meadow, awaiting its next turn of duty.

To help out with growing coach duties, the company launched the dual-purpose bus: a bus body shell, but fitted out with more comfortable seating and interior trim. The S13 had some bodywork restyling and the driver's seat was open to the passenger saloon rather than being in a separate cab. This type saw the introduction of a coach livery with a gloss black roof, which earned them the nickname 'black tops'. The S13 was the last conventional BMMO bus type built with a separate body and chassis.

A vehicle appeared in the summer of 1951 that was not given an S type designation, but two letters LA meaning Light Alloy. Looking similar to the S13 but with a revised front grille it was easily identified by its bright polished aluminium trim. It was a 44-seat service bus built entirely in-house at Carlyle Works, and was initially used as an experimental vehicle, but later found its way to Cradley Heath garage, then Wellington for monitored operational trials.

When built, it had the BMMO 8-litre engine, but as part of its experimental life was fitted with a small capacity engine, a Leyland 5.75-litre, presumably to keep the weight as low as possible. Then in 1957 it had a year of comparison tests against the new and large BMMO engine of 10.5 litres, after which it settled with its original 8-litre unit.

I have spoken to three drivers who had experience of this vehicle; they thought that maybe the company had gone to extremes with this bus, as they remembered that some stress fracture issues with the framework required attention during its lifetime. It did, however, have a life of over ten years, being withdrawn at the end of 1961. It was felt that much had been learned with the LA type, in preparation for future single-deck designs.

Another of Midland Red's experiments. Nicknamed 'the cattle truck', S13 3919 was not liked by crews or passengers. Its front and rear doors were each opened by a large floor mounted lever in the cab. Perimeter seating and copious standee capacity made this an uncomfortable and unusual vehicle for Midlands travellers. I first became aware of the cattle truck stories from colleagues who had worked on it when it was allocated to Leamington garage during 1952/3.

The push towards lightweight vehicles continued following the S5 prototype at the end of the war. Development engineers, eager to get as light a vehicle as possible, pushed on to test the limits of materials.

The ultra-lightweight LA type sitting in Central Works.

The next company-made vehicle was the D7, and over 300 were produced. The first few were built with 56 seats, but it was quickly realised that they could squeeze in more, so they were upseated to 63. These BMMO 8-litre engined chassis were bodied by Metro Cammell of Birmingham, using Midland Red's bodywork design on the basic frames, similar to those normally used on the MCW Orion body.

Three anonymous vehicles at Central Works. A C1 coach dating from 1949, a new build S14 awaiting its slot in the paint shop and, in the foreground, a new D7 chassis being parked by the standing driver. It would be taken to Metro Cammell at Washwood Heath for bodying.

Middle Left: D7 4423 passing the old Newdigate Colliery yard in Smorrall Lane, whilst operating Bedworth local services which were normally the domain of single-deckers.

Left: The lower saloon interior of a D7.

Above: D7 4499 was fitted with a new single-decker grille for evaluation, although it was thought that this design was more suited to single-deckers.

The experimental department was always up to something new, and D7 4433 was the vehicle chosen to test a BMMO air cooled engine. It proved so noisy in tests that the project was not furthered.

A Leamington garage based LD8, seen at the southern end of the 518 Coventry to Stratford-upon-Avon via Leamington, which was a regular route for the LD8s.

The oversized front grille on this experimental air-cooled engined D7 was intended to provide as much airflow to the engine as possible.

In the early 1950s it was becoming clear that in-house production of vehicles was not keeping up with the post-war increases in demand and the withdrawal of pre-war buses. It was decided to place an order for 100 Leyland Titan PD2 double-deckers with Leyland all-metal bodywork. However, as you would expect, the order stipulated that alterations to the standard model should be included to have the new look BMMO front, with the BMMO front badge fitted near to the radiator filler. The Leyland Titan is one of the world's longest-produced bus chassis, being planned in the mid-1920s and first appearing in 1927. Production ceased in 1970 even though the more modern rear-engined designs had appeared over a decade earlier. Being classed as non-standard to BMMO, they were allocated to specific garages with Digbeth taking a third of those produced, Bearwood 18 and Leamington 15, and the remainder concentrated on western Midlands area garages.

The S14

After many hundreds of hours of testing existing buses with experimental parts fitted, the company was satisfied that it was ready to launch another revolutionary design. Known as the S14, it was a lightweight bus, making it ideal for many of Midland Red's more rural routes, although it was by no means limited to easy work.

Evidence of the makings of a lightweight understructure and body framing. This is to be 4178, the prototype S14.

A number of production S14s were used for further testing. 4565 was used for extensive stress testing at the MIRA test facility at Nuneaton, and is seen here cornering at speed during the testing of suspension units, including the independently sprung front wheels. The driver looks to be having fun!

As with many prototypes, it entered proper service again at Bearwood where it could be easily monitored. After four years' service it was converted to one-man operation and had its seating reduced from 44 to 40. It operated further at Wellington garage and was withdrawn in 1967 having given over 13 years' service.

4178 (THA 778), the prototype S14, sitting in Central Works in later life. Showing Bearwood destination blinds, it could be back at Central Works to be converted to one-man operation. The single-decker on the left is a production version of the S14.

Prototype S14 fleet number 4178 was built early in 1953 and had, fitted from new, the Hobbs automatic three-speed gearbox. It was used by the development department for local testing work and for service tests at Bearwood garage. In mid-1954 it had the automatic gearbox removed and was fitted with the BMMO standard four-speed manual David Brown gearbox.

Testing a new type of bus was always comprehensive. Here, the S14 undergoes further testing at MIRA.

A further similar vehicle (fleet number 4254) was constructed one year after 4178, and the automatic gearbox that had been removed from 4178 was fitted for further testing. This vehicle saw service at Digbeth and Leamington garages. Its gearbox was changed for a manual box in 1961 at Leamington garage. It was withdrawn at the end of 1967.

S14 fleet number 4681 was a Tamworth garage vehicle. It sits in a queue, waiting to turn out of Priory Street after departing from Pool Meadow, Coventry on the rural 789 route back to Tamworth. Superintendent Jack Guest was in conversation with a lady outside the booking office and looks on sternly at the photographer. This historic shot was taken before the ring road carved its way through some of 'old' Coventry. In the distance and about to turn left is one of the rare blue Coventry Transport Daimler Freeline coaches, being used for driver training. Behind the S14 is a rare Lanchester car.

This underside view of the S14 clearly shows one of the four Metalastik rubber suspension units that, in pairs, supported the rear axle. Mounted on the front face of the differential is the handbrake calliper and disc, with some of the monocoque sub-structure above.

The S14 was a revolutionary vehicle and needed extensive testing as it incorporated so many new and advanced features. This was the first type of production vehicle to feature the new rubber suspension designed with, and made by, Metalastik in Leicester. The front wheels had independent suspension and the rear axle was held by just four small rubber units with a diagonal screw tie-bar which, when adjusted, would alter the height of the vehicle.

It had no separate chassis, just like the S5 prototype produced towards the end of WW2, although there had been intermediate testing of vehicles such as the LA type. Some parts were made from glass fibre plastics, including a pioneering one-piece roof that avoided the problem faced by many operators of leaky roofs. Indeed, following the rebuilding work at Central Works, the company introduced an extensive glass fibre department, simply known as 'the plastics shop.'

The destination blind layout was reversed on the S14 as it was intended for one-man operation: the number blind was on the driver's side so he could change both the destination and number blinds without having to leave the cab. It also featured rubber suspension as standard, disc brakes, transmission hand brake, independently sprung front wheels, and only single rear wheels to improve weight and economy. It was designed for the more rural, lightly loaded country services. The bodywork was built at Carlyle Works. The vehicle seated 44 passengers, although some were downseated and given luggage racks and pens of varying sizes when they were later converted or built new for one-man operation. One-man operation was new, and there were experiments with cab designs; some had cab entry via a door at the back of the cab. The first two vehicles were built with a 17′ 6″ wheelbase, but 216 production vehicles followed with a slightly reduced wheelbase of 16′ 5″. This S14 type was very successful; it was economical and reliable, with most examples enjoying a long life.

A Further 98 dual-purpose vehicles were required as the earlier S13 type was ageing, so two batches of S15s were built in 1957 and 1962. They had similar technical specifications to the S14, except they were twin rear-wheeled. The front dome was refined and it had slightly deeper windscreens. There was additional polished trim, especially on the second batch which had aluminium trim above the skirt panels, and this became standard on future models. Hopper windows rather than sliders were used, similar to those on the C5

The black-topped S15 class buses were useful vehicles. They were used on stage carriage work during weekdays, but on weekends they could perform any work required, like private hire, excursions, or as a duplicate vehicle on an express service.

type coach, which stopped draughts and wind noise. A small rear underfloor boot was provided but was rarely used.

These were very attractive and useful vehicles that could be used on stage carriage or longer-distance bus services during the week; they could also perform evening and weekend tours and excursions or support coaches on long-distance services. The seats for this type were to a new 'bucket' design, and the styling was in conjunction with Dunlop Dunlopillo, who suggested in their advertising blurb that the seats of Midland Red's new S15 would suit any weight, girth or bulk!

The S15s were no exception to Midland Red's practice of experimentation. Six had coach seats fitted that had been removed from lightly used C3 coaches. More than seven were fitted with various types of perforated ceiling panels, in preparation for the soundproofing that would be needed in the later C5 coach.

The C5

The C5 family of coaches and their unique development would normally follow here, but this is part of a bigger story, and can be seen in the chapter entitled 'The Revolutionary Motorway Express'.

Mr Sinclair had a dedicated and high-spirited team in the busy experimental and development departments, and it seems that there was no scarcity of ideas. Along with the numerous modifications made to existing vehicles, the introduction of new types evolving from the type before continued. But there were also more revolutionary designs from the experimental engineers, fed through the development department and design office and then onto the production shop floor.

In the last quarter of the 1950s, their sights were set on a new, large-capacity double-decker. At the time, single-deckers had seating for up to 44 passengers, but double-deckers were only seating around a dozen additional passengers due to the legislation for the construction and use of passenger vehicles that set the maximum length and width for buses and coaches. But Midland Red was always pushing the boundaries, arguing that allowing bigger vehicles was perfectly safe.

The busman's dream of home was born

The 1950s was definitely the decade of plenty for Midland Red, when giant steps were taken to put together planned designs and make the best of them. The early 1950s brought advancements in fibreglass bodywork panels, with red pigments added to make painting easier and less frequent.

Lightweight construction incorporating chassisless designs had become the norm. High-quality Metalastik adjustable toggle-link rubber suspension units brought about superior comfort and ride, while providing exceptional long service life. Driver comforts were included, too, with the introduction of semi-automatic gearboxes with two-pedal control. With all of these advances, it was time to build a most advanced double-decker incorporating them all.

As far as larger double-deckers were concerned, before it was even possible legally to build a double-decker longer than 27' 6", there existed on the drawing board plans for a 72-seater back in 1951. Plans were updated over time for the new high-capacity double-decker, and the body shape gradually improved until, in 1958, it became possible to build the prototype of a type to be known as the D9.

The long S8

Sometimes, in the need for change, the boundaries of experimentation seemed to be pushed to extremes. The company was so frustrated that their essential plans could not be put into action that a very strange bus was constructed at Central Works. A retired S8 single-decker, fleet number 3220, was cut and lengthened with wood frames and old body parts to make a bus 45 feet long, which is similar to the current maximum allowed length of 15 metres, nearly forty years later!

This vehicle was driven to the Ministry of Transport offices in Marsham Street, London, with company officials and members of the press on board, and parked up on display to show that such vehicles could travel about safely. In fact it made three return trips via the motorway. Despite having such a long wheelbase, the only place the driver found difficult was an island at the Swan in Yardley, on the outskirts of Birmingham. The company's protests were not in vain, as they likely influenced a subsequent act of parliament that increased the maximum length of buses.

This picture shows that fleet number 3220 was painted in etching primer and had no fleet names or numbers. It is seen here arriving back at Central Works after undergoing tests.

The turbocharged engine being tested, prior to fitting.

It would be the first production BMMO to have power-assisted steering, which was one of Mr Sinclair's claims to fame; the first power steering ram had been supplied on Albion Motors trucks, so its use at BMMO no doubt came about as a result of Sinclair's long relationship with colleagues at Albion where he trained as an apprentice engineer. At the time, power steering on commercial vehicles was rare.

The prototype number 4773 was a rugged-looking bus and a little angular in appearance, using body panel designs from the earlier D7 type.

After tilt testing at the Metro Cammell facility at Washwood Heath, the prototype entered service and was monitored carefully – so carefully that members of the development department became part-time drivers to experience first-hand how it behaved in real-life service. It had a turbocharged engine fitted for a time, and one of the part-time drivers managed to keep to the timetable on a late-night

A power steering ram.

Top Left and Top Right: One of the very early production D9s almost ready for its mechanical units to be fitted.
Bottom Left: Prototype D9 4773 sitting outside the works after retuning from MIRA.
Bottom Right: Production D9s awaiting their turn for completion and painting.

Saturday service out of Birmingham with a record 103 passengers aboard, and he recorded that it pulled away from stops with ease.

The D9 was another of the revolutionary types, and has long been admired by almost everyone who had an involvement with it. It was rare for new vehicle creations to be really special. All in all, it was one of the two very best engineer-designed buses, the other being the London AEC Routemaster. The D9 was nicknamed the 'Birmingham Routemaster' by some, and also earned the title 'a busman's dream of home'. It was packed with advanced features and unlike any bus before it. The type is admired by drivers, conductors, passengers and engineers alike, which is an outstanding achievement.

But this was a bus designed by Midland Red engineers to be reliable and economical for its expected lifetime, and to require minimal engineering work, much of which would be undertaken with semi-skilled workers. It brought together all the tried and tested technological advances that the company had proven since wartime, giving driver comforts, passenger appeal, features and facilities in the right place for conductors, and easy access to mechanical items for the mechanics. This made it a firm all-round favourite.

Both the D9 and the London Transport AEC Routemaster are the pinnacle of good and successful design, with the very best 'look' for a front-engined rear-entrance double-decker.

The D9 was built from 1958 (the prototype), with the last examples coming off the lines in 1966 by which time 345 had been built. The prototype remained the only 'angular' D9; all production

vehicles had very refined, stylish and curved bodywork. Like all Midland Red vehicles, there were considerable advancements and improvements to components, which were included in the various batches as they were built. Early examples had tungsten bulb lighting, and a noticeable improvement in later builds for passengers and conductors was the introduction of fluorescent lighting. Interior lighting was behind illuminated internal advertisement panels. Some vehicles had external advertisement panels that were cleverly illuminated by the interior lower saloon lights, so no additional light fittings were required. However, whilst the advertising and publicity department gained income from them, the rubber gaskets around the slightly raised exterior advertisement panels allowed water ingress which caused some frame corrosion issues in later life.

Like all types of SOS and BMMO-built vehicles, there were hundreds of differences during vehicle lifetimes as experiments were continual, to test new parts for future models and to see how differing parts affected overall performance. D9s, during their build batches, had two slightly different engines, a Mk1 and a Mk2.

The cab of the D9 where the driver could be in a world of his own. George Pittam was a part time bus driver in Hinckley, and had also been a bus driver and coach driver at Leamington and Rugby garages. His later years involved driving 5415 on special occasions whilst acting as TM for WHEELS / Midland Red Coaches.

Three D9s had an accumulator power brake fitted for experimental purposes, including an early 49xx and 5368 – as expected with such a trial, all were Birmingham-based. The accumulator power brake was later to be fitted to the CM6 motorway coaches. Most who are familiar with D9s will remember that early examples had a matt-white upper-deck ceiling. In an attempt to combat the yellow staining caused by nicotine from smoking that was allowed upstairs in those days, the company experimented with International Pinch and Johnson to produce a paint that would be protected from the effects of nicotine. Newer D9s and future double-deckers benefitted from this new pink hue.

An advertless and untidy D9 recently fitted with non-opening windows after suffering from front dome fatigue, sits in Coventry Pool Meadow ready for its 1hr 40min 658 journey to Leicester.

The D9's pink ceiling.

It seems an incredible figure, but, between 1951 and 1963, almost two-thirds of Midland Red's fleet of buses and coaches had one or more experimental items fitted for evaluation. These included brake components that were checked for wear, and experimental suspension. The merits of air brakes were checked out, and air suspension was compared to their favoured rubber suspension.

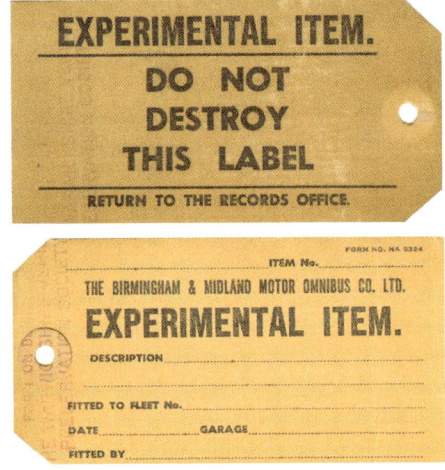

New engine types were installed in various models to assess their fuel consumption and component wear. Engines fitted with turbochargers were compared to those naturally aspirated. They investigated how other makes of engines performed in their own make of buses. They even checked out how their own BMMO engines performed in other makes of buses, like the DD11 5261, which had an upright 10.5-litre engine fitted as soon as it was delivered new, and ran with it for a six-year trial.

A bus before its time

During 1959-60, the incredible D10 arrived. This was another BMMO vehicle that shocked the bus industry, as this design of underfloor-engined double-decker had not previously been successfully exploited by mainstream manufacturers due to the engineering difficulties in maintaining legal minimum dimensions of road clearance, and upper and lower saloon gangway heights, as stated in the Ministry of Transport Construction and Use Regulations of the time. Midland Red accomplished this with 8″ to spare!

Creating the two D10 vehicles was a considerable achievement in placing the engine under the lower deck floor whilst maintaining stipulated gangway heights and keeping the overall height of the vehicle within legal dimensions. 4944, the second D10, is seen about to have its radiator fitted and the short-lived rear exit doorway installed, along with the small side window which is leant up against the rear wheel.

While the D10s used many D9 body components, there were cost challenges on the engineering side. The company was fully committed with D9 production, so the sanction of more expenditure on the D10 was not forthcoming. This was in the years before one-man operation was even legal for double-deck buses, but with the benefit of hindsight, the D10 could have been a long-term double-deck solution.

Years later, after the two D10 prototypes had enjoyed normal length operating lives and were withdrawn, one, the first built, was thankfully saved and preserved. During its retirement, it was inspected by Volvo engineers, who later brought out their own underfloor-engined model, which they called D10M! Leyland also brought a Lion model into more limited production, but other established makes and models remained rear-engined.

Changing fortunes

In post-war years, Midland Red did not supply vehicles to other associated BET operators as they had done in the 1920s and 1930s, but there were plans in the early 1960s suggesting things might change. S15 buses were involved in trials with Maidstone and District and Northern General, but this was right at the start of the staff shortages caused by quite a number of Midland Red workers migrating to The Austin to work on their new 1100 and 1300 production tracks. This resulted in Midland Red having ongoing difficulties, not only with shortages of platform staff, but also with vehicle building and maintenance staff, making it, at times, challenging just to maintain their own fleet. It was also at this time that financial pressures started to show as social trends changed. People stayed at home to watch their newly acquired television sets and didn't go to the cinema and theatre as often, and the family car became popular, meaning shopping could be more conveniently carried home rather than having to wait for the bus.

Fortunately it would be a few more years before decline would hit leisure traffic to a serious degree. Days out by coach were a very social affair, where friends would often meet up for a trip to the seaside. Coach cruise holidays were still very popular, and long queues outside booking offices were an annual occurrence as soon as word got out that the new Midland Red holiday brochure was available.

Coaches masquerade

The earlier C2 coaches from 1950, used for the company's prestige coach cruise holidays, were now over 10 years old, and the C3 coaches from 1953/4 had worked hard on excursions, private hire and express coach services for approaching 10 years. So it was decided to update the coachwork on some vehicles of each type to give them a more modern look. Some C2 coaches had new chrome surrounds fitted to the radiator grille, there were new wrap-around bumpers, and the large wheel arch valances that were previously black were painted red.

However, three C2s and seventeen C3s were rebodied for the 1962/3 touring season. They were treated to chassis refurbishments at Central Works and then taken to Plaxton's Scarborough factory to have new coachwork fitted, to give them more working years. The C2s, being just 7′ 6″ wide, were particularly useful on some of the northern Scottish coach cruises. Their new classifications when rebodied were CL2 and CL3.

Nearside and offside views of the same D10.

In an effort to convince passengers that they had a new coach fleet for the season, a new ivory livery with small red scripted fleet names was chosen. The company publicity announced that they had a new fleet of coaches, especially designed and built for the coach cruises and introduced for the 1962 season! They were really refurbished 12-year-old coach chassis, given a modified, off-the-peg, existing Plaxton-designed coach body that was described as having special emphasis on spacious seating and viewing, providing luxurious comfort and pleasure! But it was certainly the livery that captured all of the attention – even regular passengers didn't immediately notice that the coach had the same or similar registration as their tour coach last year! This ivory livery had some unintended consequences, as Harry Roake, a coach cruise driver, told me when he arrived at the prestigious Hydro Hotel in Pitlochry; when he pulled up outside the entrance and announced his arrival to reception staff they said that their accommodation was for Midland Red customers and "*that* is not a Midland Red coach!" He did eventually convince them, and all went well with the holiday, but the passengers were still unhappy with a Midland Red coach that wasn't red – and they made it clear when they reported the facts of their holiday to the coach cruise department in Bearwood upon their return. Obviously many had complained, as both the CL2s and the CL3s were withdrawn over the following winter and painted properly for the next season; it was only a slightly revised livery with an ivory waist rail band, but it *was* predominantly red.

They continued to give a 17 to 21-year service life with Midland Red, by which time they had been repainted many times in standard all-over red body, with successive changes of roof colour through black, maroon and then all-over red. Many went on to a third life for an additional three or four years with private owners. It is incredible that CL2 3352 is still with us, having spent six years with two private operators, then a jazz band in

Coach Driver Percy Taylor was a comical and well-liked Midland Red driver, based at Sandacre Street, Leicester for many years. He is now remembered in a book by his daughter, Susan Briers, called Percy's Bus, which documents his life, including his time driving in wartime. Percy stands on his wooden step alongside CL3 4190 at Leicester in July 1964, characteristically with his high trouser waistband and always with a cigarette!

Yorkshire, before being rescued and undergoing a total chassis and body rebuild in recent times by the committed enthusiast Andy Bishop. As I write this, the refurbished engine is due to be refitted, and this fine example should soon be available to see, adding yet another type to the growing list of rebuilt Midland Red vehicles.

Top: CL2 3352 stands in the entrance drive to Tamworth's Aldergate garage in 1970, with its short-lived maroon livery. The next change of livery was all-over red – another economy drive to save on labour time in the masking up stage. All vehicles could then be painted the same.

Above: After the unpopular ivory colour of the CL2 and CL3 coaches upon delivery which brought dozens of letters of complaint, the coaches all returned to Central Works when the season was over, where they received a more traditional Midland Red coach livery of red and black. But someone at the top still insisted that a bit of that ivory livery remained – as just a waistband. Two years later, the ivory band was reduced, to show just beneath the side windows only.

Middle Right: The interior of a CL3, showing the BMMO winged crest on the headrest covers.

Bottom Right: The driver's cab area of a CL3.

Going down market

After Walter Womar arrived in 1966 he eventually made some unpopular changes that would alter the look of the fleet. He decided that the black roofs of coaches and dual-purpose vehicles looked too 'funereal'. A red repaint of the roofs would make them too similar to the company's buses, so another colour was required. An old foreman working in the vicinity of the paint shop recalled that, before the war, a maroon colour was used on coaches and there was an old barrel of it in an outbuilding. More supplies of a similar colour was ordered from International Pinch and Johnson of Hockley, Birmingham and, as repaints became due, the coaches and dual-purpose vehicles had their roofs painted accordingly

Left: Showing off its smart traditional coach livery is Evesham garage based C3 4232 on a private hire, seen on the A5 near Bletchley.

Right: A coach cruise holiday in Scotland with a Leicester Sandacre garage C4 coach in 1965. The coach is standing at the front of the hotel and it is thought that the grey-suited gentleman next to the driver is the hotelier.

Production at full stretch

Bus production was instigated by sanction from the company directors, who would give authority for financial backing for the furtherance of designs into manufacture of not just each type of bus or coach, but also for each allocated batch of buses built. Not every design progressed to the production stage. Some were detailed drawings, others were ideas taken as far as the prototype stage and then 'stored' until the time was right to put a number of ideas together in a new type of vehicle, as happened with the D10. This meant that, on odd occasions, vehicles that had been assigned a type identity ended up being built/delivered out of sequence. Such an oddity was the single vehicle coded the S19.

This vehicle had many features of the later S17 type: a new larger 10.5-litre engine, semi-automatic gears, and bodywork with 52 bus seats. The S19 was used to try out more features that were planned for future models, including skylights – a feature introduced on the later types S21, S22 and S23. But the S19 was unusual in that it incorporated a 'beam' type front axle, which by Midland Red standards was somewhat old fashioned, but there were thoughts of it featuring in a future rear-engined design that was on the drawing board. The front beam axle also had suspension that was usually used on the rear axle of single-decker buses, rather than the independent front suspension that had been used for nearly ten years by this time.

This S19 vehicle was constructed in early 1963 and used for a year by the experimental department before working at Digbeth, Dudley, Shrewsbury and Worcester garages. This interesting bus gave 12 years of quite ordinary service, although, especially in its first year, it gave the development department time to assess the compatibility and behaviour of its axle and rubber suspension combination.

To an untrained eye this could easily be confused with an S17, as it was outwardly very similar. S19 fleet number 5093 is seen parked at MIRA awaiting its allocated time for testing the front axle and rubber suspension combination.

The interior view of the S19, looking forward, showing two of the three skylights fitted. Note that at this time there was no requirement for a side emergency exit window.

The innovative Midland Red engineers were continually in search of 'the perfect omnibus', a phrase first coined by Mr Wyndham Shire many years earlier. The first experiments with a rear-engined vehicle were in 1935 with the REC, but it really was ahead of its time. There were further flights of fancy with rear-engined vehicles in the 1960s, at a time when low-floor vehicles were attracting the attention of designers, and a rear-mounted engine was an obvious advantage. Leyland and AEC had brought out the rear-engined Panther, Swift and Merlin chassis, but they had various issues that made them relatively unsuccessful.

After the REC, Midland Red's first post-war attempt at a rear-engine design was during the winter of 1961/2 and involved little more than fitting an engine and gearbox at the back of a BMMO S16 subframe, and then running balance and weight distribution tests. There was another try in the second half of the 1960s, when there had been a resurgence of interest in low-floor single-decker designs, but this didn't progress further than a drawing board exercise with a short-lived designation type of S26.

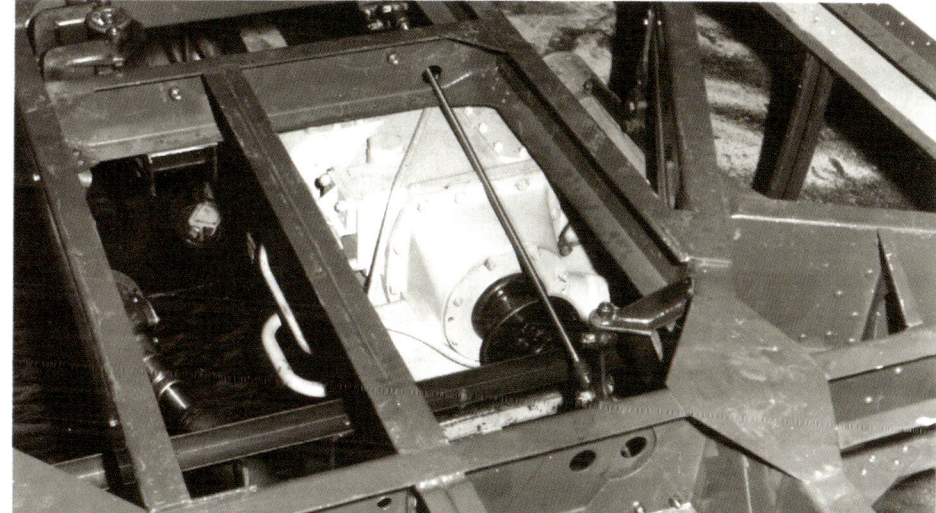

Top: A view underneath the temporary fitment of a D10 engine into the rear frame area of an S16 subframe to undertake stress, weight and balance tests in-house at Central Works. The experiments lasted one week after which the rear engine was removed and the vehicle completed as an S16.

Middle: A further experiment in 1962 looking from above, with a close-coupled gearbox fitted.

Bottom: It was proposed that a production version of this D10 engine would have been used as the power unit for the planned rear-engined single-decker.

That the company were experimenting and planning the introduction of new rear-engined single-deckers must have heightened the enthusiasm of production staff and engineers. But, as with the rear-engined REC experiments in the 1930s, the plan was not to be. This time, though, in the mid to late sixties, when this would no doubt have been furthered, it wasn't war

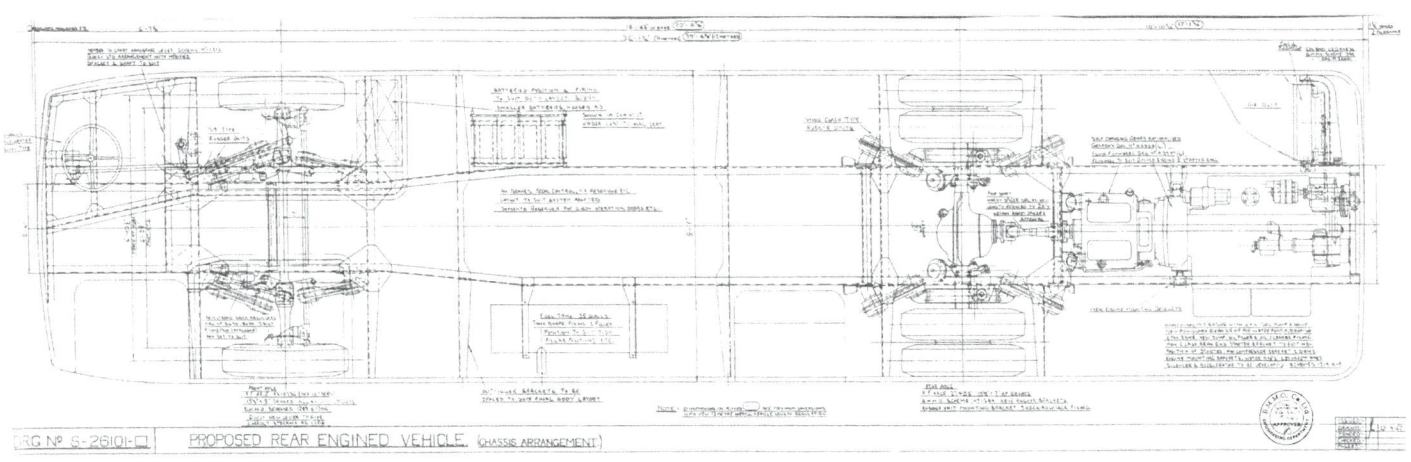

that stopped its progress, it was external forces that had other ideas on a new rear-engined mass-produced bus, built by another manufacturer.

Moving on after the S19, the next type, built in two batches, was a single-deck bus called the S16. It was built to the new larger dimensions of 36′ long and 8′ 2½″ wide, and had the small 8-litre engine and manual gearbox that was used in the earlier types. It was generally considered underpowered, although engineers were probably using up stocks of engines and gearboxes that they were committed to, whilst the company wanted to build buses to the maximum permitted size as soon as possible.

The earliest known picture of fleet number 5095, an S16, is this shot at Central Works. Note the absence of its aluminium skirt trim. It was the first built S16, but the second by fleet number.

Facing page, top left: A front view taken two days later, in February 1962, whilst being tested. It now has its aluminium skirt trim fitted.

Fleet number 5095 is seen at Metro Cammell's Washwood Heath factory where BMMO had use of the weighbridge and tilt table for 'type approval' tests.

An S16 fleet number 5537 from the second identical 1964 batch, seen in 1974 at Leamington garage, where Driver Timothy O'Connor was demonstrating gear changing techniques to a group of visitors.

S17 fleet number 5757 in summer 1970 awaits departure on the pleasant rural 588 route towards Leamington. The following year this bus would return to Central Works for overhaul and recertification, at the same time being upseated to 52 from its original one-man operated specification of 44 seats and luggage pens.

in Construction and Use Regulations regarding items like the means of escape from buses in an emergency. This resulted in three variations of bodywork, with the first batch having the entrance door at the front and standard BMMO emergency door at the centre rear. The next batch had an additional hinged emergency window half way along the offside, replacing one of the slider windows. Then later vehicles had the emergency window moved to the front offside passenger window immediately behind the driver's cab.

Below: S17 5557 with central offside emergency window.

Below: 5736 showing its front offside emergency window.

But this was soon followed by the S17, which really was a nice vehicle, well balanced, powerful and popular with most drivers. It had a similar body shell to the S16, but had a new horizontal 10.5-litre engine coupled to a semi-automatic gearbox, giving the benefit of two-pedal control and reduced driver fatigue. The gear selector switch was attached to a new-style dashboard unit moulded in fibreglass that could be seen under the steering wheel, and this was an easy identification of the type.

During the long production run of S17s, there were additional changes

S17s were converted to one-man operation and there were a number of evolving layouts, with seating for 44, 48 and 52. There were also changing layouts of luggage pens at the front offside and nearside, handed down from the days when the company carried parcel traffic and newspapers on rural services. Most S17s later settled on 52 seater one-man operated buses with no additional luggage pens.

With Central Works working as hard as it could to provide new vehicles and overhaul and maintain the existing fleet, there was still a requirement for more vehicles. In 1962, orders were placed with Leyland for 100 Leopard models (LS18s), 20 of which were delivered as dual-purpose vehicles bodied by Willowbrook with seats not dissimilar to those fitted in the S15s, and the remainder bodied as buses by Weymann. They were built to accepted BET designs. Post-war Midland Red-built single-deckers were not fitted with BMMO front badges, yet these bought-in Leylands were!

LS18 5147 waiting for its departure time for Galley Common. Nuneaton garage had an allocation of eleven of the first dozen LS18s delivered. Just visible is the BMMO badge above the registration plate.

The first S17s were built as 52 seaters for two-man operation. As approval for more widespread one-man operation was gained, S17s were called back to Central Works for conversion work. The first well-executed conversions were where seating was reduced to 44 passengers with two luggage pens, one either side of the gangway. The one on the driver's side was low-fronted and ideal for pushchairs, and the nearside was high-sided and intended for the carriage of parcels and newspapers. Other conversions had 48 seats and just the driver's side luggage pen. In later years they were used with a full compliment of 52 seats and no pens.

S17 5703 had a new, cumbersome and ugly set of seats when new which were considered for later vehicles. Thankfully this design was not furthered.

The cab of the LS18. These were cold underfoot due to their metal chequer plate floor. With their low steering wheel they were noted for having heavy steering compared to other types. The characteristic large early Leopard semi-automatic Pneumocyclic gear change pedestal can be clearly seen.

The CM6 and CM6T coaches and their exciting story would normally follow on here in the chronology of vehicle production, but due to the importance of the motorway coach development and operation it is told as part of a bigger story in the chapter entitled 'The Revolutionary Motorway Express.'

In the early sixties, with many early post-war buses being withdrawn at the end of their lives, the need for new buses necessitated buying vehicles from outside manufacturers, as Central Works was fully committed to building D9s, CM6s and S17s at the time. Evaluation of the Leyland Atlantean was carried out, and 398 JTB, one of the Leyland demonstrator buses, was tested along with the D9. "It was found to be austere, with a hard, metallic interior finish, and a poorer ride than a D9", said a Midland Red engineer.

After trials with a local chassis builder, an order was placed for Coventry-built Daimler Fleetline chassis to be fitted with bodies built by Walter Alexander of Falkirk. These of course had to have a dash

The fifty Daimler Fleetline vehicles with Alexander bodywork classified DD11 were supplied from March 1963.

of Midland Red tradition and were ordered with non-standard upper- and lower-deck screens, which were flat glass (for cheaper replacement costs). This DD11 class was delivered in 1963 and seated 77 passengers.

Further purchases of similar types were made in 1966 for DD12s, again with seating for 77 passengers. The DD12 did not feature opening front upper-deck windows, and by 1966 exterior side illuminated advertising panels had fallen out of fashion.

Two final batches of double-deckers arrived, the first in 1969 followed by the second batch in 1970 and 1971; these were known as DD13s. The second batch was built to a slightly more modern design, but still retained the flat windscreens that were always preferred by Midland Red. They had 75 seats and centre exit doors (which were little used over their lifetime). The vehicles were converted for one-man operation as soon as the necessity arose, after the operation of one-man operated double-deckers became legally possible in 1966.

In the mid 1960s the coaching fleet was in need of some modernisation. Much private hire work and coach services were being provided by an ageing fleet. Even some C1 coaches from 1948/9 were still busy. Onwards from 1967, Leyland coaches dominated the non-motorway coach fleet. The first type received, classified LC7, was a 49-seater with a body provided by Duple.

The DD12 type, of which 149 were supplied from mid 1966 were similar to the DD11 class but did not have the upper deck front hopper opening windows.

The LC7 on Hagley Road, Birmingham.

The 103 DD13 vehicles were delivered in two batches from 1969. They had rubber gasket mounted front windows and a rarely used centre exit doorway.

An LS20 operating an express service, arriving at Victoria Coach Station, London.

Its forced ventilation system was inadequate, and large glass windows made for uncomfortable travel, especially if boarding a coach that had been sitting in the sun. From the driver's perspective, the low-positioned steering wheel exaggerated their generally heavy feel.

The next arrivals were more bought-in vehicles. They arrived in 1967, this time a batch of 10 Leyland Leopards with a BET design of Willowbrook dual-purpose bodywork designated as type LS20. They were built as 49-seaters and intended for long-distance stage carriage services.

Just one smaller 30′ Leyland Leopard was bought to assist the coach cruise holiday traffic, designated LC8 with Plaxton coachwork. This vehicle had a manual gearbox, but with a two-speed back axle. It had only 36 seats with generous leg room. It spent most of its life based at the Leicester garages, but when new saw a few months service at Sutton Coldfield and Digbeth. It had a long life and was 19 years old when withdrawn.

It wasn't long before a batch of Leyland LC9 type coaches were added to the fleet. These were used to replace older touring coaches and were often seen on express services. Some of them were later converted to tow vehicles – and they certainly were fast tow wagons! I speak with experience, as I was towed, following a breakdown, with a Daimler double-decker from Bedworth to Nuneaton garage

Left: The solitary LC8 delicenced over winter and travelling on 'trade plates' takes a rest in Coventry.
*Above and Right: The LC9 coaches, new in 1966 with 36 seats, were updated to 40 in 1973. After their coaching days were over, a number were converted in 1978 to recovery vehicles where some gave almost **another** twenty years of service!*

by Nuneaton engineer Jim Newbold. It was an experience I did not want to repeat: a dark night, limited visibility, with a large tow truck just six feet in front, being towed at speeds far in excess of those that the double-decker would manage under its own power!

The buying in of increased numbers of vehicles signified the sad phasing out of BMMO bus production, but there were a few short years of new production left.

During the production of the S17 type, three vehicles were built, classified the S21a type, and although these were essentially S17s, they had experimental interior styles whilst planning was underway for the new type S21. Each of the three had 48 high-backed seats, and individual interior colour schemes to test passengers' reactions. They were delivered in the smart coach/dual-purpose livery of red with a black roof. Fleet number 5722 had fawn with grey seating, and worked from Hereford initially, then Lichfield garage. Fleet number 5723 used a black, fawn, primrose and grey scheme, and operated from Lichfield initially, then was allocated to Leicester Southgate Street garage; it had supplementary ventilation provided by roof scoops and fans with outlets in the underside of luggage racks. Fleet number 5724 had a grey interior colour with deep blue seating and was allocated to Leicester Southgate Street garage and then Hereford. All were trialled on longer services like the X91 Leicester to Hereford service, and after testing and passenger feedback were considered, the interior colours from 5724 were chosen for the production S21s.

One of the three 'confused' S17s: 5722, 5723 and 5724. First known as S21a then reclassified S22, and finally S17. Here 5723 is shown in its later years when it had standard S17 seating fitted.

All three vehicles were later classified S22 as they were deemed better suited to the long-distance bus routes of the S22 production vehicles, rather than being used on coach duties like the production S21 type. In their later years they were reseated using S17 bus seats, and the seating capacity rose to match the normal S17 number of 52 passengers, and they were again reclassified simply as S17. They were an interesting addition to the S17 type and had an operational life of almost 12 years, albeit with a confused identity.

The remaining types of BMMO vehicle production were single-deckers, all based on the mechanical specification of the S17. Their bodywork framing, however, was similar to that used for the CM6 motorway coaches, having six-bay construction with slightly larger window spacings.

Brand new and out of the box S21 5854 awaiting licencing at Leicester Sandacre garage at the end of April 1967.

Two examples of maroon topped S21s. Top: Fleet number 5864 is an Evesham based vehicle on a multi-vehicle private hire job. Bottom: A rear view of 5850 parked amidst a colourful collection of vehicles in London.

The interior of the S21. Seats were covered in a material known as Ambla, made by ICI, which was durable and easy-clean like the rest of the interior – however on very hot days passengers would stick to the seats!

In 1967, 30 semi-coach S21 vehicles were constructed in Central Works. They were slightly heavier as they had coach interiors and larger high-backed coach seats. Their frontal appearance was readily distinguished by their small number blind and the large, full-width, polished aluminium radiator grille. They had a rear luggage boot and forced air ventilation with individual passenger vents. The rear emergency door of the previous S17 type gave way to a new nearside top-hinged emergency window and an emergency door at the offside rear.

The S21s were constructed from new as two-man operated vehicles when used on service work, but were slowly converted to one-man operation from late 1970 through 1971.

The S22 type was planned for use on the company's long-distance limited-stop bus services, such as the X93-96 Shrewsbury, Wellington, Birmingham, Coventry, Northampton.

A noticeable change made to the S22 was a revised front grill, not dissimilar to the shape of the D9 grille. The small number blinds were retained and additional flip-over signs could be shown when working limited stop services. These were built as one-man operated vehicles, and had large luggage pens behind the driver's cab, and a luggage boot at the rear, although this was panelled over in later years. Midland Red still had considerable parcel traffic over the routes these vehicles operated. The luggage pen reduced seating to 45, but the seats were very comfortable, being individual bucket seats with high backs but without headrests, instead having a top handrail. Forced air ventilation was also provided to each seat. Thirty-seven were built in-house. They operated reliably on Midland Red's 'X' limited stop services and on private hires. They were even known to operate tours and excursions, and I have operated many miles of railway replacement services with them.

An S22 on the M1 at the M18 interchange whilst on a private hire to Leeds and Hull in 1979. The bus was accommodated overnight, washed, oiled and watered by East Yorkshire, a sister company of Midland Red, at their Anlaby Road garage in Hull.

The warm, inviting and comfortable interior of the S22. They had 45 bucket style seats and a large luggage pen.

A company photograph taken in May 1968 of S22 fleet number 5899 sitting when new next to the reservoir at Central Works. It would be allocated to Digbeth from June 1968 where it remained until the takeover of Birmingham area services by West Midlands PTE, when it transferred to them.

Fleet number 5901 is a vehicle close to my heart, having owned it for several years. During my ownership it returned to Central Works to have its rear suspension units replaced, where it was welcomed by remaining BMMO trained staff as the return of a BMMO vehicle to its place of creation. It is shown here at Worcester Racecourse at the First/Midland Red West event to celebrate 100 years of the 144 route.

Vehicles 5879 to 5900 were delivered new in red and maroon livery, and 5901 to 5915 were delivered all red in another livery change, made for economic reasons. Some vehicles had their small number blinds enlarged upon overhaul. The S22 class as a whole gave around 12 years of service.

The next type of single-decker was built under a proverbial cloud of uncertainty, which lasted, on and off, for the remaining years of Central Works' existence.

It was a time of significant change. The recent difficult process of nationalisation was taking hold, and uncertainty about the future role of Central Works was in everyone's mind, as they knew the S23 would be the final type of BMMO vehicle. Buying new materials and parts was difficult as suppliers were understandably cautious that their longstanding customer, Midland Red, would no longer be

Part finished S23 buses line the works' driveway.

The last S23 completed entirely at BMMO's Central Works, fleet number 5941.

A small celebration of workers at all levels involved in the production of the very last S23 fleet number 5991, one of the vehicles (5942 to 5991) sent out to Plaxton of Scarborough for completion.

Fleet number 5991 in later life, sitting in Worcester Padmore Street garage yard, awaiting its driver for its next tour of duty on service 373 to Gloucester.

During the lifetime of the S23 type there were occasions where spare parts were not easy to obtain and modifications had to be made. Here, in 1978, fleet number 5987 allocated to Wellington garage has had replacement windscreens mounted in rubber gaskets rather than in their original metal frames.

building new vehicles. New management was looking further ahead in what would be a fight for survival. Fortunately, the S23 was a basic service bus, and its frames, mechanical units and body parts were all very similar to the single-deck types built for the last seven years or so, so it would just be a matter of looking around and using up stock from the stores. Indeed, some S23s had reconditioned engine parts fitted when built, pending new stock arriving, but these were changed for new later.

Seventy-six S23s were built during 1969 and 1970, and the first 26, fleet numbers 5916 to 5941, were built entirely at Central Works. But there were difficulties with production workers leaving, fearing they were soon to lose their jobs or be offered perhaps less attractive repair roles. This meant that the remaining 50 had their subframes and body structure built at Central Works, but then had to be completed (fitted out and trimmed) by Plaxton of Scarborough. This brought to an end an extremely important part of BMMO history. Since 1923 BMMO had designed, built, tested and operated the majority of its home-made vehicles.

Living up to the old Midland Red tenet, that their vehicles should be light, fast, economical and reliable, the S23, like all other types gave a normal lifetime of around 10 years service. Of course, they would have gone on to give more years, but the pressure was on, and the lack of BMMO parts for overhauls meant that upon expiry of the second issue of their Certificates of Fitness, their time was done.

As the last years of BMMO's operations approached, their vehicle allocation was concentrated at certain garages. Towards the end, if a garage had just one remaining BMMO vehicle it could easily find its way to a garage where familiar company could be kept. The garages that were still operating an appreciable number of single-decker BMMOs were Rugby, Leamington and especially Nuneaton; these were the garages most likely to be holding the last of the spare parts and could keep the vehicles going. Double-decker BMMOs (notably the D9) and their crews were latterly concentrated at Leicester, and the final thirteen D9s were used on the Scraptoft New Parks routes. The last day of D9 service was 31 December 1979, when the six last remaining D9s were all busy earning. The last vehicle to return to the garage that night was 5314, arriving just before midnight.

Midland Red's last bus was built in 1970. Its fleet did not include own-built vehicles after 1981, apart from two withdrawn vehicles, the last S23 fleet number 5991 and one D9 fleet number 5399. Upon the big Midland Red split in 1981, these vehicles were retained in the ownership of Midland Red Omnibus Company and kept at Central Works. In a surprise move, 5399 was loaned to Midland Red North at Cannock and operated a special summer X92 Sunday service for two seasons. In 1984 it was loaned to Transport Museum Wythall, then in October 1992 it transferred there permanently, along with 5991.

If a BMMO suffered a major unit failure in its last couple of years of planned life, it could well have reached its end. But not always: I remember at Nuneaton garage we had a few withdrawn vehicles parked on the patch at the back of the garage, and over a period of time you would see headlights disappear, a driver's seat, the odd panel, a window, a gearbox, etc, all to keep other vehicles going for as long as they could.

Some vehicles aged better than others. In some vehicles there was movement in the windscreens and there was a danger that they could shatter over the driver, so front windscreens were occasionally replaced without their metal frame, and just mounted in rubber gaskets that helped cushion the glass. I experienced such an incident when driving S23 fleet number 5961 between Nuneaton and Bedworth. After leaving Hill Top the route traversed a rural section of road leading to Griff. The road known locally as Griff Hollows went over a waterway at its lowest point before climbing again towards Griff House, a property significant in George Eliot's novels.

This stretch of open road was ideal for stretching the vehicles legs, and where the road passed over the waterways of Griff Brook and the Coventry Canal (Griff Arm) a pronounced 'bounce' was felt. However, this particular day, there was a loud bang and the driver's side windscreen shattered into what seemed a million pieces. This was a very hot summers day and I was driving in an open-necked shirt which was suddenly full of glass. Amazingly, I sustained no serious cuts, just a shock to the system. My first thought was that it could have been a thrown brick, as we'd had previous such incidents on this road which runs alongside a designated travellers' site. But with no signs of debris apart from glass, it was clearly the sudden bounce that was the cause. A quick return to garage for a bus change (for the driver and passengers) and then it was 'service as usual' for the rest of the four hour shift on Bedworth locals.

The longer the remaining time on the vehicle's Certificate of Fitness, the more likely it would be that it would be kept going. This wasn't always with the knowledge of Central Works or other senior engineers, but was down to the enthusiasm of the local superintendent, foremen and engineers. The company's old watch words – simple, fast, light and reliable – were undeniable towards the end. Drivers enjoyed putting them through their paces, and even the baddies admitted they couldn't break a BMMO!

A withdrawn and cannibalised S17 type (fleet number 5610) sits out its last days at Nuneaton garage.

The vehicles received excellent care overall, with Midland Red being well known for using quality lubricants that were checked and topped-up every night. There were also four-weekly safety inspections, and brake adjustments as and when required. The day before their withdrawal, these faithful old machines behaved just as well on the road as they did on their first day out of the factory – even though they perhaps did not look quite as pristine as they did a few months or years before. I took these final vehicles on private hire and contract services, regular weekly railway replacement services, limited-stop routes, and regular bus routes, right up until they were taken from us. Most were sent to scrapyards for cutting up and recycling – who knows, there may be BMMO recycled metal in our modern-day vehicles or appliances.

The sad scene in a scrapyard in the West Midlands, showing examples of the last of the BMMO breed of vehicles.

LC10s were shorter coaches, bought in predominantly for the small roads on some of the Scottish tours. The Plaxton bodywork was to the new Elite model design. This size of coach would have had 36 seats, giving leg room of a generous proportion that was expected by the coach tour customer. However, influence was now being felt, and whether from competition or from National Bus diktats, the LC10 was fitted with 40 seats.

The next batch of coaches were LC11s: standard coaches for express work, excursions and private hire. Whether these were a cancelled order, or made up from old stock parts that were bought cheaper is not known, but they had an older design of Plaxton bodywork based on the Panorama model, and they had 49 coach seats.

The final coaches delivered new in proper Midland Red livery were of the LC12 type, again with Plaxton bodywork, and again the shorter model to ensure provision of suitable coaches for their coach tour programme. These were very similar to the LC10 model. Many of these passed to Midland Red Express Ltd and then had a further life with independent operators.

The LC10 Leyland Leopard with Plaxton 36 seat coachwork, originally destined for use on Scottish tours where narrow roads dictated the use of smaller vehicles. They were however later upseated to 40 and on occasions used on ordinary coach services, this time seen on a duplicate to the Birmingham to London 'G' stopping service which is about to depart from Coventry.

An LC11 Leyland Plaxton coach on a corporate private hire duty taking passengers to Coventry Cathedral. The coach is resting at Coventry Pool Meadow bus station.

Midland Red

A 'NATIONAL' IDENTITY CRISIS

The shares of the British Electric Traction Company had been sold to the Government's National Bus Company, despite valiant protests by Midland Red. These protests carried on even after the deal had been done – a bit of an embarrassment for J. W. Womar, the general manager. He finished his days working in an office at the back of NBC headquarters in Buckingham Palace Road, London.

D9 4868 went to London in a coordinated protest with other BET subsidiaries, bedecked in posters, to sit outside the Marsham Street offices of the Ministry of Transport. Local service buses also carried side adverts against Nationalisation.

Much to NBC's embarrassment, Midland Red's landmark coaches, the CM6Ts, were running up and down the M1 motorway and through London to Victoria Coach Station multiple times a day – no wonder National Bus didn't want the CM6s on the motorway!

These were uncertain times for a proud organisation like Midland Red and, as we all know, the identity of most of the old BET bus companies that the National Bus Company recently took over was washed away in a coat of white paint for all coaches.

Buses were changing too, with a new livery of corporate poppy red (mainly from BET-originating companies) or leaf green (mainly from the Tilling group). In a sense, Midland Red remained red, but of a more orangey hue. The last of the BMMO S23s even had to be finished by Plaxton of Scarborough due to staff shortages and the general winding down of their building activities. This allowed Central Works to prioritise existing staff for maintenance and other projects. Midland Red didn't want to standardise their bus fleet on the new upcoming Leyland and National Bus Company joint project that was the Leyland National bus. They decided to circumvent the system in order to reduce the number of Leyland Nationals being forced upon them, and purchased many more traditional dual-purpose vehicles from Leyland, with bodies to the same basic BET design but built by Willowbrook of Loughborough and Marshall of Cambridge. These formed the classes S24, S26, S27 and S28.

Midland Red bought many traditional Leyland Leopard vehicles in an effort to prove that they didn't need so many Leyland Nationals. S28 fleet number 331, a Worcester based vehicle, shows the BET designed dual-purpose bodywork that was common to S24, S26, S27 and S28 types.

Midland Red, though, did get their first Leyland National delivered in proper Midland Red colours. Traditional fleet numbers were now gone too, and the Leyland Nationals started at 101, which had the old-style gold Midland Red underlined fleet name. The rest were delivered with corporate insignia in poppy red. The era of enterprise, passion and independence had gone!

Fleet number 101 has enjoyed probably the most 'celebrity' life of any Midland Red Leyland National. It made visits to various locations in its original livery, attended the Midland Red 100 Celebrations in 2004 at the Black Country Museum, and is now preserved.

The first Midland Red Leyland National number 101. The only one to be delivered in original Midland Red livery. All future Leyland Nationals were delivered in corporate poppy red.

But the early 1970s was an interesting period, and sometimes humorous in many ways to an avid internal observer, as each attempt at control was stubbornly batted away by Midland Red.

The steady uptake of corporate livery took a long time, and some buses would come back from Central Works' paint shop with corporate body and Midland Red wheel colours, a corporate paint scheme and old-style Midland Red transfers, or other strange combinations.

A rather scruffy vehicle was transferred from Stafford garage to finish off its last months in service at Leamington garage, but Mr French, the long-serving and proud garage engineering superintendent, did not have scruffy vehicles at *his* garage! Still, his request for a repaint at Central Works was turned down. Stubbornly, Mr French refused to let it out on regular service until it was painted, so he instructed his bodyman 'Root' Fletcher to go into the boiler room, fetch some paint and set to work painting it in the garage. This was done, and the bus entered service with a fresh coat, but with tell-tale traces of its earlier life. Although it was in poppy red it had its old-style fleet name transfers. Leamington did not have any old-style fleet names in the stores, so he cleverly masked around them before painting, so the old-style Midland Red fleet names were on show until the very end. This bus was the very last S16 produced, fleet number 5545, which survives today after first being bought by our local preservation group at Leamington garage and later passing to BaMMOT, now Transport Museum Wythall.

Top Left: The 1970s in particular was a time of confused identity. Here's a Leicester D9 in Midland Red livery but with NBC stipulated grey wheels. Supposedly as an economy measure and no doubt due to staff shortages at the time, the later Midland Red livery had painted over the illuminated 'MIDLAND' sign above the destination display, although the BMMO radiator badge was still clear and visible.

Top Right: The very first Midland Red bus to be painted poppy red was D9 4851, a Leamington bus. There was no white band at this stage, but there was a white NBC logo, fleet name and legal lettering – the latter would later be grey.

Right: It's surprising how a livery can change the appearance of a vehicle. The NBC dual-purpose livery was tried on a small number of vehicles, but it was considered unsuccessful on the S21, and they were painted to all over poppy red within months. These were the last BMMO vehicles to have the classic red with black roof livery when new, except for the very last S21 which was delivered in red with maroon roof livery under Mr Womar's diktat.

That hard-to-define but stubborn Midland Red spirit kept the company alive and going forward, and rather strangely, vehicle experiments were still going on into the 1970s – after nationalisation and even after their own vehicle building had ceased!

In mid-1971, S17 number 5772 had a Leyland engine fitted for assessment over a four-year period, after which it was replaced by a standard BMMO engine. Only a couple of years before this, the company was taking another look at rear-engined single-deck designs, trying no doubt to avert the inevitable: the arrival of the Leyland National which was then in its planning stages.

Bottom Left and Right: What a difference a colour makes! Red was the only colour that suited the CM6 type after the much better, classy 'black top' coach livery was no longer applied. Here, 5660 looking smart is about to leave Victoria Coach Station, bound for Coventry and Nuneaton. Some coaches at this time were still showing their true and traditional liveries, making for a great spectrum of colour, and also making it easy for passengers to find their familiar coloured coach that would take them home! The bland, uninspiring appearance of 5665, sitting in a line up in Digbeth Coach Station. Just visible to the left is an un-refurbished CM6T, looking equally naked, and dare I say 'dealer white-ish.'

THE REVOLUTIONARY MOTORWAY EXPRESS

Perhaps the motorway express era of Midland Red's great history shows the biggest leap of faith in their abilities and the greatest act of boldness and confidence in a product which was totally new and untried. But it had to perform flawlessly from the very first day that the M1 motorway was opened. It was a remarkable show of prowess and a massive investment in a completely unproven area of operation.

The outstanding design of the two versions of coaches that were produced within a ten year period, the CM5 and CM6 classes, really were a revolution, and were hugely successful in their performance and reliability. Their astonishing speed, coupled with driver and passenger appeal, led to considerable growth in the service between the capital and the second city for business and leisure, and the day-trip market.

The motorway coach story begins with Mr Donald Sinclair being briefed on the Government's plan to build Britain's first proper motorway, the first part of which would be constructed from north of London to just outside Rugby, with further plans to extend it north. Midland Red's daily Midlands to London services were important, and some ran jointly with associated operators like Ribble, North Western Road Car and Standerwick. But they only ran on 'A' roads with their concomitant speed limits and various intermediate calling points, so this network of services took between five and six hours of journey time.

Mr Sinclair looked into the plans and immediately realised that the new motorway would have no maximum speed limit. This could be a great opportunity for him to make some giant steps, with immense risk, to invest in a special type of coach for this new route that would serve England's second city, and then run non-stop to the capital. He was well aware that he was in a good place at Midland Red for his plans to materialise, with designers of remarkable ability, a great experimental and development department and in-house production facilities. Even so, the plans had to be kept as secret as possible for some months while preparations were made.

Sinclair first met with Jack Ransome, who was head of the experimental department. Jack had had a long career with the company since 1930, and had been involved with every type of vehicle produced since then. He then held detailed discussions with his experimental department team, the results of which were reported back to Sinclair.

Before the motorway had been considered, it had already been decided to take the last S14 single-decker sub-frames into the development department workshops, where they would be transformed into the next new type of Midland Red coach, destined for general use in private hire, express coach services, tours and excursions.

Humour took the subject of a non-stop coach service to London to the extreme! Would a non-stop Midland Red coach pick up its passengers by snatching them from a hook by the roadside in a similar fashion to that of the mail trains?

The prototype C5 coach in its original form and, unusually for Midland Red, fitted with a curved windscreen.

This photograph was taken in April 1958, before it entered service at Digbeth garage where careful monitoring and evaluation work was undertaken.

Another cartoon image used internally to amuse staff. It shows a C4 coach, the forerunner to the motorway coach, heading down the M1 with Mr Sinclair, the general manager, at the wheel. "How fast shall we say these coaches go?"

But the development of this basic coach came at an opportune moment. In the confines of the workshop, away from prying eyes, variations of this new coach could be easily uprated to make it suitable for operating the newly planned London motorway non-stop express service.

The same prototype coach with a revised front bumper moulding and the familiar 'lantern' style windscreen which was fitted after comments were received during testing of the former curved screen. The angle of the lantern screen was found to help reduce reflections from the interior lights by reflecting them downwards rather than back into the driver's eyes. Midland Red's contractor for window provision suggested this type, as they were at the time looking to provide it to operators in Holland, Australia and New Zealand.

Don Shepherd and Bob Richards recalled that, within a month, behind-the-scenes discussions were held, and Mr Sinclair let the development department staff know that he wanted to see this new type so finely tuned that it could gain the recognition of being 'the fastest coach in the world'. Sinclair was then in internal discussion with the traffic department to assess what speed would be acceptable to the travelling public – his plan would fail if passengers were deterred by a high speed that was deemed dangerous. It should be remembered, at that time, buses and lorries were not allowed by law to exceed 30mph (40mph after 1961).

Bob Richards, who was a member of the development and experimental team, recalls that he and colleague Jim Pearson were aware of discussions about maximum speeds ranging from 50 to 100mph, but they eventually settled for 80mph. Obviously, such an innovative coach startled the industry, and there was conjecture on the matter of what top speed was indeed possible from its uprated BMMO engine. Ford engineers declared that it was impossible for the BMMO bus engine to achieve such an excessive speed, but at that time a Ford coach could not even contemplate continuous high-speed running. (Ford and Bedford coaches were seen as 'lightweight' coaches and favoured by many, especially smaller, local coach companies for general coach work). Midland Red's pioneering motorway express project was even brought up at The Institute of Mechanical Engineers in London, who would have liked Midland Red to have performed more exhaustive tests, but Jim Pearson, who was a member of the institute and introduced the paper to other members in a presentation, said that it worked for Midland Red so they were not going to pander to others' conjecture.

Midland Red had been pioneers for years in the designing and building of buses and coaches, but in order to design and build a coach destined for non-stop high-speed motorway use when there were no actual motorways in existence, many new factors needed to be taken into account for this unproven task.

Firstly, specialised tyres needed to be produced. With a maximum speed limit of 30mph for large vehicles, there was no need for commercial tyres to be available for greater speeds, let alone for prolonged use on a motorway where heat build-up would be a significant consideration. Greater braking distances at such high speeds were an important aspect, too. So, separate discussions with tyre producers took place and they decided that steel should be introduced into these road tyres, as was done in tyres used in the aviation industry. Versions of these became more widely known in later years as steel-braced radials. Trials of these new tyres, fitted onto Midland Red coaches, took place discreetly at the MIRA test facility, and their performance characteristics were carefully monitored by officials of the tyre companies and Midland Red's engineering teams.

Consideration also had to be given to the braking system, which must be able to safely stop a vehicle that was travelling at over 80 miles per hour. However, BMMO already used a constant flow hydraulic system, the pressure coming from a pump driven from the output shaft of the gearbox; so the faster the speed, technically, the better the brake. To the company's great advantage, they had already undertaken extensive trials with disc brakes – something of a novelty in the commercial vehicle world at this time – and they had provided many millions of miles of problem-free service on Midland Red buses for over seven years.

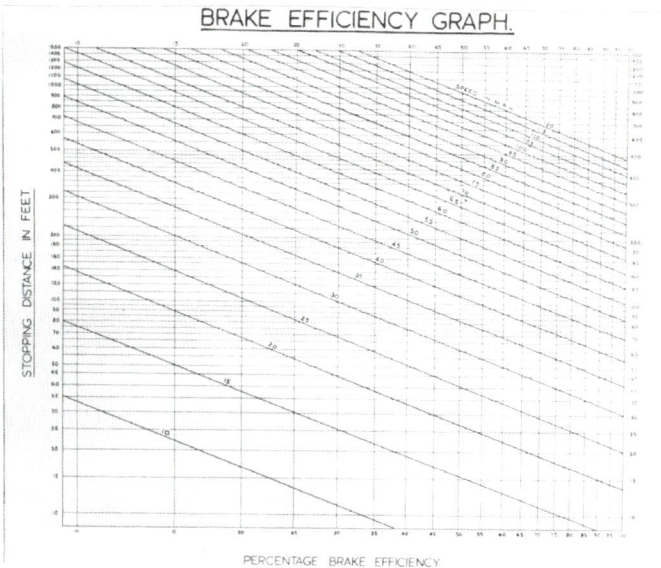

The official BMMO braking speed/distances chart – note that it shows speeds up to 120mph!

Existing services to London had refreshment/comfort stops along the route, but as this new service was being planned as a non-stop service, some of the new coaches would have toilet compartments to satisfy the needy customers' comfort demands.

Initially, a standard prototype coach known as C5 (the fifth coach type produced since the war) was completed, swiftly followed by some of the production vehicles for normal coach duties. A number of vehicles from the production batch were taken aside for further development to become the prestigious motorway express coaches. These had modified and uprated engines, new high-pressure fuel pumps and fitted turbochargers, all for increased power. Overdrive gearboxes and a variety of back axle ratios were used, depending on the variant of the C5 type. These were tested without any motorway being available, so some very fast running on the A45 between Dunchurch and Coventry took place at quiet times, to avoid unwanted attention.

The tests were carefully monitored and Mr Sinclair was kept informed of the results, any unplanned delays (and the reasons), and if vehicles were stopped by the police. He had to receive a written report from the test driver on the same day. BMMO were members of the Motor Industry Research Association (MIRA), based at the old wartime aerodrome at Lindley, near Nuneaton, where a new high-speed curved section of banked roadway had been recently built, mainly for testing racing cars. Midland Red made full use of this for their coach speed tests, and it proved useful for testing wheel bearings and suspension tolerances under such extreme use. Tyres were also tested here. There was a front wheel tyre failure at over 75mph, but the vehicle was brought to a standstill under full control. After investigations into this failure, the reinforcement material of the front tyres was changed from rayon to nylon.

The Midland Red motorway coaches were the first large vehicles to use this high-speed banked circuit. Previously the domain of racing car manufacturers, many thought it was quite a novelty to see *buses* storming round at such unheard-of speeds.

The main understructure had been proven at MIRA test facilities some seven years prior, with the first S14-type buses. This is where the structure experienced severe stress tests on surfaces including the Belgian Pavement, and a variety of other appropriate tests. The running under-frames, basic 8-litre engine and rubber suspension had all proved themselves suitable. Some items, including engine and suspension, needed uprated units, but the S14 type of lightweight bus certainly was a good base for the development of the motorway express. Behind the scenes at Central Works, an upgraded interior specification was progressing to make this coach the height of quality for its time. There was leopard skin patterned moquette, additional soundproofing, some wood veneer trim panels, seats with adjustable head restraints and much more.

Contributing members of MIRA, who were mainly vehicle manufacturers and members of the motor trade, paid for use of the site's facilities, and Midland Red made good use of them. It was an important proving ground, and, together with mileage on ordinary roads (the A45 being favourite), around 10,000 miles of motorway coach test work was clocked up.

Looking rather like a couple of toys, two CM5T coaches travel at high speed around the banked circuit. You can just make out a camera in the rear window of the first coach filming the second coach for publicity.

Below: This is the view from that first coach. The coach here is being driven by test driver R. E. S. Richards, with General Manager Donald Sinclair sitting on the front passenger seat.

One problem that proved quite tricky was the ingress of water into the luggage boot at the back of the coach. Previously, this had not been a serious issue on other vehicle types, but now, when travelling at such high speeds, the air pressure at the rear of the vehicle was allowing water to penetrate the ordinary boot door seals. After a number of door seals had been tried, the development team contacted aircraft engineers to see what their solution was to prevent water ingress. They suggested that the only successful approach was to pressurise the boot to an extent that the water could not penetrate. This was not an option on a coach.

High-tech research and development was needed (remember, we are in the 1950s), and the solution was to install Bob Richards, a well-built man, along with some basic tools into the luggage boot. This wasn't the most pleasant place to be, even for a few short minutes, but he had to face a much worse ordeal. While the bus hurled along the A45 through the pouring rain at unspeakable speed, he was shaken around on the hard wooden boot floor while simultaneously trying to find a solution to the problem. He had a hammer, a screwdriver and a couple of new boot door seals. After enduring this performance three times at short notice (whenever rain was forecast), and replacing the seals on many occasions, frustration was understandably taking its toll. It was dark, dirty and extremely uncomfortable, and Bob was unable to be in anything other than a horizontal position in the main boot, flanked on his right by the workings of the toilet compartment which was just above, in the rear corner of the saloon. But then, in a fit of pique, he lashed out his arm whilst holding a screwdriver and struck the thin walling of the base of the toilet compartment which contained all of the toilet workings – and the problem immediately improved! The equalising of the pressure between the boot and the coach interior (via that unintentionally created ventilation hole), meant that he would no longer have to travel in the boot! And as a result of all of this high-tech R&D work, all coaches were built with a small ventilation grille, and some had small fans fitted to assist in balancing the pressures.

This issue of water ingress was of great importance as the company could not afford to have their good name tarnished by passenger complaints, or claims for damp or wet luggage after the journey on this new, prestigious service. But, on very wet days there were still issues, and so finally to solve the issue, the engineers fitted light duck boards on the base of the boot and some drainage holes at the lowest part of the boot. They also fitted a fixed vinyl sheet which folded out of the coach boot door when loading, and was then placed over the luggage to deflect any water down into the bottom of the boot and out through the drainage holes.

Of the ten coaches involved in the test work, some underwent multiple tests that involved more than one vehicle, while others simply did tyre testing. Two particular vehicles did most of the high-speed work and had many engine modifications undertaken at the local Hinckley bus garage, as it was near MIRA. Not all testing was highly technical, for example, ensuring that the windscreen wiper blades were sufficiently sprung to prevent them from lifting off the windscreen when travelling at high speed.

Security at MIRA was always tight regarding who could get in or out through the gate house of the main site. It was even more tight on who could gain access to the track, where access and monitoring were done from the control tower. Slots had to be pre-booked by the manufacturing company and due consideration was given to who else would be there and what they were testing. This generally was not an issue for Midland Red as they were likely the only bus and coach manufacturer there, but it certainly was between competing car manufacturers. Drivers had to be approved and pre-registered. There was an underground tunnel to access the main track, but it wouldn't take a large bus. Post-war, when the test track was being converted from the old aerodrome to provide high-speed facilities, coach racing was probably not on their list of priorities, so coaches and buses had to take a longer route, joining via the loop track.

A couple of famous characters from the motor industry who were often at MIRA when R. E. S. Richards, one of Midland Red's test drivers, was on site were Norman Dewis and occasionally 'Lofty' England. They were from Jaguar Cars in Coventry; Norman was their highly experienced and accomplished test driver, and Lofty was, at that time, the head of Jaguar Racing. Bob Richards and Norman became good friends, and their regular meet-ups were often in the canteen at MIRA, where the two would enjoy meals and endless cups of tea, and often deep conversations while waiting for the control tower to authorise them to access their testing slots on the track. Visitors to MIRA were always briefed by their bosses about employee confidentiality, as the business of innovative product technology was highly sensitive, but of course, they were only human, and conversations about work were all too easy.

Norman was a small, but very self-confident man. One day, in the canteen before work, he told Bob that he was involved in testing a new superior type of brakes for the E Type, and they were disc brakes! "Oh," said BMMO Bob, "My company developed disc brakes for buses years ago, and now they are standard fittings on Midland Red buses. We tested the early ones here at MIRA for our integral S14 bus. We developed them with Girling." Ironically, Girling was the original pioneer of the racing car disc brake. It wasn't often that Bob could get one over on the usually very self-assured Norman!

Midland Red was the pioneer in the production of passenger vehicles using disc brakes, later to be followed by Setra.

When the motorway coaches were in service, close attention was paid to drivers' end-of-day reports, engineers' inspections, and especially tyre condition and behaviour, so that alterations and modifications were continual.

The front passenger seat view of the motorway. This photo was taken by the late Richard 'Rob' Paramor who was then in charge of the passenger chartroom at Victoria Coach Station and an invited guest on one of the coaches used on the first day of operation: 2 November 1959 – the day the M1 was officially opened by Earnest Marples, Minister for Transport. Rob Paramor, after a successful career in travel was instrumental, along with me, in the formation of the Wheels organisation in the 1980s.

In the late 1950s and 1960s, news was provided by newsreels at the cinema, early home television or newspapers, so not all gossip was widely spread, but, interestingly, Earnest Marples, who had a background in accountancy, was also managing director of a construction company called Marples Ridgeway who were contractors used in building the M1 motorway. This could be seen as a severe conflict of interest in holding such an important government post.

Like any other Midland Red bus type it is highly unlikely that any two of these coaches were really identical. Drivers' reports led to bigger driver's mirrors. On some vehicles, twin headlights were introduced, some horizontal and some vertically placed, where high beams were set independently of the running headlights, providing much better driving conditions in unlit areas. Engineers' reports resulted in the fitting of additional gauges in the cab, whereas previously

BMMO vehicles were so well trusted that the fittings were basically a speedo, light switches and a horn! There were three departures from Birmingham per day, with up to four coaches allowed on their route licence for any one departure, so there could be over 130 passengers on each departure slot.

The company regime was for the motorway coaches to be inspected after each trip. This was known as a 'turn around check', and this was handled, along with other light maintenance, at the operating garage – so Bearwood, Digbeth and later at Nuneaton. After a spell of operation, Central Works called in a number of vehicles for in-depth tests; any significant issues discovered would lead to modifications. Radiator shutters were experimented with, first under the control of the driver and later operated by a thermostat where the fins would open at a preset temperature, all in aid of getting the engine running at optimum temperature. It was found that water from spray on the motorway was affecting some electrical items, including the speedo drive – so a nice simple solution was to put the affected item in a plastic bag with a heavy duty elastic band around the top! Oil spray could find its way onto the handbrake disc, and had affected one vehicle's rear suspension unit where the rubber had delaminated, so shields were put in place for protection. Running at such high speeds for long periods also encouraged the ingress of dirt into the engine, so modifications were affected for that too. Boot doors at the rear were modified from an upward opening single door to two side-hinged doors.

Things were going well into the Swinging Sixties, and the motorway express services were enjoying greater patronage than expected, but problems loomed when British Railways objected to Midland Red's application to the Traffic Commissioners to increase the number of vehicles on each departure. British Railways was state-owned, and if the increase went ahead, it would allegedly suffer a loss of revenue to a private company. The objections were aired at a court hearing, which resulted in a maximum of four coaches being allowed on any one departure. The Birmingham to London coach called at Coventry and then ran non-stop to London, so, cleverly, to provide additional capacity, a new service was licenced from Coventry to London – this operated from Nuneaton garage, and so the service was extended back to Nuneaton.

The Birmingham service was given the classification ME1 and then operated from Birmingham directly to London Victoria, and the Nuneaton-based service ME2 had additional calling points at Bedworth and Coventry before operating non-stop to London via the M45 and M1. A booking agent was provided in Bedworth opposite the picking-up and dropping-off point: the old Market Place. The booking agent was Bunny's shop, where locals could buy tickets.

The splitting up of services gave much-needed breathing space, with additional capacity and the ability to run duplicates on both services. Up to now, these services were operated by the original CM5 type coaches, which were racking up incredibly high mileages.

Below: This coach started life as a C5, became a CM5 motorway coach and in later life became a CS5. Fleet number 4837 with horizontal twin headlights sits in Paignton among lots of coaches taking a rest whilst on express services.

Bottom: CM5T fleet number 4807, with vertical twin headlights, during a special test to monitor a downrated engine and to check fuel consumption. Sitting at the bottom of the slip road on a summer early-morning test, in the early days of motorways when its rules of use seemed more relaxed, enabling a casual chat at the start of the hard shoulder. Notice that there were no crash barriers.

CM5 motorway coach fleet number 4837 is about to enter Victoria Coach Station in London, ready for its departure to Nuneaton via Coventry. The wooden destination boards above the side windows were interchangeable and on vehicles allocated to motorway duties would normally be showing 'Coventry London Motorway Express' for this service, or 'Birmingham London Motorway Express' or 'Birmingham Worcester Motorway Express'. When the C5 coaches were working on other duties like private hires, express services or tours and excursions they would show the boards pictured here which covered overall use.

Later, and no doubt to monitor and upgrade the motorway coaches efficiently, Nuneaton's motorway vehicles still had their turn-around checks done at their garage, but for other work, they were driven to Wigston Garage, which was the area dock shop, where full facilities were available, including a fibreglass shop, a trim and body shop and a good range of engineering facilities. So, they were able to keep all but serious engineering work away from Central Works. Les Ayres was the foreman, and he had a long BMMO pedigree behind him. His story is in my previous book, *Midland Red and its People*.

The experience and knowledge built up from running these coaches highlighted common faults and led to various modifications. Central Works had received multiple concerning reports of how fast some coaches were being driven on the motorway. It was decided to reduce the maximum speed by governing the fuel pump, reducing the uprated engines from 2,200rpm to a more sedate 1,950rpm. This improved fuel consumption even more and reduced wear on timing chains and tappet rattle.

Clocking up 75,000 to 100,000 miles each in the first year is some going, and being on the road in all weathers brings problems: in winter from road salt, and in hot weather from damaged oil seals allowing oil throwback. Road dirt being thrown up under the bus at high speed was getting into the brakes, causing disc pad wear, and also finding its way into lubricants. All these things were rectified as a priority.

In real motorway service, these coaches had hard lives with incredibly high mileages, and in their later years, as was usual with some coaches, they were used more locally on bus services. The cascading of old coaches to provide bus services had always been an issue. Many disliked their use as one-man bus services because of the door arrangement, and for two-man buses, navigating the narrow gangways was a problem for the conductor in busy times.

Mainly, the plan was to use them on more rural, sparsely used services because their large seats and narrow gangways was a big issue with the trade union, and trouble often brewed regarding their new use.

Whatever your thoughts or feelings on coaches travelling at such high speeds, what is certain is that the first type of motorway coach, the CM5, would travel at well over 80mph on many occasions. When many of the C5 family were cascaded to provide local services, there were changes made that might not be immediately apparent. Some CM5Ts during their conversion work will certainly have lost their 'T' (toilet) compartment, with seats added in its place; but some certainly retained their motorway spec engine gearbox and/or axle ratio and high-speed CAV fuel pump. Various combinations of other components might be changed too.

Some coaches, like the one mentioned below, had only internal alterations; for example, the outward opening entrance door was changed to an inward swing-opening type, and a small number blind was fitted into the destination roof box. It should be remembered that at this time, there were severe shortages of workers, including engineering staff, so it's quite likely that low-priority alterations that would not be noticed were just given a miss. The C5 family, during its main lifespan, had a number of variants anyway, from the basic C5, CM5, CM5T, CS5, and then the C5a which was a hybrid version of any of the original models.

At Nuneaton garage we had a number of the C5 class vehicles, including the demoted C5a – a classification used for any variety of the C5 family. One of these had a long history of motorway operation, and was one of the ten used for testing trials during its earlier years. I was a conductor on it when it was operating Humber Works and Keresley Pit bus services. The journey to the factory or colliery was operated 'private', often from the garage, and this is where the speed of the vehicle was often tested, after the crew had perhaps been spending too much time in the canteen! Some of these vehicles did reach 80+mph even in their later twilight years, and allowing for speedo calibration errors!

Fleet number 4809, one of the motorway test coaches used at MIRA. It is seen here after being demoted to a C5a designation. For the majority of its life, it had been one of the smartly presented 'black tops' but Mr Womar made the change to maroon tops and then all-over red (for economy). This is how 4809 was photographed in the summer of 1970 on the patch at Nuneaton bus station, about to go on stand to operate an evening rural stage carriage service that would see its remaining service days out. It was converted to one-man operation, but due to union resistance it was rarely used as such. It was this vehicle, along with one or two others no doubt, that still achieved high speed in its later life. It was sold after withdrawal and became a film demonstration vehicle in Lichfield, and then sold again to a private buyer in the Black Country. It was scrapped in 1976 at over 17 years old.

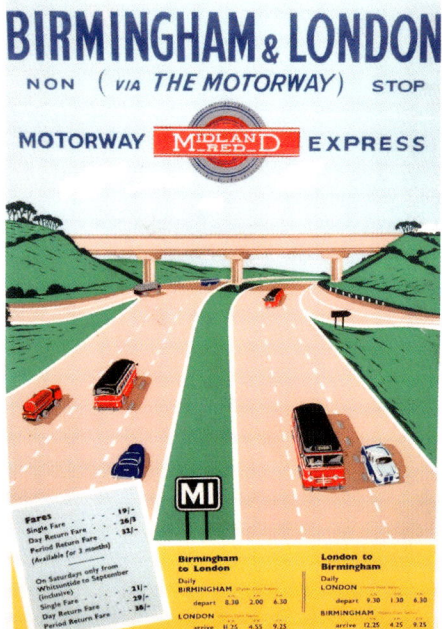

One of many posters promoting Midland Red's high-speed motorway express services.

Bigger and Better: The CM6 Story

After protests by Midland Red, along with their crude looking 45´ long battlebus, the government sanctioned in a new Transport Act that the maximum length of public service vehicles could be increased: double-deckers from 27´ 6" to 30´ and single-deckers from 30´ to 36´.

The newly permitted dimensions would allow Midland Red to build a new coach with 44 large, comfortable seats and a toilet, rather than the 34 seats of the existing 30´ CM5T. In mid-1962 designs were laid, and construction planned for a new, bigger prototype for the next phase of motorway coach development. Subframes were rigorously tested with the aid of concrete ballast to simulate laden and unladen weights. After these had proved satisfactory,

Running on trade plate 064 HA, one of many held at Central Works, is the beginnings of fleet number 5295 which became the prototype for the CM6 type motorway express coach. It boasts an employee's second-hand blue sofa as the passenger seat, but the low windscreen would be little protection for those braving the elements during this important test work. The test driver's long overcoat was actually a driver's great-coat — a well made and warm, lined coat made by a firm of Edinburgh tailors. The photograph was taken just north of Carlisle, on one of its many similar test journeys.

the running frames were back in the works to be bodied, and they needed to be type-approved, starting with a tilt test using the facilities at the Metro Cammell factory.

The visual appearance was, at first look, confusing for a 'new' coach: it looked just like a lengthened CM5T coach, still with a lantern windscreen and a manual gearbox, but with a new 10.5-litre engine. This prototype had 46 seats of an aircraft design and a rear-mounted manual flush toilet, just like the earlier motorway coaches. One double seat was subsequently removed, but the aircraft-style seating remained unique to this particular coach. At first the coach was in a flat grey/mustard etching primer finish and was tested at night on the M1. This led to a bit of premature publicity, when an article appeared in the press declaring that a mystery 100mph 'ghost bus' was seen in the fast lane of the motorway.

Various modifications were carried out, and in 1963, the coach returned to the bodyshop in Central Works, where its appearance was altered considerably. It lost its earlier windscreen design in favour of a four-piece screen with curved side glasses. It also had two engine changes, and was fitted with a 5-speed semi-automatic gearbox. It had been planned that this coach would have a semi-automatic gearbox from new, but Self Changing Gears of Coventry could not supply a suitable unit at the time. The gearboxes they supplied to Midland Red were operated by oil rather than air pressure and so were 'special order', although they were derived from the DMU train gearbox design. It temporarily had a 10.5-litre turbocharged engine fitted in the experimental department for testing and evaluation before it reverted to a standard motorway specification CM6 naturally aspirated version.

5295 (5495 HA) as originally built, looking every bit like a lengthened CM5T.

The same vehicle taken to be photographed in the same road but in its modified and final prototype form, with what became the standard CM6 windscreen layout.

The prototype was not as frequent a visitor to MIRA as the CM5 vehicles, as the technology had been proven, but the CM6 testing was just as exciting for those involved.

Then came testing at MIRA, and everyone was impressed. On one of its outings there, Bob's friend Norman Dewis from Jaguar was on site, and it was arranged for Norman to accompany Bob and his assistant on board the new coach for a ride high up on the curved bank of the high-speed circuit. Norman stood at the front of the gangway near the cab and added another thrilling episode to his career, exclaiming "You're doing more than 80!" Bob replied, "Yes, but that's the maximum shown on the gauge. We usually count the fence posts on the edge of the track to gauge the speed." Then Norman had an idea. On site this particular day was one of his favourite cars, 77 RW, which was an early E Type and a well-known test car. He decided to drive it around the track, accompanying the Midland Red prototype coach and matching its speed. He said, "I'll give you the thumbs up when you touch the ton!" – and that's exactly what happened. Bob remembered this as the best and proudest of his days at MIRA. There were rumours for years about a 'ton-up' coach; the denials that this was possible may have something to do with it often being confused with the earlier type of CM5 coach.

At MIRA. The early test car, an E type Jaguar 77 RW with Jaguar test driver Norman Dewis, and the prototype CM6T 5295 (5495 HA) motorway coach with Midland Red test driver Bob Richards.

On entering service in 1963, the CM6 prototype was allocated to Digbeth and Bearwood garages. From spring 1965 it appeared at Rugby garage, where it ran as a standby coach, being near to the motorway. It served at Nuneaton on normal ME2 duties in 1971 and 1972, and again was at Rugby until it was withdrawn in 1973. A photograph taken in late summer 1972 of this coach leaving Coventry for London whilst allocated to Nuneaton garage is featured as the front cover image of my book *Midland Red and its People*.

Fluorescent lighting was fitted as standard after an earlier experiment on a CM5 coach. Modern forced air ventilation was also fitted to CM6s after a system was successfully tested on CM5T 4830, a vehicle that held a unique place in motorway coach life as it was used as the directors' coach for some time.

CM5T 4830 was probably the best of the C5 coaches. It was used as the directors' coach for many years.

Above: The first production CM6T.

The CM6T interior, showing the electrically operated roof vents of the original build.

Most were fitted with toilets of a more modern type, with a stainless steel bowl and electric flush. There were five CM6s built without toilets which allowed for 46 seats. These were built for the X43 and X44 Birmingham to Worcester via the M5 services, for use with a conductor due to the manually-operated entrance door.

Worcester garage based CM6 5668 stands in the city's Newport Street bus station.

On CM6s the forced air system took some time to perfect. The earlier coaches had a front air intake but there was no room for the blowers without affecting the destination blind equipment. They were placed on the roof curve above the front window, but later experiments found it much more effective to place them further back on the roof, above the rear wheels. The CM6 roof was finished with a streamlined peaked dome at the front and at the back to assist with air flow.

The visual appearance of the production CM6s was a step change, and here the link with the C5 type was lost. These smooth, streamlined coaches were allocated initially to Bearwood, Digbeth and Nuneaton. They were very impressive and always looked comfortable performing their work. They were sleek, aerodynamic and businesslike, and looked unlike any other coach of the time. They were a great step forward from their predecessor CM5 coaches.

The crack team of motorway men who handled these coaches were picked from the best, with safety record, attendance and appearance all being considered. In fact, all drivers were excluded from the CM6 type unless they were specifically appointed as a motorway driver. The type was also expressly excluded from the inter-company coach loan/assist arrangements where Midland Red would loan a vehicle to an associate company if they suffered a breakdown whilst travelling in the Midland Red area. The only exception to this was if a Midland Red motorway express trained and approved driver was at the wheel.

I have yet to meet a driver who had experience of the Midland Red motorway coaches who didn't love the CM6 type, and there were some who had their favourites. Once on the motorway, it was usually full speed ahead, in and out of the outside lane as appropriate. Sports car drivers doing 80mph were left open-mouthed as the Midland Red purred past them. There was no such thing as road rage. If car and van drivers looked in their mirror and saw a red coach approaching they moved over and allowed it to pass. These superlative coaches enjoyed a particular reputation and respect.

Here's a note on CM6 tyres from Alan Eatwell, former Midland Red Engineering Superintendent:

"The CM6s were still in front-line use in the early 1970s. Tyre contracts were generally let for around five years, as I recall, and whereas smaller companies would have one contract (e.g. City of Oxford Motor Services dealt only with Goodyear from around 1924 through to 2012, when they were displaced by Michelin), the larger companies including the 'Red' would have a number. I seem to recall that BMMO's tyre business was allocated on a division basis. During my time, the Birmingham garages (i.e. Digbeth and Sheepcote St, with probably Bearwood before it closed) were Dunlop; whereas when I was foreman at Redditch that was Firestone, being a Worcester division garage; and when I was superintendent at Shrewsbury that was Goodyear, being in Cradley division. All of which necessitated tyre swaps upon a bus being reallocated to a garage in another division, of course.

"The contracts were priced on a per-mile basis which included initial supply, replacement and fitting by the contractor. Contractors therefore had more interest in tyre longevity than the operator Midland Red who were going to pay the agreed mileage rate regardless. The contractor had to get as many miles as possible out of each tyre to reduce the replacement cost which they had to bear. With that objective, their tyre fitter was required by them to undertake a rigorous regime of tyre pressure monitoring, tread re-cutting (on buses), and wear compensation by swapping the tyres around, front to rear and side to side. Associated with these mileage aspirations, the tyre contractors were also keen to maintain awareness of rubber compound characteristics, and often the work we were doing was to ensure that the longer-lasting rubber that they proposed didn't jeopardise handling and braking."

A CM6T coach having a turn-around check between runs to London. It is based at Digbeth garage in Birmingham.

It was only three years into the life of the CM6 when Nationalisation reared its head and, along with some other BET companies, Midland Red mounted a serious campaign against the prospect of the company losing its independence under government control. With Midland Red being something of a 'stand-out' organisation, especially with its unique Motorway Express operations, it soon gained notoriety with coaches emblazoned with protest banners.

Here's another photo of the first CM6T fleet number 5646 (BHA 646C) having dropped off its passengers at London's Victoria Coach Station in 1968. The eagle-eyed reader will notice that, besides its side protest slogan above the windows, a modified radiator grille has been fitted that has larger ventilation gaps than in earlier photos of the same vehicle.

Refurbished under wraps

With these high-performance coaches almost exclusively used on the motorway express services for which they were designed, they racked up very high mileages. But, there was strong affection from everyone for these very special coaches. The iconic CM6 type represented the pinnacle of BMMO vehicle development. It was one of those types that was almost perfect, from its design and businesslike appearance to its power and capabilities. When it was new, a vehicle's Certificate of Initial Fitness was for a seven year period, so the CM6s would normally have needed an extensive overhaul for continued use. Pressure from above, perhaps attributed to these cost-conscious times, meant it was difficult to justify an expensive overhaul to keep them going, but few people inside the company wanted to see them gone!

But opposition to their use on the London services was brewing in higher places. Nationalised corporatisation was taking hold, and new Leyland Leopard coaches with Plaxton bodies were bought to bring things into the new NBC white coach regime. Whilst the Leyland Leopard is a perfectly good coach, it was no match for even a seven-year-old CM6T. Drivers were actually *disappointed* when new coaches arrived, a most unusual occurrence, as most drivers are very pleased to receive new vehicles, but the CM6T was special in so many ways.

Even considering the stress of fast-lane running, seven years is a very short life for any vehicle. But having had high-speed running for all of their lives and racking up half a million miles they had, compared to a bus, done their bit! The undersides had a lifetime of exposure to winter salt, grit and wet and needed remedial work. As there were vehicle shortages, a plan was hatched that they could be converted to one-man operation for the X43/44 Birmingham to Worcester motorway service, and other limited stop or long-distance bus services, and perhaps routes like the X99 Birmingham to Nottingham. That was the plan proposed, but was there another agenda?

Soon, the first CM6T was called to enter Central Works and had an appropriate overhaul. I remember being surprised by the incongruous appearance of the new front roof dome that housed the destination box – it didn't look as good as the curved aerodynamic dome of the original CM6 design, which housed only a single track blind. It was later explained to me that a grant had been available from the NBC for vehicles to meet their one-man bus specification. Allegedly, a loophole could be used to secure the grant which had helped with the CM6 refurbishment costs, but in order to qualify the vehicle had to have a bus-style destination box and other fitments. Another condition was that it had to have a power entrance door, and this was duly fitted, ready for approval.

Now classified CM6A, 5654 with a rather clumsy-looking destination box on such a gracious coach. After demotion to stage carriage work for a time, it gets another chance to feel at home on work it was built for – high speed motorway express duties. Drivers told me they thought that the big rooftop destination box cost them up to 10mph in a headwind.

For reasons unknown, only the first vehicle that was converted for official approval, fleet number 5654, had the power door – the others that were modified all retained their original manually-operated door, and then gained wide, stainless iron, brightwork trim. Could there really have been a plan that they were not being refurbished for bus work, but for front line express work?

Again, to comply with the NBC's one-man operated bus specification, the first vehicle re-entered service and was seen on 'X' services, including the X99 and 765 Coventry to Lichfield runs. When it had been visible for some months on 'bus' work, it was then surreptitiously used again on motorway services.

The same vehicle CM6A 5654, around 1974. Although it was supposed to be demoted to bus work it had to be painted in white National Express colours. Between fast services to the capital, it was still doing an occasional stage carriage service. It was never officially allocated to Nuneaton garage, but has a full set of Nuneaton blinds; it was on loan there shortly before withdrawal. The driver is Nuneaton-based, motorway-trained Bernard Ellis.

The company issued some press information on the newly refurbished coach which reveals that the real intention was to enable the vehicles to continue as motorway coaches rather than buses. Here is an extract: "The addition of stainless iron banding increases the appearance a good deal – and at high speed on the motorway the coach looks most attractive… A new type of windscreen wiper is being fitted, and at the request of drivers, a new wiper and screen wash is fitted at the back to clear the rear window of motorway mud."

But also note that the 'official' publicity image is posed, showing a limited stop service number X68, the Birmingham, Coventry Leicester route – a route it never operated.

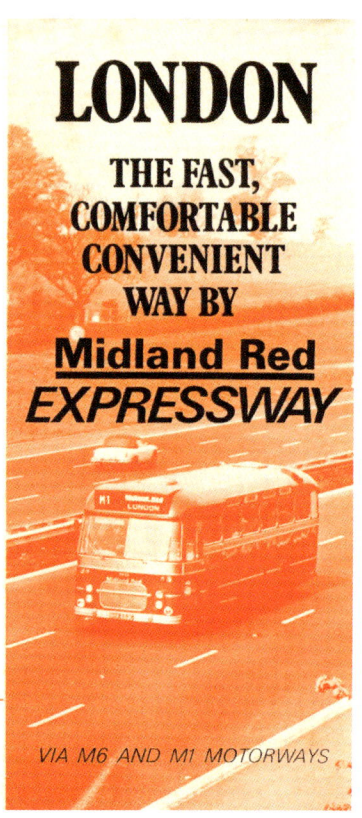

When a number of these vehicles had been treated to their refurbishment and upgrade Midland Red re-branded them the 'CM6T Superfast' coach, and they were smartly outshopped in red. A press launch saw fleet number 5653 take a coach load of journalists for a spin along the motorway. The destination was, of course, a day out in London. This press photograph was also used for the cover of a new timetable leaflet for the service.

The newly refurbished Coach Under Wraps in early 1972.

Within days of the completion of the first coach conversion, I was visiting the publicity department of Central Works for a meeting with Gordon Diggle and Haydn Wootton. During the morning break, one of the attendees showed me into the old chassis shop where I saw a vehicle covered with a white sheet, and I was enigmatically told that, at the moment, it was "not for everyone's eyes!" Curiosity got the better of me, so at lunchtime while the foreman of the body shop had gone to the work's canteen, I ventured back to the body shop and quickly removed the white sheet. There, to my astonishment, was a gleaming, newly refurbished motorway coach – not in NBC white, but in proper Midland Red all-over red livery. I had to be quick as the canteen was in the building opposite, so I hastily photographed it, and with the aid of an accomplice and some large wooden step ladders we managed to pull the white sheet back over the coach, and it was hidden once again.

The CM6s that were chosen for refurbishment were brought into Central Works for mechanical overhaul, and fitted with new polished chrome body trim, new 'compliant' destination blind boxes, a new interior floor and a retrim to the interior and seating. The electrically-controlled skylights, which, by this time, had become unreliable in operation were retrofitted with conventional, manually-operated push-up roof lights. All of this to help keep these vehicles on the road for a few more years. The first few appeared in Midland Red's livery and looked very smart, but this didn't go unnoticed, and NBC gave instructions to paint them white.

The plan must have been to wear us down and eliminate that strong Midland Red spirit. When vehicles were outshopped in white, the owning company's fleet name (in this case, Midland Red) was allowed to appear just above the front wheel arch on the body, but NBC were not happy with its size, and instructions came to reduce its visibility, which meant, at the speed of a CM6 coach, it was unlikely to be seen at all!

Left and Right: The shrinking fleet name above the wheel arch.

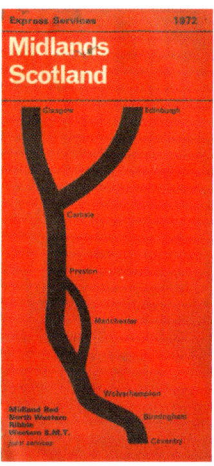

After a further couple of years service, they were withdrawn, which was surprising, as two years of service after a refurb at Central Works was not long to benefit from the costs involved. But even after this initial spell of extra life, there was still hope. One day, when there were only a couple left running, Dave Haughton, the well-known ex-foreman at Digbeth Coach Station, told me that even after some had been withdrawn and parked pending disposal down at Worcester garage, he had been in discussion with his area engineer, and it was agreed to get some of the better examples quickly brought back into operational condition and MOT'd to do more work, as they could now prove that they had a severe vehicle shortage. This was much to everyone's delight. In fact, it was not unheard of for drivers to make special requests to the foreman engineers to ensure that they had an old CM6T allocated to *their* motorway duties.

Eventually, the National Bus Company did not want these 'time expired' Midland Reds on the London service, but a Birmingham-based Midland Red official said defiantly, "We weren't prepared to stop using the CM6s while they were fit for work, and on the numerous occasions we were told to stop allocating them to the London route we would send them twice as far when we allocated them to the Glasgow and Largs Scottish motorway services – an even longer route than Birmingham to London!

The CM6Ts did, however, continue to appear on occasional London services, if it was deemed necessary to cover a breakdown or to replace one of the new Leylands signed off with a fault by the driver, who much preferred a shift with an old friend!

But eventually, when they were really tired, and as spares became harder to find (particularly non-standard BMMO CM6 engine spares), instead of withdrawing them, they were used on local, mainly contact work. This was often Austin factory runs, or off to Winson Green prison to take prisoners to Warwick for the county court.

Eventually, however, they were again retired to Worcester Padmore Street garage parking compound. Two found their way, via a dealer, to further extended lives, and another was preserved, details of which appear in my previous books. We are extremely fortunate that we can still see, and even take a ride aboard, the preserved example running on special event days at the Transport Museum Wythall.

Dave Haughton, Digbeth engineers' foreman, was an advocate of keeping CM6Ts on the road as long as possible. Reflecting on his time there, he said, "Everybody liked them – drivers, passengers and engineers, so why not keep them going as long as possible. I'd fetched them from Worcester yard when they had been withdrawn, brought them back to Digbeth garage and given them a thorough check over, got them MOT'd and made motorway coach drivers happy for a bit longer! Eventually, the problem was that they had some specialised parts that weren't made any more, and eventually they met their end."

The coach that replaced the CM6T on London motorway work was the C15, a standard Leyland Leopard with Plaxton bodywork. It was just like the coaches used by any other member of the National Bus Company, with the aim of bringing Midland Red into line.

A couple of withdrawn CM6s, parked and awaiting their fate at Padmore Street parking area, opposite Worcester garage. Had Central Works still been producing parts for their vehicle range (or had more extensive stocks of the specialist parts that were exclusive to the motorway coaches), and still been using their full overhaul facilities, these special coaches could have achieved a normal post-overhaul life.

Most only had a two to three year post-refurbishment life. White paint made these coaches look bland and banished their previously classy appearance. The steel band trim was not to everyone's taste; I've heard comments that it 'americanised' a very British coach, but it wasn't the first time that steel brightwork had been used. American influences can be found in a number of previous SOS and BMMO types. Wyndham Shire produced designs for prototype rear-engined single-deckers after visits to USA. Also, Sinclair, influenced by visits to Greyhound in America, brought out the 'American S9' fleet number 3441, which is featured on page 50 of my book Midland Red Influence, and the LA type fleet number 3877, featured on page 34 of this book.

Right: A memory of those great motorway express drivers is captured in this photograph of Driver Chris O'Flaherty who sadly passed away in January 2025. The coach, fleet number 5648, was freshly out of Central Works after its overhaul and refurbishment, and looking as good as new. Driver Chris had worked out of Midland Red's original garage at Bearwood and Digbeth and was highly regarded by his colleagues. He thought these coaches were exceptional. As an example to some modern day drivers, he proudly jumps on board in immaculate uniform and polished shoes, ready for another exciting ride. It is hard to accept that it is fifty years since CM6s were regularly used on motorway services.

Motorway Express

Test driver Bob

Bob Richards came to Midland Red by way of a family connection. He was dating a young lady who happened to the daughter of Midland Red's traffic manager, Roy Brandon. At the time he was happily completing a railway engineering apprenticeship with GWR and seconded to Tyseley Works, Birmingham. Once he had his papers, he was strongly encouraged to join Midland Red's development department which was about to move from Bearwood to Central Works. He quickly settled in to Midland Red ways and was extremely proud of his time in the Experimental and Development department. I was extremely pleased to be able to call him a friend, and felt fortunate to have been told first-hand stories and received some of his reports, documents, and photographic material from his working days. He also provided the foreword for my second book, *Midland Red Influence*.

He was involved in the company's final attempts to be a pioneer bus and coach developer.

In 1967, the 70mph speed limit was introduced to motorways, and most of the exciting work was over. When we met in later years, we used to travel together to the twice-yearly gatherings of Midland Red alumni at a pub just south of Banbury. I would pick Bob up from his then Coventry home, and on the journey of just under an hour he would recount stories of his career, which I would later hastily write down. When Bob retired, he moved from Coventry to Devon, just a couple of streets away from the Peco model railway headquarters in Beer, where he wrote regular, lengthy, handwritten letters expanding on his earlier tales and adding others. These were highly detailed stories, and some were supplemented by examples of his test reports. They highlighted how many of their earlier experiments were performed with the most ordinary of tools and equipment – but the exercise was to prove a point and not to impress!

One memorable tale involved an investigation to see if the black-painted roofs of coaches were causing uncomfortably hot temperatures for passengers during hot summer days, especially on the motorway services. This involved two large Crawford's biscuit tins, one painted black, the other white. A hole was drilled in the centre of each, into which a cork was fitted. The cork had a central hole that held a glass thermometer that monitored the temperature inside the tin. The test results led to the roof panels being painted white to reflect the heat of the sun. It was important that this could not be seen from street level, as it would spoil the smart coach livery, so only the central area of the roof was painted white.

"There will never be another coach anything like the CM6T," explained Bob, "It is a coach of its era, absolutely the best and at the top of its game – and so comfortable to drive." Every CM6 coach had a rigorous testing program, starting when bodied but not yet trimmed. The development team members had the pleasure of putting them through their paces for their first 1,000 miles on the clock. Engines for the motorway coaches were part run-in before being fitted to the vehicles. Achieving more 'managed' mileage on each vehicle before it entered service involved a number of journeys, leaving Central Works after 9am, then up the M6 from Stafford to Charnock Richard Services in Lancashire, an early lunch, then returning to Central Works in the early to mid-afternoon. When the mileage had been built up, the vehicles would go into the body shop for internal trimming and the fitting of seats; then they'd be sent out to their garage of operation for their excitingly fast and rather special service life.

After the morning run up the motorway, this unidentified CM6 coach sits at Charnock Richard Services, where it rested before another fast run back to Central Works.

The first production CM6T 5646 journeys through the Lake District on a crisp and snowy day in January 1965, before returning to the works to have seats fitted and internal trim completed. From February 1965, this coach enjoyed a life working from Bearwood garage.

Bob thoroughly enjoyed his time at Midland Red, saying that he was involved with things he could hardly have dreamt of – and many that certainly couldn't be done now. But experimental work was severely curtailed after 1969, and then ended a few years later as nationalisation tightened its grip. After his time at MIRA, meeting other brilliant engineers, and with his work at Central Works approaching its end, Bob felt that Great Britain was losing its pioneering ethos. He always said that Midland Red had its own special spirit, which was absorbed by many of its people. And so Bob allowed himself to be poached away from Midland Red to work with the Swedish company Sandvik, until his ultimate retirement. He enjoyed a long and busy retirement until his sad passing in 2016 when he returned to Midland Red territory, and his ashes were scattered at the Heart of England Crematorium in Nuneaton.

The lucky ones

You can read about the afterlives of a small number of CM6Ts that escaped the cutter's torch in my earlier books, but there were others that had interludes of more relaxed work. The CM6 coaches were designed for one job – a job they did superbly well. But in later life, and with general vehicle shortages prevailing (especially during the 1970s), CM6s found work in a more diverse range of areas. These included workers services, operated from Digbeth, travelling to and from car factories on routes known as 'Austin runs' that had an 'A' prefix to their service numbers. There were also more interesting runs, such as the high security Winson Green to Warwick runs, taking prisoners from jail to crown court.

There were also lucky passengers who had a CM6 allocated to their coach service or private hire; and sometimes coach holiday passengers, at the start or end of their holiday tour, were shuttled by CM6 between the National Holidays tour base of Sheffield and their Midlands home. There was one Digbeth coach service from Birmingham to Bristol which often had a 'short working' attached when resting in Bristol where it would be called upon to "do a quick Cheltenham and back". The white-painted CM6s never looked good, but I wonder if the passengers realised how lucky they were to have travelled on these iconic coaches, no matter the colour.

After its refurbishment, in the drab white National Travel livery, modernised CM6T 5666 is seen near Worksop on a National Holidays feeder service. At the wheel is Nuneaton motorway coach driver Brian Stokes.

A Nuneaton based CM6, fleet number 5670, having an easy day allocated to a private hire duty in Nottingham.

Modernised CM6T 5674 (the last built CM6) sitting at Digbeth, all set for a private hire departure to Alton Towers.

CASUALTIES

It's not often that you can study the underside of a bus. Here, a member of the D5 family has unexpectedly gone off-roading whilst operating the long Hereford to Shrewsbury X34 route. The breakdown crew on site have already attached a steel cable in preparation for the bus to be hauled back onto its wheels.

Midland Red was a proud operator, and that brought with it the need to protect their reputation and image. They had systems in place, developed over many years, that encouraged drivers to be safe, and instilled in them their prime objectives: the safety and comfort of passengers. This started with training to do the job 'the Midland Red way!' The training school was a strict place for, what would be seen today as, a rather extravagant six week course (detailed in 'The Driving School' on page 101). Each year, drivers would be rewarded with a safe driving bonus, more correctly termed 'drivers free of a blameworthy accident'. This would accrue a medal, or year bars to be added to an existing medal, and a certificate would be issued every year by the Road Operators Safety Council (ROSCO), a scheme that Midland Red participated in for many years and which was firmly part of the Midland Red social calendar. Presentation evenings were enjoyed with a three-course meal at a good local hotel or venue, where certificates and medals would be presented by a local dignitary, perhaps the chief constable of the police. Staff transport would be provided free of charge, along with a bar at the venue too!

Operating almost 2,000 buses is hard enough, and for any bus or transport company ongoing incidents and accidents are simply occupational hazards that have to be well-managed when they occur; such events were part of the strict record-keeping process at Midland Red. The company kept league tables of which garages had the most accidents, and these were published for all staff to see. Of course, such figures required close attention. A city garage with a high passenger count and higher traffic volume would be classified as a greater risk than a rural, sparsely populated country town garage; nonetheless, it was interesting to see variations in the tables over time.

When anything went wrong, there was an established, slick and well-oiled procedure put into action which was tailored to any event, to minimise impact. The entire era of Midland Red was without mobile telephones and internet communications, so instead of recording an incident on their phones, passengers and onlookers would be helping each other, allowing the driver to ease the problem and to get help as required. A driver would, in the first instance, check on his passengers, then call emergency services if they were needed, followed by a call to his garage. The garage staff would action any breakdown or recovery vehicle and the men required, and provide a replacement vehicle for ongoing passengers if needed.

If the accident was serious, the garage superintendent would immediately inform head office, who would arrange for senior staff to attend, along with any heavy equipment that may be needed from Central Works. They would manage the situation, along with the emergency services, and get passengers on their way as soon as possible. A bus involved in a serious accident or collision would often be moved to an inconspicuous spot near the incident location – a team from Central Works with a full recovery outfit would see to that. In some severe cases, it has been known for the team to use a roll of brown paper to tape over the damaged area of the bus and paint it red; they would return later, usually in the quieter twilight hours, and recover the bus to 'the works'. There were occasions when a large sheet of fabric was used to cover the vehicle for its journey. These may seem extreme measures, but they were all to preserve the reputation of the company, and to maintain the image of public passenger transport as one of the safest ways to travel. It was often people's *only* way to get about!

Nevertheless, the overall safety record of the company was exceptional. Staff were trained well. Buses were well designed and built, and maintained under a strictly managed regime of inspection and rectification. There were costly mid-life overhauls too, from which an almost new vehicle would emerge. The bottom line is, just as with any industry, we are dealing with machines and people, so something will go wrong at some time. Midland Red drivers' records of being free of blameworthy accidents were impressive, but there was an increasing number of vehicles on our roads, weather conditions were variable, and bus drivers were (back then) expected to be out in all weathers, including snow and ice.

Above: Probably the most feared of road conditions for professional drivers is black ice. It can hide beneath a film of rainwater or a layer of snow. The scene facing the driver of this Oldbury bus shows nearside body damage after it slid into a lamp standard. This is wartime, so notice the white-painted corners and wheel arches.

Top Right: An accident in icy conditions, believed to be in August 1947 near Sheldon, Birmingham. A Digbeth garage based S6 single-decker has slipped/skidded on the road and turned over. Whether the Digbeth based pre-war FEDD double-decker fleet number 1575 was involved or had just pulled up is not known.

Middle: A winter wonderland. It happens to even the experienced drivers, and this time to coachman Jim Wimbush who was on a normal weekday bus driving shift, operating route number 550 back from Southam to Leamington, driving down the steep Ufton Hill. There was black ice under the snow and, despite his years of experience, the Leyland LD8 type double-decker slid on the road and ended up in an adjacent field.

Bottom: This early post-war S8 type bus on a local Shrewsbury route during a very wet spell had to pull over to the left to avoid a larger lorry coming in the opposite direction. The bus continued under its own momentum further than the driver intended, and despite his efforts he could not get it out of the ditch. A walk to the telephone box and a call to the Midland Red Shrewsbury garage soon got things into action, and a company recovery vehicle was sent to get the bus back on the road.

Left: Merry Christmas! The Driver of S14 bus 4284 doesn't look very happy after he avoided a lorry coming the other way. He ended up sliding into a ditch in the snow. A driver's worst nightmare is being virtually helpless. All Midland Red garages had a supply of shovels, usually all smartly placed in their holding clips on the garage wall. In severe winter conditions, the driver could take one with him, and should he need to clear the snow from around the bus wheels to get extra grip on the country roads, his trusty shovel would help the bus service get through. Sometimes, however, a shovel wasn't enough.

Above: An early wartime image near Kings Heath in South Birmingham in winter time. This is BHA FEDD fleet number 1793 on its side after skidding. It's a busy scene, but just one policeman is visible amongst numerous uniformed ARPs.

Right: On 3rd October 1953, nearly fifty passengers were injured and one passenger and the driver died when fleet number 2504, a double decker, turned on its side on Groby Road, Leicester, right on the city boundary. Local residents provided sheets for bandages and cups of tea for the passengers, who remained calm throughout. Three county ambulances and four from the city ferried the injured to the infirmary. The fire brigade attended to ensure that the bus was safe. Midland Red brought their heavy vehicle recovery truck to put the vehicle back on its wheels. The bus was officially withdrawn a month after the incident.

Motorway prestige - an incident on the first day

Midland Red's Motorway Express routes were, pretty much, their highest profile services, and it was vital that their image remained untarnished. But these routes were pioneered by Midland Red, so no one had any previous experience.

High-speed road tyres for anything but racing cars were in the very early stages of development, and buses travelling at over 80mph was certainly a novelty. On the first day that the M1 motorway was opened, 2 November 1959, there was an incident on the first departure. This was a press event just before the regular passenger coaches set off. Two coaches left Digbeth, one carrying company VIPs and the other members of the press and several management officials. A front tyre on one of the coaches failed at around 65mph, but the driver kept the vehicle under control and brought it to a standstill on the hard shoulder.

Unfortunately this was the coach carrying members of the press, who would be writing-up reports in the national papers and magazines about this fabulous new method of transport between the second city and the capital. Fortunately it did not do much harm, as the situation was handled quickly and efficiently. A call from an emergency telephone on the side of the motorway led to swift action from Midland Red's garage at Rugby, where a replacement motorway coach was despatched for the speedy transfer of the passengers, along with mechanics and a new wheel and tyre that made sure the original coach was quickly back on the road. What could have been a negative response from the passengers on board was instead praise for the driver for bringing the coach to a safe stop on the hard shoulder, and the assistance swiftly provided that allowed the service to arrive on time in London.

Accidents

The first six or so years of motorway services saw growing passenger numbers and increasing motorway traffic. There were a number of accidents involving the motorway coaches; some were quite severe, but others looked worse than they actually were. It was perhaps inevitable that there would be occasional incidents on such a pioneering operation, but with the incredibly high mileages operated, accidents were extremely rare.

On a mid-March morning in 1965, motorway coach driver Eddie Finch reported to Padmore Street garage in Worcester a little after six in the morning for just another day's work. He was allocated CM5 4836 for a duty up and down the motorway express route along the M5 between Worcester and Birmingham, with service numbers X43 and X44. His first journey was the second timetabled departure of the day, the 0640hrs to Birmingham. His conductor, Jack Willis, was on board along with just eight passengers. The service only had a couple of stops along its route, but these coaches had manual entrance doors and so conductors were required.

Before the accident, and looking very smart. CM5 type fleet number 4836 had, until a few weeks before, been on loan to Digbeth garage where it is seen here, parked at the side of the garage in Mill Lane.

The start of the journey was uneventful. With the early morning dew still around, they joined the M5 going north towards Birmingham. They were passing the Droitwich junction near Wychbold when a car that was joining the motorway emerged from the slip road. It immediately pulled out to overtake a slower vehicle, straight into the

path of the coach. The driver was forced to take evasive action, but lost control of the coach. Like a nightmare fairground ride, the coach careered across the central reservation, across the other carriageway, through the crash barriers and rolled down the embankment. It came to rest in the garden of a bungalow called The Lawns (since demolished when the M5 was widened in the early 1990s). It was cruising at 65mph at the time. There was considerable damage to the front of the coach, but the main structure remained intact. As fumes were present, probably from leaking oil and fuel, the fire brigade attended the vehicle and watched as it was righted. An ambulance also attended: one passenger received a rib injury, one a broken arm and the others had cuts and bruises, mainly from some of the windows breaking along one side of the coach. The injured passengers were taken to Bromsgrove hospital for outpatient treatment before all being sent home the same day.

The company protocol swung into action for this kind of incident the moment it was reported, and Bearwood (the chief traffic offices) was notified. High-level staff were despatched to the scene, and the 'white elephant' recovery vehicle that was based at Central Works, and capable of sorting almost any incident, was summoned. Mr Davenport, the company photographer, recorded various images of the coach as it was found and during its recovery.

The coach was put back on its wheels with the help of the white elephant, then covered with a sheet to hide the damage (and the company's embarrassment), and prepared for its journey to Central Works for assessment. It was initially parked up, awaiting a space in the body shop, where Bryan Gwynne, who looked after special projects, investigated the damage and made notes.

Looking at the images, it would be reasonable to think that this would be the end for this coach. It had crossed over the carriageway, rolled down the opposite embankment and ended up on its roof. The integral construction held up well; in fact, the integrity of the passenger compartment was sufficient to protect passengers from serious injury – this was 16 years before rollover cage construction regulations were introduced. Despite Central Works being busy to capacity building the last of the D9s, S17s and CM6s and undertaking mid-life overhauls of older vehicles, Bryan thought that this coach was worth rebuilding, so he scheduled its work and arranged for parts. Over the following months, the coach was demoted from its motorway coach status and rebuilt as a C5A variant. It then rejoined the operational fleet, this time moving to Malvern garage where it continued to perform occasional private hire work, excursions and bus services. The vehicle saw service at Sheepcote Street and Hinckley after that and for its remaining years. It was withdrawn at Easter in 1971 and sold to Margo International Coach Lines in London, that bought many of these vehicles after withdrawal by Midland Red.

Whilst not wanting to make light of any accident, we were living in different times back then, and the reaction was just to get on and sort it! The relatively relaxed nature of how these incidents were handled seems very different from the long delays, investigations and red tape of today – yet the result was much the same. The company investigated and learned from each incident, and even if it was caused by others it taught drivers to be more aware of what other road users might do.

MR. FRANK TROMANS.

On another occasion, a CM5T coach was on a journey from Birmingham to London under the control of one of the first and most experienced motorway express coachmen, Frank Tromans, who worked at Midland Red's Digbeth coach station.

It was the 1830hrs departure of the ME1 motorway express from Birmingham on Friday evening, 25 November 1960. The fully-laden coach had been making good time in the fast lane of the motorway. A passenger sitting behind the driver related what happened next. A car travelling in the middle lane pulled out in front of the coach to overtake another vehicle, causing the motorway express driver to take evasive action. In doing so, his front wheel touched the grass at the side of the central reservation (there were no central crash barriers in those days). The front offside wheel dropped slightly where the concrete road surface met the grass. The coach rolled onto its side, slid onto the central reservation and came to a standstill facing the opposite direction. Fortunately, only one passenger, a 73-year-old printer from London who was returning from holiday, was taken by ambulance to Dunstable Hospital, but he was released a short time later. Police on scene ensured the traffic flowed safely while the Midland Red recovery truck arrived, and a lane was cordoned off for a short time while the coach was put back onto its wheels.

A passenger said that there was no panic, nor any time to think. "We were in a jumble with all the hand luggage coming off the luggage racks. We soon got ourselves sorted and stayed on the overturned coach as no one wanted to go outside – it was raining! The driver checked on all the passengers and then went to telephone for help. The Midland Red quickly sent a big recovery truck from a local garage which uprighted the coach and we went to the nearby motorway service area where we all had a cup of tea and refreshments while we waited for a replacement coach, and then we carried on with our journey to Victoria." Those were the days!

Besides accidents affecting the more prestige routes, there were, of course, those day-to-day bumps to keep the local garage bodyman in employment.

S16 5519, a Leamington allocated vehicle, was operating on 'The Track' series of routes connecting the outskirts of Leamington with the outskirts of Warwick. It left The Rushmore estate in Leamington travelling to The Forbes Estate just off the Stratford Road in Warwick. Entering Warwick Square, an estate car hit the offside of the S16, causing the lower panel (which was a removable) to fall off, along with the adjoining support pillar. The local beat bobby was quickly on hand to record the event.

5519 in Warwick Square where the conductor seems to be more involved in events than the driver who is looking out of his cab window, concerned at the damage to his bus.

S17 fleet number 5710 had a rear end collision with a lorry in the Coalville area, causing considerable damage. Another S17 fleet number 5555, allocated to Nuneaton garage for its entire 15-year life, had a similar but front offside accident with a large farm hedge cutter in Fillongley, Warwickshire, where the farmer continued to pass alongside the bus, not realising his cutter arm was directly in line with the roof of the bus. Fortunately no one was injured. It was repaired at Central Works and returned to service.

THE HUMAN SIDE

Midland Red grew rapidly in the inter-war years. Early growth led to employees joining Midland Red from the returnees of WW1; then the depression and great recession from the late 20s into the 30s brought willing workers to join many of the prosperous employers at the time, including Midland Red.

The post-WW2 years have been different, and the bus industry generally has had continual issues with shortages of staff. Midland Red needed to reinstate those services that were curtailed or withdrawn in wartime conditions and also needed to expand to match the new housebuilding boom of the 40s and 50s, but the difficulties were accentuated in 1947 when the weekly hours of work were reduced from 48 to 44.

At the end of WW2, Midland Red had 1,400 vehicles, with total staff of 6,700 and annual mileage of 45 million. Just seven years later the fleet stood at over 1,800, with 9,000 staff and 73 million miles were operated. Recruiting enough staff to keep up with the company's expansion must have been tough. The company maintained an appreciable number of loyal staff, many of whom would work many hours of overtime to keep services running, but it was clear that the training schools for both conductors and drivers were perpetually busy to replace those employees who couldn't see bus work as their career; many of them were ex-servicemen who couldn't settle.

Three quarters of all employees were drivers and conductors, and clearly the unsociable hours of work over a seven day week and a semi-outdoor life with long and sometimes split shifts did not appeal to everyone, but some would give it a go until something better came along. Drivers and conductors were regularly working around 60 hours a week, and more in summer months. Midland Red promoted careers with the company, emphasising all of the positives.

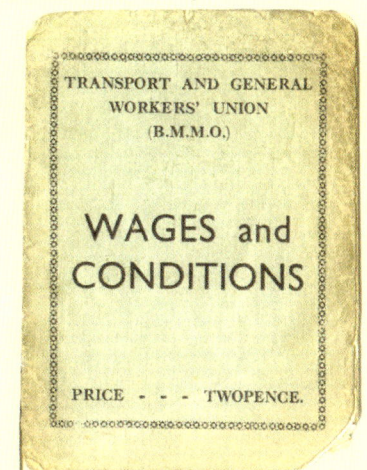

It was a well-paid job, especially with overtime constantly available for those that wanted it. The job offered security, an open air lifestyle without constant supervision, free uniform and travel concessions and the opportunity to meet a wide variety of people. People who considered themselves 'real' busmen said they would never change jobs with any other workers, and this was borne out by 1,000 of its staff who qualified for 25 years long service awards, and almost 100 who received 40 year awards.

After the war, the person with overall responsibility for staff was the staff officer Mr L. H. Youngs, who himself had a long service with Midland Red. He directed policy with regard to recruitment and retention of all staff. It was decided to pay particular attention to employees who were planning to leave, and enquire as to the reasons why. If an employee was worth retaining, a personal letter would be sent to them in an effort to persuade them to stay. The company looked further afield, to foreign countries, and nearer to home in Ireland.

To help, a number of hostels were opened, including at Dudley, Sutton Coldfield and Leamington, each with a matron. The appointment of a welfare officer, Mrs M. Griffiths, also helped workers to settle into both their new accommodation and their job. Employees were paid during their training in a further attempt to lure bus crews into a more attractive life on the buses.

Even so, the shortages continued. In the late 1960s, a crisis was declared when the shortage of platform staff was at its most acute, at 400 short. This affected the reliability of services, made more serious by the maintenance issues of the time, including parts shortages.

Decades of service

Although the recruitment of staff was a continuous process, there were many long-serving employees, and they never seemed to be camera shy. Enjoy this look through the decades, but spare a minute to imagine what it was like doing their job at that time. Employment conditions have changed considerably. It would be no good a driver signing off the heaters for 'not working' in the first picture!

The company needed to maintain enough staff to operate timetabled services, so publicity and recruitment was important. A retired pre-war single-decker was used as a publicity vehicle and was regularly seen at Leamington Pump Room Gardens on job recruitment duties, where this picture was taken.

A three-horsed omnibus at the time BMMO was formed, in the early 1900s, outside the stables in Bearwood Road.

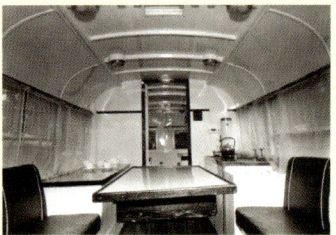

The publicity vehicle parked at Central Works in 1964, awaiting sale. The wooden section at the entrance folded down to form a ramp. Inside was all the new recruit would want. A sit down and a cuppa – it would be the only free one he would get! The bus was originally delivered early in 1935 as a petrol-engined ON type. A year later it was converted to have a new diesel engine as a CON (Converted ON). It was converted to its new use as a publicity/recruitment vehicle in May 1955, when some others of the type were being withdrawn. This one just missed the preservation era and was sold in May 1964.

A rather nostalgic picture of a Leamington and Warwick tram in the early years of the 1900s. The crew are Edmund Ayton and Frank Warner, both of whom transferred to BMMO when the Leamington and Warwick Transport Company became part of the BMMO empire. Edmund was an electric tram driver and during WW1 saw active service in the Middle East and Egypt. He returned to tram driving in 1919, and when the trams ended in the 1930s, in favour of the green motorbuses, he became a motorbus driver. Late in 1937 he joined Midland Red, operating from the same tram depot in Emscote, Warwick. He became a coach driver and was popular with his passengers. His son, Bert, followed in his footsteps and was retiring from long service as engineering foreman when I began working at Leamington garage.

Frank Warner, whose career is mentioned in Midland Red Influence, had a lifetime on the buses. His father drove the first tram in 1905 and Frank joined in July 1919 as a conductor. He, like Edmund, transferred to Midland Red employment in 1937 and progressed quickly, becoming traffic superintendent in Leamington. He collected £3,000 during WW2 for the Midland Red Red Cross fund which he said was to repay his debt to them from WW1.

At the short-lived Burgage Walk depot in Nuneaton, just after BMMO took over the North Warwickshire Motor Traction operations. A Tilling Stevens single-decker with five drivers and conductors posing for a what might have been a rare photo opportunity in those days.

During WW1, some buses were converted to run on town gas. This Tilling Stevens TS3 single-decker had firm side boards to hold the gas balloon and prevent it falling over the sides or front as it deflated. Lady conductresses were employed during wartime.

A gas-powered single-decker bus operating at Atherstone in 1917. The driver standing by the bus is Maurice Perry (1883-1926) who lived in Croft Road, Nuneaton. He worked for North Warwickshire Motor Services and subsequently for Midland Red for a total of over 18 years.

MIDLAND

A wonderful scene in the Worcester area of the well-liked QL type. The driver is wearing gaiters over his lower legs that provided some protection from the draughts that came from the holes around the foot pedals in these early buses. The conductor is wearing his Bell Punch ticket machine.

The 'M' type (Madam) was designed with lady shoppers in mind to encourage them to travel off peak. A partition was fitted to keep smokers to the rear of the bus. HA 4920 was new in May 1929 and was withdrawn in December 1949. This photograph was taken in Rugby, just prior to WW2.

Staff were rewarded for their loyalty and benefited from many activities. Here is an account of an annual staff outing from the 1920s:

"The annual office staff outing has grown each year in popularity. On Tuesday 21 June 1927, the destination was Symonds Yat, and six large pneumatic-tyred saloon buses were needed to accommodate everyone that wanted to go.

"They set off from Bearwood at 8.30am for a scenic ride, stopping off for lunch at the Garrick Hotel in Hereford. On arrival, a telegram awaited the passengers from their boss, the traffic manager O. C. Power, declaring that urgent business had prevented his attendance but he wished everyone a jolly time. Arriving at Symonds Yat, the party at once entered into the many delights there: some went boating, others crossed the ferry for rambles amid the woods, while the more thoughtful rested a while in contemplation of the sylvan scene.

"When at 5pm it was time to return it was declared that the stay was far too short; a week would be too little to take in the beauty. A ride through lovely country brought the party to a tea stop at Ross. Great Malvern was the next stop for 45 minutes, for a stroll or ramble on the hills. There is no more beautiful country in the world than this England of ours. Truly it is the gem in the silver sea and Symonds Yat is one of those beautiful facets."

Coach Driver Ces Reeves of Nuneaton garage stands proudly by his QC coach. The QC was the first proper Midland Red coach, developed from the Q (Queen) bus, having a central gangway and an entrance door opposite the driver. The fixed side screens and rear dome gave better protection for those aboard, and the driver could operate the canvas roof from the central gangway. It ran along a channel in the side screens and could be closed or opened in a few minutes.

A crew from Banbury enjoy a long-distance day away on a two vehicle private hire to Weymouth in 1938. The coach on the left is a new SLR (Saloon Low Rolls-Royce) and the vehicle behind the drivers is a CHA registered SON (Saloon ONward) with English Electric bodywork and a sliding entrance door immediately behind the engine.

A wartime Leyland TD7, having been rebuilt in later life, stands at the terminus. The conductor has a pre-war style summer jacket and is wearing a harness for the Verometer ticket machine.

Three drivers from Wolverhampton garage take a rest on a summer's day in 1955, by the side of a pre-war single-decker.}

Hereford garage's longest serving staff. Driver Thomas, on the left, was the first driver at Hereford garage. He joined Midland Red in 1920 at the original and short-lived garage at The Black Lion. His conductor joined a year later. The photograph is taken in Hereford garage in 1950, in front of an S6 bus.

Coach driver and coach conductor pose in their white smocks whilst on a 'Road and River Cruise' excursion in 1959. To reach the status of coach driver these men would have already given considerable service to the company. In the era of this photograph, bus drivers normally had to achieve over eight years of service before they would be considered for coach work.

Above: A jovial Pat McCumisky of Nuneaton garage stands by his S17 in 1970.

Left: Banbury D7 fleet number 3363 in the garage doorway in 1962, with crew discussing their schedule and working out the tea breaks.

Bottom left: Midland Red were never shy of sending their vehicles anywhere. This two-year-old service bus was about to depart with company staff from Leicester Southgates garage for Scotland in 1952. The three-day trip went without incident and the bus was back on ordinary Leicester local services the following day.

Conducting a Midland Red bus

The vast majority of bus services, and indeed some coach services, had bus (or coach) conductors on board. In the 1920s, even on charabancs the conductor had a seat, with its own entrance door just forward of the offside rear wheel, that was partitioned off from the passengers. Coach conductors were not required after the mid 1960s.

During WW2, with many men being conscripted to the armed forces, there were staff shortages at most garages, and so, many women were recruited for the important task of collecting the company's bus fare revenue. But the collection of fares wasn't the only duty the bus conductor had to perform. The bus conductor was the person in charge of the bus, and they were responsible for its safety and its running to time.

"There's always an excuse for running late, but NEVER one for running early!" the recruits were told during the start of their induction to become a Midland Red bus conductor or conductress.

The first week of training began in the classroom. Sessions included safety issues, and it was the safety and comfort of the passengers that were the prime objectives of those hoping to hold a PSV licence.

New conductors and conductresses are shown the workings of a ticket machine by the chief training officer, Mr Hill, at the Bearwood training school.

For 'raw' recruits to Midland Red, it was time to be measured for the company uniform. Then came a little information about the company: how it all worked, where everyone fitted in, and how the new recruit needed to get up very early in the morning for early shifts one week, and then work very late shifts the following week. Reliability was at the heart of the job.

It often took time to understand and get used to the complex shift arrangements, and the bus bell codes: one bell to stop at the next bus stop, two bells to start the bus away from a bus stop, three bells meant the bus was full and the driver should only stop if someone wanted to alight (not to pick up more passengers), and four bells was the signal for an emergency stop. They also had to become acquainted with the various ticket types, and the use of the ticket machine. These were complex things in their own right, and involved checking the date, and setting the inward or outward direction of route and the type of journey, such as single, return, child, adult, worker, scholar and 'anywhere' (i.e. the popular 'day anywhere' ticket).

The bus conductor also had to be trained on the 'extra' category of tickets that were used for accompanied dogs and the carriage of goods and newspapers on Midland Red's extensive parcels network. There were also transfer tickets where passengers had to change buses mid-way to complete their journey; for example, a service I conducted was the Nuneaton to Ashby service 697, where sometimes a Nuneaton garage bus would travel as far as Measham and passengers would transfer to a Coalville garage vehicle to continue to Ashby.

Destination boards used on pre-war buses, or roller blinds on more modern vehicles, needed to be changed at each end of a route. If you were allocated to an older bus with wooden or aluminium destination boards, you had to make sure that you went to the store and collected *all* of the boards that would be needed by the bus for the whole day - not just for the time you were allocated to it. The boards would be stored in the luggage racks and hung at each end of every route.

While the bus was travelling on its route, various items of information had to be recorded on the 'waybill', which was the daily report sheet. The number of passengers on board was noted at each 'fare stage'. Fare stages were places along the route where the fare changed, and they were usually indicated by the words 'fare stage' printed on the bus stop sign. Also recorded on the waybill were the ticket serial numbers issued up to each fare stage, and the accumulated takings at the start and end of the journey, which were copied from the ticket machine's readings.

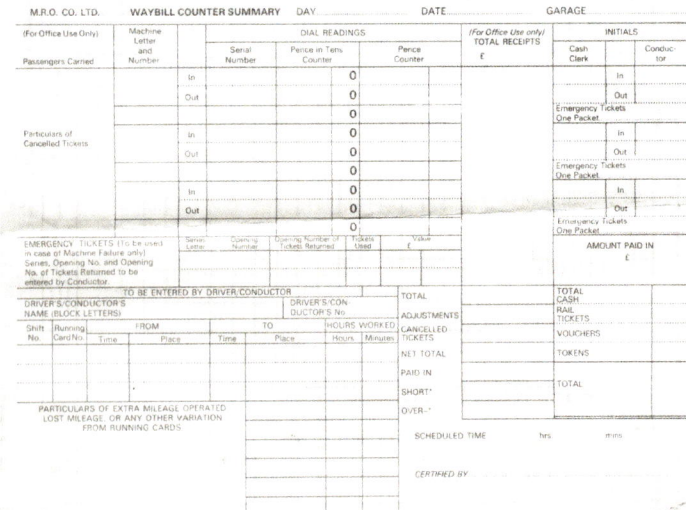

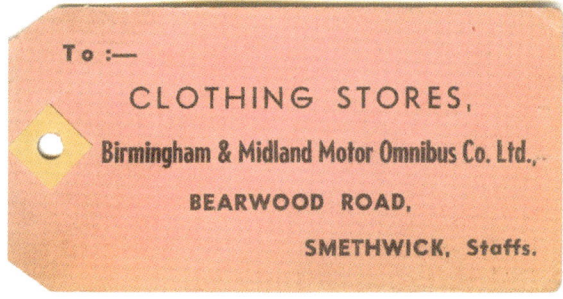

The back of the conductor's waybill document, showing space for three sessions of duty; this could have been a three-part split shift or a normal two-part shift, with space in case overtime was worked. It was the back of the waybill where the ticket machine counters were added-up to calculate the amount of money the conductor had to pay-in at the end of their shift.

The 'real' task for the conductor was, of course, to collect bus fares (the company revenue), besides providing local and travel information, and carrying the Midland Red timetable that would assist passengers requiring information on other routes and connections.

The new recruit would report at the depot for their assigned shift. They were introduced to their chaperone, and then it was off to the canteen for a cup of tea. The driver would probably be there already!

Left: A trainee clippie with her chaperone, giving advice on ticket types to be issued.

Below: A rather quaint scene in the lower saloon of a FEDD, with the clippie busy giving change to a passenger. Actually, this was 'posed' for a wartime publicity photo – all the 'passengers' were office staff from Bearwood garage!

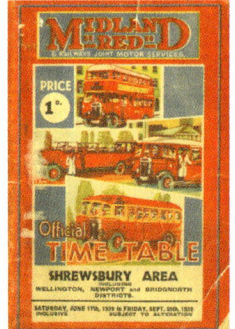  

After a week in the school it would be time to go out with an experienced clippie to see how it was done for real! And by this time, your new uniform would have been delivered from the uniform stores at Bearwood.

Who would think that changing the destination blinds would involve some serious climbing. Wearing the correct footwear always helped. This wartime view shows the SOS radiator badge that was soon to be replaced with BMMO insignia. The lights have tin masks to prevent light being seen from above.

To become a bus conductor, a licence had to be obtained from the Traffic Commissioner, where the good character of the applicant was checked. After about three weeks of working with the experienced conductor, and assuming good progress was made, their name would appear on the rota of shifts, and a new career had begun. Their new conductor licence would be issued and their numbered badge would arrive from the Traffic Commissioner's office in Birmingham (for the West Midlands Area) or Peterborough (for the East Midlands area), and in their smart uniform they were ready to start.

There have, in fact, been one or two famous Midland Red bus conductors. Sir Edward Downes, born in Aston, always said that his conducting days started at the Midland Red. He went on to conduct over 1,000 performances at the Royal Opera House, and conducted the first-ever performance at the new Sydney Opera House. But his beginnings as a conductor were with Midland Red during WW2, when he also had a second job, performing fire-watching duties for the City of Birmingham Fire Brigade during night air raids.

Inside a typical conductors' room at the garage, with spaces for conductors and conductresses to count the contents of their cash bag, which would hopefully tally with the figures taken from the ticket machine for the value of tickets sold. Up until the 1950s, this was paid-in directly to a cash inspector who was part of the garage traffic assistant team at each garage. In later times, a night safe was provided and conducting staff placed their calculated takings in the safe, ready for counting the next morning by cash clerks.

A conductor's paying in slip, completed at the end of each day and presented with the cash for checking. If the amount of money paid-in did not tally with the amount required, the conductor would find their name on a 'shorts and overs' list and any discrepancy would be corrected in their pay packet. Should this occurrence become more frequent, the employee would be called for a disciplinary interview.

The conductor at the end of his shift. When in later days the offices were unmanned, he would place the takings into the night safe which was built into the wall of the despatch office.

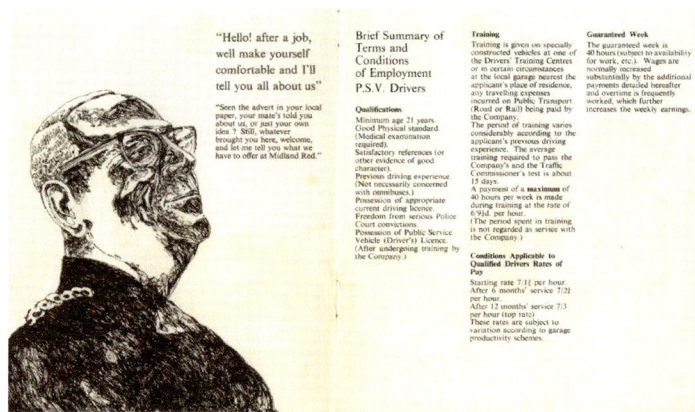

Part of a recruitment brochure that appeared around the same time as the famous 'Frank, Bill, Percy and Fred' staff recruitment advertising campaign. This was at a time when garage superintendents still wore uniforms.

On the other side of the wall was the safe, encased in concrete, with the chute leading directly inside the safe. The early morning despatch office clerk is seen taking ticket machines from the conductors' lockers to prepare them for the next day's work. This involved checking the dial readings, and adding new waybill sheets and ticket machine paper rolls etc, before issuing them to their new users as they arrived for their shifts.

The increasing need to save money brought the introduction of one-man operation. This gathered pace. From 1966, one-man operation was allowed on double-deckers, and by 1979 the role of the bus conductor at Midland Red was all but over. Over the previous few years, the company gave conductors the opportunity to train to be drivers; those that refused or were not suited to driving were offered redundancy.

The author, as Leamington garage's last newly-employed bus conductor. Having worked for the company for a few years in office positions, he was anxious to see life as a member of the platform staff. Here he is working a favourite route on an early D9, on a late evening shift, running from Whitnash to Cubbington via Leamington town centre.

The Driving School

The usual way of applying for a job, whether as a driver or conductor, was by applying at your local Midland Red garage.

Midland Red had a regimentally-run central driving school, located in a building at the rear of its main garage premises in Bearwood, Birmingham. New driving recruits, or conductors upgrading to become drivers, were sent to Bearwood for six weeks of structured training. It should be bourne in mind that new recruits in this era would likely never have driven a vehicle in their lives before, unlike today, when you are required to have held a full car licence before upgrading to larger vehicles. But there were some exceptions. Midland Red recruits who joined perhaps after military service could well have been trained to drive some form of mechanically propelled vehicle during their service. However, their previous experience was not a 'free pass' to any part of this training. Everyone who entered was taught to drive 'The Midland Red way!'

The division of the engineering and traffic departments that was so prevalent at Midland Red was no different here: the driver training school was administered by the engineering department.

After initial formalities, applicants started with two weeks of classroom tuition. Mr Hill, the chief driving instructor, had a formidable reputation and would not tolerate latecomers to his class, sending them home to try again on another later course. And this was in the days when Midland Red didn't pay trainees during their training, as those who were successful in passing their test were gifted a job and career for a lifetime!

One candidate who was late for his class was trainee driver Harry Roake, who, in late 1945, had been released from his army service and applied to Midland Red for a driving job at his local garage in Rugby.

Harry set off very early in the morning on the 586 bus from Rugby to Coventry (a 50-minute drive), then caught his planned 159 bus from Coventry to Birmingham (taking just short of an hour); then he walked across Birmingham to catch his bus to Bearwood, a 20-minute ride down the Hagley Road. The walk took a little longer than he had expected, as he had never been to Birmingham before. The service along the Hagley Road was frequent, but he missed the bus he had planned to catch, and then had to walk from his alighting stop at The Kings Head along Bearwood Road. He could clearly see the large letters 'MIDLAND' standing proudly on the side of the building, but the walk seemed to take ages. On arrival he then had to find out where the driving school was. The result was that he was 10 to 15 minutes late, and Mr Hill had started talking. Harry knocked on the door, entered and apologised for being late. Mr Hill was clearly unimpressed, and told him that if he turned up at the garage late for his shift as a bus driver, his passengers would be inconvenienced, and perhaps he should consider this on his way back to Rugby, where he could apply again to join a future training course!

This, of course, was a stern lesson, not only for Harry but also for the other recruits who were sitting there witnessing this harsh start to their six-week course. They certainly paid attention after that, and Harry went back to Rugby garage and asked to be given another opportunity. He attended on time for the next course, and went on to have a successful 30-year career – including being my driving instructor in the early 1970s.

Harry Roake, a trainee driver in 1945 and my driving instructor in the early 1970s. The photograph was taken from a video recording that I made of him discussing his career. He was proud to wear his many safe driving medals, along with his long service brooch. Harry was a character with many humorous stories to tell of his time working for Midland Red as a bus driver, coach driver, coach cruise driver/courier and driving instructor, before his retirement in 1988.

Driving students would learn how important it was to understand time and timetables and to take care of the vehicles and related equipment. To help them understand what they were driving and how the bus worked, they were taken to Central Works in Edgbaston to see how vehicles were made and maintained, how to change wheels, etc. They also learned of the importance of their Midland Red uniform and the wearing of their uniform hats. They were allowed to remove their hats when out in the countryside, but when re-entering a built-up area, town or city, they risked being reported if their hat was not worn.

After their two weeks of classroom instruction, it was time to hit the streets. The trainees were given two weeks on one of the fleet of dual-control training vehicles. These were specially converted vehicles that were drawn from old single-decker buses or coaches that had been withdrawn from their main duties. The conversions were comprehensive and undertaken at Central Works. This involved fitting two steering wheels and two complete sets of pedals so that the instructor was totally in control of the vehicle when a trainee was in the driving seat. This had many advantages, including the trainee drivers learning their new skills in the safest way possible. In times gone by, most trainee drivers would not have driven a vehicle before – cars were only for those fortunate few! But if you could master driving one of the training vehicles, you felt you could drive anything.

Another advantage of using such well-converted vehicles was that the instructor could take the trainee out of Bearwood garage and into central Birmingham on their first day. The instructor was able to control the vehicle while the trainee learned how far he had to turn the steering wheel, and how to control the gearbox, clutch, brake and accelerator pedals.

Administrative tasks included completing paperwork, defect forms, reading schedules, and accident reporting, if you were unlucky enough to be involved in such incidents. It certainly paid drivers and conductors not to have accidents as the basic pay was enhanced by bonuses, including a payment, usually made quarterly, for being free from blameworthy accidents. Records of individual garage accident rates were kept and published yearly. Those fortunate drivers not to have had a blameworthy accident would be given an additional payment in their wages, and an annual certificate and a medal presented at the annual Safe Driving Awards. This was usually held at a large hotel or civic suite, with the medals presented by the local mayor, chief constable or other dignitary, and with senior management from the company in attendance. There was usually a three-course meal provided too.

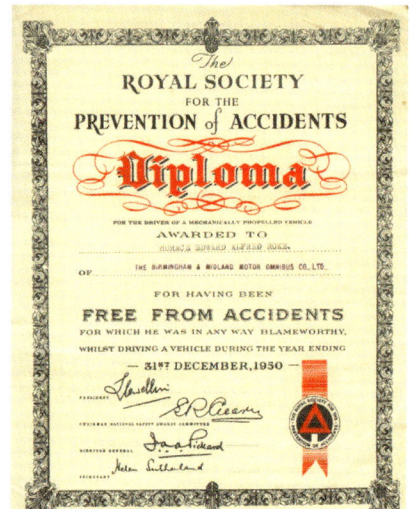

Top left: The early dual-control vehicles were converted from vehicles made in the 1920s, where the instructor sat behind the trainee. The fuel tank, originally under the driver's seat, had to be moved back to accommodate the instructor, and is just visible. There was not much comfort provided with these seats.

Below left: In the mid 1960s, the C1 coaches that had entered service immediately after the end of WW2 were being withdrawn. Several were chosen to undergo comprehensive conversion to become the new driver trainers. These were the last of the full conversions. Trainees were told that if they could drive these old timers, they would be able to drive anything in the future. It certainly was a good grounding, especially in mastering the now lost art of double-declutching. These C1s were withdrawn in 1976 and replaced with S16 single-deck buses, where the instructor was perched on a seat mounted above the entry steps and had only basic controls.

Dual-control driver trainer C1 number 3311 seen in coach livery when just converted, at work in Leamington. This vehicle later went on to another life with a building contactor which allowed it to be around long enough to be of interest to preservationists; it is now restored and in running condition.

The training vehicle that the author had experience of driving – fleet number 3327. At the time this photograph was taken, it had been repainted all-over red and was allocated to Bearwood garage.

The final BMMO type to be converted for driver training use. The S16 service bus was the last type built with manual gearbox and conventional clutch. This vehicle was fleet number 5517 and it spent many years at Leamington garage. It was based at Nuneaton driving school where its young driver was visiting on an enthusiasts' trip from a preservation group based at Leamington garage in the 1970s. When the S16 trainers were withdrawn the company bought second-hand Leyland or Bedford coaches for the Nuneaton training school and hired-in a double-deck Bristol FLF, owned by an ex-driver, which was used for double-decker experience and for the trainees' actual driving test.

These were the days of double-declutching and listening to the tone of the engine for the right time to change gear, when the gears would 'mesh' rather than 'grate'. At the same time, the trainee had instilled in them, "your prime objective is the safety and comfort of your passengers." This was especially important when learning how to do emergency stops. There was a certain technique for stopping the bus very quickly, yet keeping passengers safely in their seats and avoiding injury. This technique of brake control wasn't just for emergency stops, but to bring the bus to a controlled stop at a bus stop when passengers were likely to be standing up or walking along the gangway towards the platform doors.

Bus drivers had to report the condition of the bus at the start of each driving period, so to avoid drivers being penalised for the occasional scratch in the paintwork, it was common for the old-hand drivers to carry a red lipstick of a similar shade to the bus colour. They would furtively rub it into the scratch to make it less conspicuous, thereby avoiding the loss of their quarterly bonus for accident-free driving. During my early days at Leamington garage I witnessed this first-hand by a driver of many years' service (bus and coach driver Sid Jackson), who was then in the later part of his working life.

After the two weeks of dual-control training and continual assessment by the instructor, the trainee would either be sufficiently competent to be promoted to the next stage of training or, on rare occasions, sent back to his originating garage as 'unsuitable at this time'.

The next stage was a considerable step up: a double-decker. Here the trainee was isolated in the cab, and the instructor had no separate controls, so this experience would initially test you, and more than likely *make* you a driver. As a trainee, you were told that you are in charge of the bus, not the bus in charge of you! There was usually a means of communication with the instructor through a window space in the back of the cab; either the window had been removed, or a small slider was open.

Left: A delighted driver being issued with his paperwork by the examiner after successfully passing his PSV test. Right: In the 'cheap and cheerful' paint era when red covered almost everywhere. D7 4397 of the training fleet rests in Coventry in spring 1976.

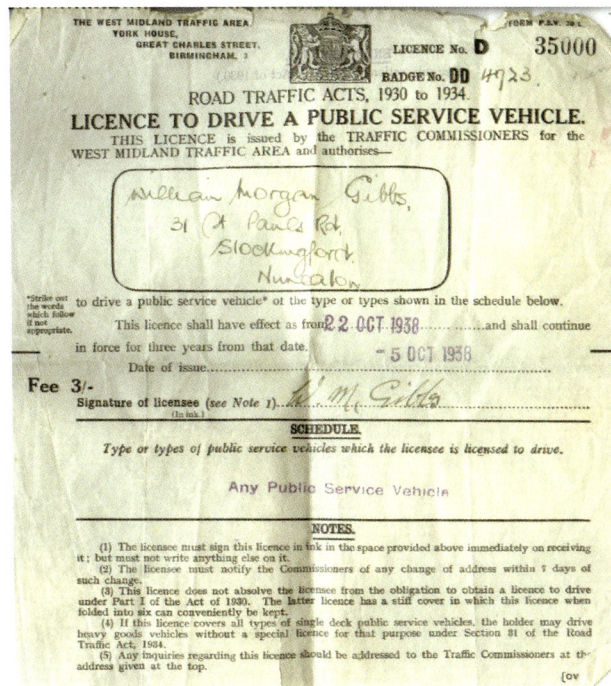

A copy of the paper driver's public service vehicle licence.

A driver's badge, identified with red border trim (a conductor's trim was green). This badge shows signs of its age, having belonged to a driver with over 40 years of service.

The remaining two weeks of training were brought to a conclusion with a driving test. If you were one of the fortunate majority who passed their test, there would be the customary waiting time for your licence and badge to be sent from the Traffic Commissioner in the area where you were working. This time was filled, back at the garage, with what was known as 'all types' training. This was an opportunity to gain a little experience in driving the different types of vehicles that were allocated to your garage. Besides the all types training which could be done in a day or so, it was also time for learning the routes, where the driver would be expected to operate almost as if he had done it a hundred times before! This was very valuable training, as it never enters a passenger's mind when they board the bus that it might be their driver's first day out with 'real' passengers on board!

Accurate form filling meant accurate wage payments. There seemed to be a form for everything. This trainee driver's route learning card was mostly used for the period between passing the driving test and the arrival of the official driver's licence, during which the new driver would learn the routes at the garage where he was employed. It would also be used for drivers who already had a licence, but were moved to a new garage.

Here is an account from a colleague who reveals some tips that he picked up from the highly experienced Midland Red driving instructors during his training:

"The next stage came when I drove, in turn, three types of double-decker: the BMMO type, an AEC Regent, and a Daimler fitted with fluid flywheel and Wilson gearbox. The vast majority of vehicles operated by the BMMO are, of course, of their own design and construction, but they have a few AEC, Leyland and Daimler vehicles acquired during and immediately after the war. On double-deckers, it was necessary to watch more carefully the distance from the kerb, to counter the road camber and to clear telegraph poles, overhanging trees and even shop blinds and signs. Ordinary bus routes for double-decker buses were clearly marked on the daily running card. Instructions and deviation from set routes was strictly forbidden.

"And now for some of the points which struck me during the training. First and foremost the good humour of the instructors despite all the wrong things that the trainee driver does – faults which must, on occasion, make the instructors feel like giving up in despair. Another thing, too, was the importance attached by instructors to courtesy on the road, and I began to realise during my training that it is at this stage that the slogan 'The Friendly Midland Red' is instilled into the staff. The passenger must always come first, I was told. When taking a right corner, don't accelerate round it because passengers may be waiting on the platform to alight at the stop just round the bend. I was shown that, even with an emergency stop, the thought of the passengers must come first. Brake by all means, and as quickly as possible in an emergency; but just at the last moment, as the bus is almost at a standstill, release the brake and then re-apply it again so that this cancels out the natural 'settling back' of the vehicle. In this way, passengers who, in an emergency stop, will have been thrown forward in the bus will not suddenly be jerked back again as the vehicle comes to a standstill.

"I discovered that cornering was a matter of geometry and that as long as one delayed turning the steering wheel until the eyes could see the full length of the kerbstones in the side street, it was possible to get around a corner without running the back wheels over the kerb, which was severely frowned upon. By using this technique I found that it was possible to get around seemingly the most impossible corners."

Something to consider

The pass rate of trainees who had been through Midland Red's rigorous system of driver training was excellent, with 96% being successful. It's interesting to compare these figures with those of today. Both training and testing have changed considerably. Training has been split into the two parts of theory and practice, but the emphasis is on passing the test rather than teaching someone to drive a large vehicle with consideration, responsibility and understanding. Testing is no longer just a pass or fail – you can pass with up to 15 'minors' (mistakes), but you must not have more than three of the same minors. A 'major' will result in failure. We no longer have double-declutching between gear changes, and you are not supposed to use the gears to slow down. How things have changed – but for the better? The pass rate in recent years has been between 49% and 63%, hardly an improvement, but with the expense of training at today's independent PCV driving schools, it is more cost-effective to train to pass a test, rather than train to comprehensively understand and learn to drive and control a large passenger carrying vehicle. It's rather telling that what used to be termed a public *service* vehicle is nowadays called a passenger *carrying* vehicle.

Today, a person aged 18 years who has held a car licence for one year can apply to become a bus driver. In the days when I joined Midland Red, you were allowed to conduct a bus at 18 years old and could apply to go driver training at the age of 21. I remember walking through the garage at Old Warwick Road, Leamington, accompanied by my instructor, who remarked, as we passed a coach parked inside the garage, "Never get on a coach until you have bought a ticket or been invited on board by the coach driver. And if you want a coach moved because it's blocking access, it must be moved by a coach driver or a mechanic."

It was usual to be considered suitable to make an application for coach driving after you had completed around eight years of suitable service as a bus driver. When appointed, you were issued with a white coach driver's smock and a white top cover for your driver's cap. Then, after you had been a coach driver for a period of time to prove your worth, you might be considered for the three C's: Coach Cruise Coachman. The coach cruises were away for 5 to 12 nights and you were expected to be available at all times for your passengers' needs. You were provided with a tailored dark blue suit, three white shirts and a company tie, at which point you had made it!

Tips from coach cruise holidays were almost always much higher than your wages. You would be accommodated and fed in the best hotels and have morning coffee and afternoon tea, all in. Friendships struck up between drivers and very loyal coach cruise passengers were often long lasting, with passengers checking what tours their favourite driver was doing this year before deciding which of the tours they would choose.

How times and attitudes to service have changed over the years for many modes of travel. For example, in time gone by, three-course meals were served on flights, but today's meal options on holiday travel could range from a sandwich and chocolate bar to nothing at all.

A static driver trainer

In the years of the 1960s and 1970s when the C1 coaches from the late 1940s were used as driver training vehicles, the development department were working out how they could save the company money on gearbox and clutch repairs by manufacturing a special 'static training vehicle' which would be used after the initial classroom sessions, but before the drivers were taken out on the road in the dual-control vehicle.

There is no doubt that a 'crash' constant mesh (rather than synchromesh) gearbox is an art to be mastered. The training school with its dual-control training vehicles allowed trainees two weeks to get used to gear changing, which may well have been possible, but each vehicle handles differently. An engineering foreman raised concerns, suggesting that damage to gearboxes may be lessened if trainees could practice putting vehicles into gear in just one static practice vehicle, so that by the time they went on to the road, they were more competent. The idea was floated with the development department at Central Works and a handwritten initial report was forwarded to Jack Ransome, BMMO's head of the experimental and development department. You can see from both the report and the response that considerable thought had gone into the project. At the date of the response, in 1958, the Tilling Stevens generators from the petrol electric vehicles of the 1912 to 1920 period were still being used on the test benches. However, the plans were shelved when it was decided that the costs of the project would exceed the costs of the gearbox repairs.

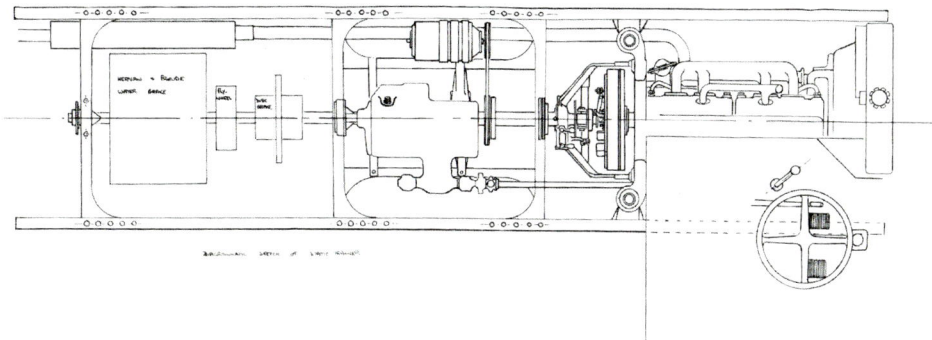

The blueprint for the proposed Static Trainer to avoid new drivers wearing out the clutch on existing trainer vehicles. This was just an exercise and was never actually built.

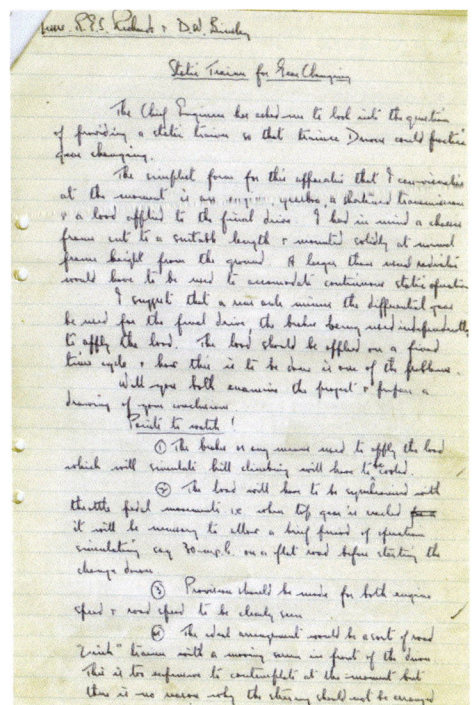

RESPECT OVER A LIFETIME

Colin Webster has been around for my entire working life with Midland Red, even before I became an official employee. He employed me and promoted me when the opportunity was right. He and I left the company's service when we realised it was heading in a different direction to that of our earlier days, and when we were, perhaps, not getting the same satisfaction from our time spent at work, although we left Midland Red South at slightly different times. In my later ventures in life, Mr Webster has kept in touch and, rather like his days as an inspector, he would turn up when least expected. When I 'early retired' from buses, I had time to organise a number of reunions for old company employees, and Mr Webster was the regular guest of honour.

Despite numerous reminders for me to use his first name, it was something I found very difficult for a number of years. Many old colleagues have told me similar stories, and that was due to the immense respect we held for him. Now in his late nineties, in poor health and housebound, he enthusiastically, and with just a bit of emotional nostalgia, shares some salient points of his long career with Midland Red.

A press photograph taken at the launch of the first phase of the Wheels business when it was a transport emporium with model shop, coach hire agency and themed restaurant based in Leamington Spa. Colin and his late wife Jean with author Ashley pose with a tray of coffee and trains in the model railway shop on the opening day.

Colin's Story

My career with Midland Red began way back in 1949 as a newly recruited conductor in Leicester, initially based at Sandacre Garage. As was the way, everyone was encouraged to join the sports and social club with a small deduction from your weekly wage. There were many sporting opportunities throughout the year, with inter-garage games and a large Midland Red company sports day in Birmingham each year. The members were also able to attend many social events and dinner dances that were arranged.

Many of my working colleagues had made careers working for Midland Red, and some who had completed 25 years service plus were eligible to join the 25 Club – a company-wide club of long-serving employees who had regular dances and visits throughout the year, and no doubt many will have heard of this. But, at Sandacre garage we additionally had the 40 Club, which was not so well known – not because fewer staff had completed 40 years of company service, as it was not based on length of service, but on 40 being the full complement of membership of the club. It could have been named such as it was the approximate seating capacity of vehicles used for outings, so, in the interests of everyone being involved, could not exceed the number that could travel together. There was more to this club, as membership was very tightly controlled, and there was always a waiting list. So you waited until someone either died or left the company before another from the waiting list was considered for joining. Then, every member had a vote to either vote in or out any applicant. I was not accepted first time, probably because I was relatively new to Midland Red and not enough of the 'established' members knew me well enough.

Three photographs of the Sandacre 40 Club.

One of the 1951 outings I recall being at Christmas, as the weather was cold. It was a trip to London, with a visit to the theatre to see The Crazy Gang, but before the show, a visit to Worthington's Brewery had been arranged. It was a very memorable trip, as not only did the beer flow well for all participants, but an amazing and comprehensive buffet meal was provided with as much food as we wanted. We hadn't seen the likes of ham since before the war, and personally, probably not at all, but they were carving it off the bone until everyone had had enough. Pork pies were another novelty on offer. We do somewhat take things for granted these days! Rationing did not end until *nine* years after the war, in 1954, with meat being the last thing to be under tight control.

Many things that I recall clearly will have little significance to the more recent, younger readers, like Bell Punch ticket machines and preprinted tickets in racks, so best not to dwell, but after the Bell Punch came the Verometer. This was a chest harness-held, ticket roll printer, with press buttons to enter the ticket value, and then a crude slider lever which issued the paper ticket – and if you completed a shift conducting with a Verometer without getting ink all over your hands and uniform, you had done well. The Verometer machines were phased out from the early 1950s to be replaced by the more well-known Setright ticket machines which lasted until the end of proper Midland Red days. So onwards, and from a conductor, the company trained me to be a bus driver in 1951.

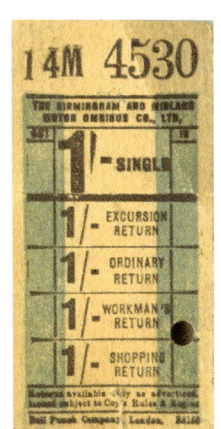

A Bell Punch ticket.

A Verometer ticket machine and a ticket produced by it.

A ON type pre-war single-decker, seen here in 1952, after entering service with the driving school at Bearwood garage. It had been converted from its original half cab layout to full front design and fitted with full dual-control facilities. This vehicle remained with the driving school until 1962.

Driver training was taken very seriously by the company, and a trip to Bearwood garage and the main driving school, which held regular driving classes, was the order of the day. Firstly there was an examination by the company doctor to ensure that you were fit enough, then came learning basic driving etiquette and technique. Filling in time sheets and report forms was all done in the classroom. Then we went out, usually six or seven trainees at a time, in a very old dual-control bus with two steering wheels and two sets of pedals.

When confident enough on that, we were often taken out on other buses used for training, starting with single-deckers and then progressing onto double-deckers, and when you were considered good enough by your instructor, you would be advised of the date of your test. If you passed the test and theory, all done together, you would have the opportunity to drive what we called 'all types' which were the many different types you may be called upon to drive. This would be buses only, not coaches, as coaches were only for experienced drivers who were deemed suitable for coach duties after about eight years service. Then, as soon as your drivers' licence and badge came through, you would be allocated driving duties at your local garage.

I have never been one for knowing intimate details of buses – they are either single-deckers or double-deckers to me – but I do recall the AD2s. These, I have learned, were AEC double-deckers with bodies to a Midland Red design, and they made an impression on me that has lasted all these years! They were lively buses and nice to drive. One type I didn't like were the Guys; they wouldn't pull the skin off a rice pudding, and many a time, when on rural Leicestershire services, going via Bradgate Park and on to Copt Oak, passengers would have to walk behind the bus on steep hills, or would be entertained by some noisy gear crunching as first gear was trying to be engaged, or missing a 'snap' change from first to second gear – all these things making the driver look very embarrassed. I recall a number of occasions when my new wife was a passenger sitting next to our neighbours on their way home from Leicester to Newtown Linford (as newlyweds we lived with my wife Jean's parents while we saved for our new house), and it was on these days that I dreaded having a Guy allocated to me for those journeys. I would look in the rear view mirror into the lower saloon of the bus, imagining everyone talking about me not being able to drive!

Within two years, being newly married, and being out on late turns more than I would like, I left Midland Red to seek other (van) driving work with better social hours, but I was never able to settle. Then, to my delight, in 1957, Midland Red opened a newly built garage in Station Street, Wigston, that was not far from where I had moved home to (our first home together). So, despite the unsocial hours, I gladly sought re-employment and was accepted back into the Midland Red family. There was always overtime available too, to add additional money to the weekly pay packet – of course, paid in cash in a small brown pocket envelope.

I was, of course, aware of inspectors boarding and checking buses, and noticed that their work seemed much less stressful than mine as a driver. It was also noticeable that some of our more rural routes were gradually transferring to one-man operation, and that was not for me, so with support from the company I quickly gained an RSA diploma in passenger bus management. In 1962 I was made an inspector at Southgate Street garage, then moved back to Wigston in the same role. Whilst I was an inspector, I couldn't help but notice that the life of a traffic superintendent seemed like 'the life of Riley': office-hours start time, long lunch breaks, and home pronto at 5pm or earlier! I would like some of that, and I made it known that I would like to progress in my promotion.

In 1967, I was offered the position of traffic superintendent at Hinckley Garage, and with this place on the management ladder, I was able to buy a new detached home in the town. What I didn't quite grasp at the time was that the role of superintendent was becoming more rigidly organised. I found it wasn't possible to go home for lunch any more, and that I might be called out of hours to attend to problems – but I had now made the leap. Within two years, I was moved to Nuneaton garage, where, as written in my foreword to the book *Inside Midland Red*, I came across Ashley – and the infamous Adrianne Wilson.

A set of circumstances and placements of people at that garage made my time at Nuneaton what could accurately be described as dreadful. By this time, the trade unions had gained so much power that regular strikes became the norm, being called for the most trivial of matters, and situations were made very much worse by poor leadership from senior management appointed during the period of nationalisation.

However, I survived that ordeal and moved on to be traffic superintendent over Coalville and Swadlincote garages, which was a much more peaceful and enjoyable place to be. After this pleasant spell came my move back to Leicester, but this time to divisional headquarters in Peacock Lane.

Of course, during all this time, we as a company had seen big changes. We had become part of the National Bus Company which saw us lose a lot of our independence, although certainly a period of stable funding existed, until politics changed and we were then involved in de-nationalisation, where the company as a whole was split up into six separate companies and spelled the end of what was probably the finest and best operated bus company in the world – the Midland Red.

During this period of change, I did move around a little, from the divisional office in Leicester to assistant divisional manager at Cannock, then to Rugby with Midland Red South as operations officer and staff officer, and then after a further five years was hastily made redundant in a badly managed situation where other staff knew I was going before I did! The company was being prepared for a buyout, and as a senior manager, but one who did not wish to contribute finances to the new buyout, I was not to be added to the 'costs' of the management buyout (which incidentally failed). Midland Red South was subsequently sold to Western Travel Group, and its cost subsequently covered by two garage sales: Stratford and Leamington Myton Road. Later, its fate fell to Stagecoach holdings. Strange how it was once a very large private concern, then after much upheaval, it returned to being a large private concern – but in a very different organisation and with different aims and values.

I have, of course, never lost contact with Ashley, and while reminiscing during a recent meeting with him, I realised I had made some official connections with 19 of the 34 Midland Red garages that existed at the time. In a career spanning over 40 years there has been contact with a whole host of colleagues, mostly wonderful and interesting people. I am quite sure that we had the best years of a company we were both very proud to be part of.

Top Right: Colin always said that the Guy double-deckers would not pull the skin off a rice pudding and often embarrassed him with crunchy gears when trying to ascend steep hills. Guy Arab fleet number 2555 HHA 7 was part of a wartime allocation of vehicles delivered in 1944. It is seen in St Margaret's Bus Station, Leicester in 1956 and was finally withdrawn from service in 1956.

Middle Right: Another Leicester-based Guy Arab, fleet number 2589 HHA 84. Both Guys are shown after their mid-life rebuilt.

Bottom Right: Colin's overall favourite vehicles in this period were the AEC Regent Mk2s, classified as AD2, delivered during the late 1940s and having bodywork similar to the wartime prototype D1. The crew of AD2 number 3124 are in conversation in this early 1960s view taken in St Margaret's Bus Station, Leicester. Note the new D9 sitting on the adjacent stand.

Below: Two ladies wondering which bus to board in St Margaret's Bus Station in Leicester. Fleet number 3126 JHA 27 is about to depart for Loughborough in 1957.

HOW DID IT ALL HAPPEN

You will have noticed that the writer of the foreword of this book also contributed the foreword of my very first book, *Inside Midland Red*. I am pleased that Colin Webster has done this, as it closes the circle. You see, Mr Webster has known me the longest of any of my Midland Red colleagues, even from times before I actually worked for the company, when a persistent nuisance of a school lad would stand at the bus garage doors, waiting for permission to step inside and breathe in the whole Midland Red atmosphere that existed within those garage walls.

As I stood outside the doors, there came the gentle voices of the crews, taking down their duties from the rotas that hung in wooden cases on the garage wall. There was the banging of tools over in the engineers' side of the garage, the characteristic tones of the various bus engines running in the garage, the clanking of buckets being used by the cleaners, the bouncing of the odd bus tyre being taken from the tyre store to an awaiting bus for fitting by the Firestone, Dunlop or Michelin tyre man – whichever was in contract to the company at the time. And the smell of over-used oil – not from the engineers, but from the canteen's array of large frying pans that cooked the endless supply of sausage, bacon and egg sandwiches for the crews, engineers and garage staff.

I sometimes arrived at the garage after being allowed 45 minutes to go bus spotting (supposedly in the bus station) whilst Mum and Dad were shopping in town. On other occasions, I would supposedly be out playing when, in reality, I was sprinting up the road to the bus stop to catch a bus with a friendly crew who would let me travel on long bus rides. Sometimes, depending on the conductor, they would let me play at being a conductor with the ticket machine, collecting the fares from passengers and issuing tickets. Occasionally, the driver would let me stand up at the front and change gear for him. But most of the time, it was to be dropped off at the garage. While I stood by those garage doors, one of the GTAs (Garage Traffic Assistants) would pass by, perhaps going to give the engineers a message or to see how long a particular bus would be before it was repaired and ready for service, and sometimes they would be asked "Excuse me, can I come in to take some numbers of buses please?" They would almost always reply, "Yes, but keep to the sides of the garage."

The surprising thing is that I wasn't ever really interested in the bus numbers – I just seemed to have a talent for absorbing and recalling them. I only noted numbers when there was something interesting or different to see – perhaps a bus with a different seating layout to normal, or more likely, the oldest bus in the garage, as I knew it might not be there next time I visited.

If I knew a particular crew, I was often invited into the conductors' room, where they would cash up their money and place the bag in the chute of the safe after their duty. The conductors' shifts were on rotas displayed in the conductors' room, whereas the drivers were out on the garage wall, between the offices and the garage doors. I found it interesting that the drivers' rotas were split across four different cabinets. There was the main rota, which was for ordinary crew-operated bus duties; there was the growing list of one-man bus drivers, and there was what was known as 'the old man's list' which was a shorter rota for some drivers who were approaching retirement age or had returned to work after illness. These were usually lighter duties, such as rural country services where there was less stress than driving heavily loaded town services or inter-city routes. However, most duties included a mix of routes so there was usually a good variety to a day's work. The final list, consisting only of around a dozen or so men, was the motorway list. This was for the men who were hand-picked for the company's prestigious motorway express services and had permission to drive the CM5 and CM6 vehicles that were specifically designed and built for those highly respected services to the capital. These men were the equivalent of the fast steam train express drivers who were known as 'top link' men, and without much effort, I can recall names from this list like Malcolm Day, George Sabin, Geoff Wormleighton, Eric Packer, Brian Stokes, Roger Brotherhood, Roy Eltenton, Bernard Ellis, Johnny Quick, Pete Kenny and Trevor Whitmore. Gone before them were names like Fred Izzard, who became a well-liked driving instructor, and Alan Walker, in an earlier life a queen's guardsman and still looking the part and later the well-known inspector based at Pool Meadow, Coventry and at Digbeth, Birmingham.

Alan Walker was promoted to motorway express driver in earlier times, when CM5 coaches were the regular performers on the ME2 (Nuneaton Coventry London) service circa 1962-5. Alan emphasised, during a conversation with me, that a written report had to be prepared, handed in and sent to the general manager in Birmingham the same day if any motorway coach was delayed or stopped by anyone whilst in service. One day, he was speeding up the M1 and overtaking everything in sight when he noticed he was being chased by a police Jaguar. He allowed the police car to overtake and pulled over. The Buckingham Constabulary motorway officer told him he was going too fast, although there was no speed limit on the motorway at that time. Alan's report went in as soon as he returned to the garage. Some years later, when Alan and I were both based at Pool Meadow in Coventry, he as an inspector and I as travel sales supervisor (a new position replacing the traffic superintendent), he was pleased to show me a letter of reply sent by the relevant constabulary to Midland Red's general manager, Mr D. M. Sinclair. The letter began "Dear Donald" and went on to apologise for the unnecessary stoppage of one of his specially designed express coaches, assuring him it would not be stopped again, and that notification had gone to traffic officers on the motorway to tell them of the special design of these motorway coaches.

Motorway drivers were picked out as suitable candidates, tested on relevant parts of the Highway Code, and then taken out onto a motorway for assessment. If successful, you were then an approved motorway driver, but you would first be allocated 'duplicate' coaches to drive, rather than the main 'service' coach, so that you would be in the company of a more experienced motorway driver. After a spell doing this work, you could be promoted to the main motorway list when a vacancy arose.

There were also those wannabes who had a genuine desire and aspiration to be a Midland Red motorway express coach driver and join that elite team, but for some reason, just didn't make it. Mick Gilbert was returning one day from Lichfield to Nuneaton on a 765 bus service when, just four bus stops short of the end of his run, he clipped the curb when pulling out of the bus stop lay-by. Unbeknown to him, he was being assessed by a plain-clothed Midland Red road foreman (engineering inspector). His report noted this 'relatively minor' mistake as being the driver's error, and sadly, Mick never made it to the motorway list. A moment's lack of concentration led to a lifetime of disappointment to have never belonged to this 'crack' team of drivers.

One of the conductresses at Nuneaton garage, a lady of Tibetan origin, used to save me copies of the *Midland Red Staff Bulletin*. She would give me a copy when she was on one of the shifts that included our school bus run; or if at the garage, she would pop into the conductors' room to pick one from the pile that usually sat there; or she would pull one out of her bag if she saw me in town. The information in these magazines really helped my knowledge grow as it taught me just how big and incredibly self-sufficient Midland Red was. It gave details of happenings in the garages and offices all over the Midlands, including Bearwood Chief Traffic Offices and Central Works, and information about the latest vehicle specifications etc. The front page almost always included a letter, mainly from the general manager, advising everyone of the difficulties facing the industry and how Midland Red must strive to maintain revenue and passenger numbers. Of course, this publication was really a very successful propaganda machine that praised the advances of the company and encouraged all employees to push hard to maintain services and perform well. The back page was always devoted to complimentary letters from passengers, praising the efforts of staff who went that extra mile. The staff magazine had existed pre-war, when it was sold by conductors to passengers, and league tables to see which conductors could sell the most were common. These pre-war magazines had a wider appeal, with topical travel stories and adverts promoting other Midland Red services like private hire and longer distance journeys and coach holidays (coach cruises) – by Midland Red bus and coach of course! After the war, the magazine became the *Staff Bulletin* and was only an internal staff magazine.

The company had in place many layers of organisation in order to control its operations. Particularly important in BMMO's case was its distinctly separate traffic and engineering departments; and bridging the divide were the accounts and financial controllers at head office, who had sight of both traffic and engineering finances.

The engineering typist/clerk is in the engineering superintendent's office to check the details with him before sending the fuel records to head office.

Mr Webster was transferred from Hinckley to Nuneaton as traffic superintendent in the very late 60s, the latter being the nearest of the garages to my home that I visited. At that time, he was just over half way through his long career with the company. It pays to know a bit about such a person and their experiences and career path – especially when they go on to have a role, as Mr Webster did, as company disciplinary officer. If you were hauled up in front of him for any offence you might have committed, it was absolutely no use trying to bluff your way out of it. Mr Webster had done every job and knew all the tricks of the trade. He appreciated honesty. Even if it was an error that resulted in the sack, you may be fortunate to get your job back after time had passed, due to the strong trade union. Sometimes, for a less severe offence, you may be lucky enough to be just suspended from work for a number of days.

The company was run along similar lines to many of the large organisations of the time, with many of the directors, management and workers coming from a forces or military background (both WW1 and WW2). This gave a certain level of expectation of discipline and, therefore, respect. Many employees would have benefited from national service; this, for some, was the grounding needed for a successful future; for others it just continued to provide a stable and organised lifestyle. Respect was built up in Midland Red over decades, and that respect came from both outside (the wider PSV industry) and within the company itself.

At local garage level, both departments had separate divisional control mechanisms: North East Division, South West Division, Central Division and so on. They also had separate traffic and engineering superintendents, local administrative staff, inspectors, and platform staff (drivers in engineering, conductors in traffic). Consequently, there was often a lot of duplication of functions and staff, though less so in the very smallest of garages. Kineton, for example, especially in its later years, worked under the control of nearby Stratford garage; only light running repairs were carried out at Kineton, with scheduled maintenance undertaken at Stratford. It should be borne in mind that Stratford Blue was a wholly-owned subsidiary of BMMO but was allowed to trade and operate under its own management. Stratford Blue also owned a row of five cottages next to the main Stratford-upon-Avon garage, and the rent from the tenants was paid each month to the booking office staff at the garage office.

WHERE THE MAGIC HAPPENED

Engineering mattered to 'non-standard' Midland Red in a slightly different way to other bus and coach companies, as it was a very big department within the Midland Red business. It dealt not only with the garage engineers, the foreman and the superintendent for each of up to 35 local garages, but the entire Central Works operation. Many of the larger companies had a central workshop but it was mainly for repairs and refurbishments whereas Midland Red's Central Works was all of those, plus a design, development and manufacturing plant too. This included the procurement and provision of raw materials and parts, and the many job roles of designers, developers, testers, vehicle production staff, skilled and semi-skilled workers, foremen, labourers, progress chasers, stores men – and even the directors' chauffeurs had their base here. All had their associated costs.

In the inter-war years the company generated income from engineering sales by supplying considerable numbers of their SOS own make of vehicle to a number of associated companies from Newcastle upon Tyne, Peterborough, Llandudno, The Potteries, Staffordshire, Derbyshire, and the Nottingham areas of the Trent and PMT companies. However, after WW2 they were only providing for their own needs. The pre-war income from vehicle sales was no more, unlike the traffic side of the company where most departments continued to generate income.

Engineering at Midland Red was first controlled from Bearwood, then on completion of the rebuilding of Central Works in 1954 its control was moved there, neatly bringing together the company's principal functions at the Central Works and Midland House site in Edgbaston. This control hub was outwardly assisted by the divisional engineer level of management, for example North East (based at Leicester), South West (based at Worcester), etc.

'The Works', 'Central Works' and 'Carlyle Works' were all names associated with the Edgbaston plant, where the magic happened and where the evolution of the Midland Red bus was seen at first hand. Bearwood garage had handled engineering matters since the horse bus era. It grew in size by the acquisition of adjoining properties and this made the garage a confusing place, with partition walls supporting endless extensions. So, over more than 20 years, various engineering departments were moved to Central Works which itself required modernisation under Mr Sinclair's tenure and became the most advanced bus plant in the country. A celebratory opening ceremony of Central Works was performed in 1954, on the Silver Jubilee anniversary of the company, where great play was made over both its facilities and its future. In the previous book, *Midland Red and its People,* Alan Eatwell told us all about his apprenticeship and later engineering managerial roles at Midland Red. It is a fascinating story of how a teenage lad, originally wanting a job on the railways, was introduced by his father, a chief inspector of Midland Red, to Central Works as the company's last fitters boy and their first indentured apprentice. It is a personal story of the working relationships of his workmates and how the magic of Midland Red's unique spirit was passed from one generation to the next. In *this* book, we take a look at some early images of the inside of Central Works – normally only seen by those working there, or those lucky enough to be taken around on a rare conducted visit.

Six 'Lancashire' boilers down in the cellars were kept in immaculate condition and, as Alan Eatwell writes in his 'Fitters Boy' section of Midland Red and its People, having "a presentation that would have impressed any ship's engineer." Fred Porter, a long serving engineer for the company, was in charge of this department. The boilers were piped through the entire site, providing all of the hot water. They generated steam for the heating radiators, but by the time it had travelled to the extremities of the heating system and returned to the boiler house it had mostly condensed to hot water. But it was still of a sufficient temperature to make Fred's tea – it didn't seem to concern Fred much that the water he was using had been circulating since 1951, and that it was about the same colour as tea even before he had added the tea leaves!

The Design Office was situated above the entrance to what was known as 'The Tunnel'. This was a busy office where buildings, new vehicles, spare parts and everything else was imagined.

Designs, once manufactured, would go to the team in the Experimental and Development Department for testing and monitoring.

The Chassis Shop, with what appear to be D7 chassis being assembled. The monochrome photograph on the right is taken looking in the opposite direction, and shows an early C5 subframe on the left with a D7 next to it.

The Stores department was vast, with 20,000 storage bins for parts. It reached from the basement area up to the roofline. The stores clerk checked and monitored requisition paperwork to ensure nothing left without the correct request and signature.

The Plastics Shop, where fibreglass parts were moulded, including one-piece bus roofs. The upturned roof is for a C5 vehicle.

When the D9 was being produced, the Plastics Shop was constantly busy as there were many fibreglass parts needed. Here two ladies are producing the D9 staircase as a clever two section unit.

Above: The Electricians Shop. This is where Alan Eatwell spent half of his electrician's posting when he was at Central Works. He unexpectedly supplied some timely and detailed information about this department: "The chap at the back on the far left was Norman, the works convenor for the Metal Mechanics Union which was later subsumed into the TGWU. This department is where starter motors, door motors, stop solenoids, wiper motors, dynamos, and subsequently alternators were overhauled. The shop was sited next to the Setright shop where conductors' ticket machines were repaired. Unusually for this area, the Setright shop was not under the control of the chassis shop superintendent, as others were, as the Setright shop was a 'traffic' activity. The Electricians Shop had two chargehands, both called Dennis; one is second from the right in the picture and in the lighter cow gown (signifying his status). He looks to be checking something prior to being tested on the 'Octopus,' a multi-purpose electrical testing machine to his right, with its ammeters and voltmeters just in view."

Top: Lower saloon interior ceiling panels were made full-width in colour impregnated sheets. Here the ceiling is being fitted.

Vehicle production in full swing. Above: Motorway Express coaches in 1959 have skylights fitted into the glass fibre roof. Right: D9s in the finishing area that will soon be carrying passengers.

Left: One of the most advanced features of the refurbished Central Works was the new Paint Shop facility where buses were spray painted as they rose from below floor level, after the roof had been painted. It enabled buses to be painted in minutes rather than days, which was typical with brush painting, and helped the company to maintain the vehicle overhaul program. Buses were prepared with any necessary body repairs, and masking-up was done in adjacent areas.

Top: To service the needs for the hundreds of staff employed on site, the catering department had a commercial kitchen built onto the back of the canteen building. The kitchen serviced two eating areas. One was the workers' canteen with meals being served at kitchen hatches, similar to the style of school dinners. The smaller of the eating areas was for the management and had waitress service.

Above: An early picture of the manual workers canteen, with forms and benches. These were later replaced with Formica tables and chairs. Visible in the background are the serving hatches.

Above: Over the years, Midland Red had an extensive fleet of vans and goods vehicles. There were local delivery and parcel vans, lorries for taking engineering spares to garages, and even a fuel tanker.

Signwriters were employed from the very first days of operation through to 1980. Fleet numbers were rarely applied by signwriting; they were usually transfers. But this late afterlife paint job came after the old style transfers had come to an end and had been removed from stocks.

Painting an all-over advert was a three-week job on D9 fleet number 5412 to promote the use of the new postcodes being introduced by the GPO. These days, all-over adverts are usually wrapped using pre-printed vinyl.

Right to the end there were celebrations at Central Works, some seeing longstanding colleagues retire, others to mark significant milestones in the company's life. This group, including members of the Experimental and Development department (particulary those involved in the revolutionary Midland Red motorway express vehicles), say goodbye to Jim Pearson who joined BMMO from Leyland Motors in the 1950s for an exciting ride in the development of many Midland Red buses and coaches. He left to take up a position with Birmingham City Transport. Also in the photograph are John Morley, Ron Freelove, Bob Moore, Bob Richards, Robert Morley, Trevor Yeo and Doug Watkins.

Publicity and advertising was originally managed from Bearwood, but once everything had moved to the Central Works site, the department occupied what appeared to be a pre-cast concrete building, easily accessed from the side pathway between Midland House and the works or via the main drive from the gatehouse. Outside were usually stacked new concrete bus stop poles, waiting to be sent to any part of the Midland Red operating area and set into concrete bases. Design work was carried out here for timetables, excursion brochures and tours booklets, and a publicity van delivered them to individual offices and garages.

Midland Red had a long association with James Upton, the renowned firm of Birmingham printers, typesetters and wood engravers. At their Baskerville Works in Cambridge Street they printed vast numbers of Midland Red local bus timetable leaflets, area timetable books and the *Midland Red Gazetteer of The Midlands* for many years. They specialised in theatrical printing, and became famous for printing LP record covers and CD covers. The company was founded by James Upton in 1852. It is likely that their Baskerville Works was named after John Baskerville (1707-1775), also of Birmingham, who designed the renowned Baskerville typeface and also inspired the title of Arthur Conan Doyle's story *The Hound of the Baskervilles*. James Upton's grandson was also named James Baskerville Upton and died in 1973. The company later moved to Barford Street, and the site was finally closed in 2007.

In most businesses of mass employment there were pilfering and theft issues to varying degrees. This was no exception at Midland Red's garages, offices and factory. On many occasions, items not meant for buses or coaches were being soldered, bolted or polished and then smuggled past the gatehouse and homeward bound. Whilst not wishing to make light of this practice I would like to recall a story told to me by a colleague working at Midland Red's Central Works.

A lady who was working in the trim shop was off sick and, with work piling up, her absence was noticed by her department's superintendent. Concerned for her welfare, he decided to enquire after her health and take her a box of chocolates. He knocked at her door and was invited in by her husband who explained that his wife was upstairs at the moment, and showed him in to their living room. The manager was open-mouthed as he looked around. The lady cheerfully entered the room and said hello, but then the awful truth dawned upon her as she saw the expression on his face. Their entire three piece suite was fully covered and professionally trimmed in Midland Red's burgundy leathercloth, the likes of which was fitted to the saloon sides of the early D9 double-deckers – and very nice it looked too! There followed a polite but awkward conversation. The manager made his excuses to leave, and popped open the kitchen door to say goodbye to her husband, only to find two kitchen stools covered in brown leatherette, a covering used in earlier D7 buses. He made a hasty departure without venturing to look any further. It is not known whether she enjoyed the chocolates, but her employment was certainly short lived!

A sad day in Midland Red history was marked by this group photograph, featuring all levels of the workforce, on the day that the very last BMMO-built bus was made. In fact the bodywork trim would be completed by Plaxton of Scarborough. This was fleet number 5991. It entered service in June 1970 and worked at Cradley Heath, Stourbridge, Tamworth, Swadlincote and Worcester garages. Its ownership was with Midland Red Omnibus Company and it was parked at Central Works. When the site closed, it passed to the BaMMOT trust at Wythall for spares, and has since moved on.

5991 was withdrawn from service in 1980 and is seen here some time later at Central Works parking area.

Such an integral part of the Midland Red business, Central Works wanted for nothing. Even when things went wrong, they had the medical centre with nurses on duty. Not only did they look after accidents at work, but they monitored workers' existing medical concerns and prescribed medication for employees' longer-term conditions, which helped take the strain from local doctors and hospitals.

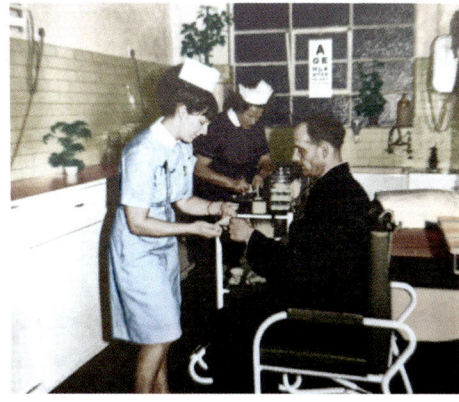

The proud site that created so many 'highs' in terms of its designs and experiments, and advancements in vehicle technology. It really was the centre of much of Midland Red evolution and revolution. Access to the site was only for staff and invited guests, and getting past the gatehouse during opening hours was not easy, although many an enthusiast has climbed the gates and evaded the night security man to discover exciting sights of something new.

One of the not-so-pleasant jobs at Central Works was the steam cleaning of vehicles, normally performed when the vehicle arrived from a garage for overhaul, before old parts were renewed, or as part of re-certification or pre-MOT inspection. Steam cleaning was also performed at some garages like Wigston and Leamington (Myton Road) which had ramps constructed usually at the back of the garage yard.

The steam cleaning facility being demolished at the sad closure of Central Works.

A ghostly reminder of what was a fine bus building facility. These are views after partial demolition. A sad end to a facility which could, perhaps, have met the coach manufacturing needs of National Express, yet ended up as a pile of rubble. It is now just another housing estate, without a single street name to recall its past important contributions, not only to Birmingham's industrial past, but to transport and social history.

For many years Midland Red had a photographic department and film unit. This was originally based at Bearwood, like other head office functions, but later moved to a laboratory in a basement at Central Works. Midland Red made travel films to assist in the promotion of coach cruise holidays, and maintained a comprehensive collection of filed photographs, taken from multiple angles, of each new type of bus. Mr Davenport who ran the unit told me that Kodak invented colour Kodachrome film in 1935 and when it became generally available for prints, a couple of years later, Midland Red began using it when colour was required.

Not often considered, there was also a properties department that looked after all of the owned and leased infrastructure and buildings, and the land they stood upon. Thirty-five garages alone is quite a property portfolio, but added to that was the considerable area of land, factory buildings and plant at Central Works in Edgbaston, the adjacent Midland House complex with its computer centre, the bus stations including the large Bull Ring under-cover site, and general infrastructure including bus stops spread throughout the Midlands. BMMO owned a large number of properties including several houses in the vicinity of Central Works and adjacent to other garages, including a row of cottages adjoining Stratford Blue's main garage. Not all were adjoining properties, such as those around Central Works and the staff hostels etc. The extensive Digbeth property with its garage and coach station also had commercial offices and shops that were let out to tenants. Rental income from all of these properties helped offset the considerable operating costs of the company's bus and coach operations.

There was also the considerable costs of running Midland House, adjoining Central Works, that looked after the administration and legal matters not only of Midland

Red but also its subsidiary companies like Stratford Blue Motors, Leamington and Warwick Transport Company, and others.

Midland House is where the main company telephone switchboard was situated, just inside the main entrance door, which also acted as a reception point. Bearwood garage had extensive offices that acted as the company's chief traffic offices, but after Midland House was acquired in 1952 functions were transferred there; this included the main switchboard, which moved from Bearwood upon its closure in 1973, together with its well known operators Pat Trigg and the very theatrical Barbara Taylor.

The property department collaborated with company architects regarding any refurbishments or alterations to existing properties, and negotiated with suppliers and builders when any new properties were required.

The property department was in the line of fire when the finance department needed savings. This came to the serious attention of employees on 24 August 1971 when it was reported that the BMMO sports ground in Quinton would have to be sold for housing to raise funds for the company. The Sports and Social Club decided to buy the actual club house, and it was then just the sports field area that would be involved in the sale. For years Midland Red football and cricket teams played here, and the annual Midland Red sports day took place, where employees from all corners of the Midland Red area came together. Mr Womar, the General Manager at the time, said that replacement sports facilities would be found, but within two years this became irrelevant when Midland Red lost all of its Birmingham operations to the new West Midlands county boundary changes and the formation of West Midlands Passenger Transport Authority, with services run by West Midlands Passenger Transport Executive.

Coseley Buildings of Wolverhampton provided the Ludlow garage building. The firm's publicity shows an LD8 and D5B in the garage.

WHERE THE MONEY CAME FROM

The traffic department brought in cash not only from its main occupation of running local and limited stop longer-distance bus services, but also from its extensive coaching activities – all collected by bus conductors or by staff in the company booking offices and garages. The traffic department also had expenditures: it operated training facilities at head office and at some divisional areas or local garages, such as conductors' training school facilities. And, of course, there were the costs of the organising and formal planning of tours and excursions, and giving advice and planning details for private hires to their organisers.

There was also the important coach cruise department which developed, planned and organised the highly successful inclusive holiday program by negotiating with hotel providers, and restaurants for morning coffees and afternoon teas, besides planning which venues they would visit. The tours department planned the once extensive day excursions, morning tours, afternoon and evening tours, trips to the races and road and river cruises.

The staff department looked after staff employment levels, recruitment, retention and the welfare of all staff. Each department had its own superintendent, secretarial and admin teams – all with access to the central typing pool if they didn't have their own secretarial staff.

Looking after the local income stream were the inspectors and traffic inspectors, usually a team of four or five at each garage, who were used primarily for revenue protection duties. But they also had a multitude of other activities, including despatch office work, garage duties, bus station supervision, investigation of complaints, visits to customers' houses, and resolving all manner of issues from overcharging to incorrectly issued bus and coach tickets. There was also a chief inspector role based at head office.

Each garage had a traffic superintendent, a secretary/typist, a senior admin assistant (SAA) and various garage traffic assistants (including the despatch office clerks, wages and schedule clerks, cash office and waybill clerks and the booking office and enquiry clerks).

Nuneaton's Coton Road garage traffic superintendent Jack Randall and his secretary/typist.

The waybill office clerks undertaking daily waybill analysis.

Much detail was collected each day. Mileages operated were recorded in great detail as buses did not have milometers fitted. There were recognised mileages for double-deckers and for single-deckers, as there were often routes where only single-deckers could venture; the presence of trees or the many low bridges which existed back then for collieries, quarries, and the main and branch line railways would prevent double-deckers being used.

Conductors had to carefully record any deviation from their daily running card so that, back at the garage, the waybill office staff could add or subtract any mileages. These adjustments were used in the monitoring of fuel usage, and eventually to update the overall bus mileage records over in the engineers' department.

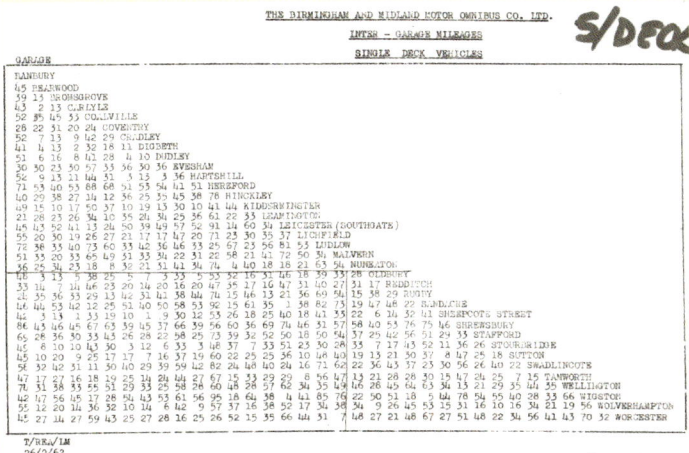
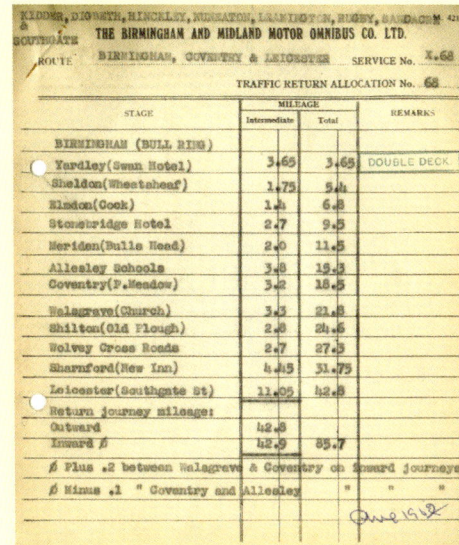

A route mileage card for the X68 service Birmingham, Coventry and Leicester. It is typical of those used for all services, showing intermediate and cumulative route miles.

Single-deck and double-deck inter-garage mileage charts. The waybill clerks checked daily mileages against the official mileage cards, then the engineering clerks checked and recorded the actual mileages against the fuel usage and updated the vehicle files. Each route had mileage cards to help calculate accurately any lost or additional mileages operated.

A metal plain clothed inspectors pass with chain link - dating from 1929.

Inspectors were given instructions from the traffic superintendent of their local garage, but also had to work to instructions from their local or district senior inspector or head office based chief inspector.

Most passengers would see a lone inspector boarding a bus to check tickets, but at the same time they would be monitoring the condition of the bus interior, adverts and notices, and ensuring that the bus was on schedule and had the correct destination blinds showing.

Some inspectors also worked in pairs (for reasons that will become clear) and had a company van, usually an Austin A40 Farina, painted in livery; later, Ford Escorts were used for a time. These were known as the 'flying checkers', or by their correct name, travelling inspectors, and they could appear anywhere to catch out bus crews who were not expecting any such intrusion into their activities, especially out in the countryside. They would also be used for special operations where a particular employee (more than likely a conductor) had, perhaps, been reported for failing to collect fares in due time, issuing incorrect tickets or numerous other possible infringements.

Outer turning points of routes were always worth checking up on, especially during evening licencing hours, where either the driver or conductor (often both) would leave the bus and pop in for a quick half. Being caught on licenced premises was often terminal for your job, but crews had clever mechanisms in place, often in cahoots with the landlord, where on first sight of an inspector, the crew would disappear out of another door and hopefully not find the other travelling inspector waiting outside the door, ready to pounce as they departed. It was a cat-and-mouse business because all of the inspectors had previously been drivers and/or conductors, so they knew the score well. Sometimes a customer would tip them off that inspectors were about, and the landlord would rush the crew out of a back door, through a toilet window, or even via the cellar. One crew member even donned a customer's coat and hat, and, with the brim pulled down, bid the inspector a good evening as they briefly passed in the busy pub. The inspectors found them back on the bus and were none the wiser.

It seems that there were also unwritten rules too. Most of the main towns had a Midland Red club building where crews could visit almost without fear, or some other popular haunt. In Nuneaton, it was Bond Gate Social Club, just a stone's throw from the bus station. Leamington's was an actual Midland Red club building in High Street, opposite a calling point shared by many of the main services, the Crown Hotel, where crews would often change over in mid-service. These were probably allowed because they offered food and, of course, non-alcoholic refreshment – but little of the latter was consumed!

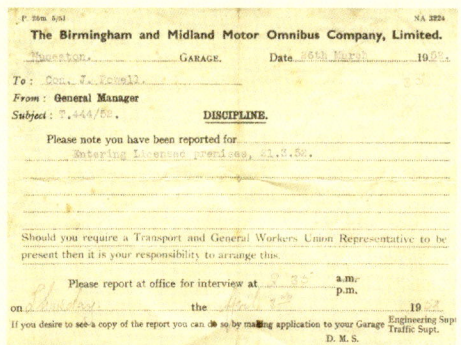

A piece of paper that no employee wanted to see, but no doubt expected on the occasion of a crafty visit to a public house: a disciplinary sheet for 'licenced premises'.

And when things went wrong there were the arbitrators: the disciplinary officers. The list of offences that could be committed by bus crews was almost endless, but in the company's heyday, the person in charge of the bus was the bus conductor – and they were a *traffic* department employee. The driver was under the supervision of the *engineering* department, which had its own layer of inspectors who were controlled from divisional level by a chief engineering inspector at Bearwood.

There were also inspectors who settled into more or less static locations, such as bus station inspectors. One of the smartest and most liked of these was Inspector Alan Walker who for many years was to be seen as duty inspector at Pool Meadow in Coventry, looking after the many coach and bus departures seven days a week. Alan was one of a team allocated there throughout the 1970s. He had previously worked as a driver and motorway coachman. Other inspectors in his team were Jack Collett, Derek King, Derek Blower and Jim McDonald. In an earlier life, 6′ 7″ tall Alan had been in the Queens Guards and always wore mirror-like polished shoes, and his uniform hat with the peak facing down. In later years, Alan transferred to Birmingham's Digbeth Coach Station until his retirement.

Inspector Alan Walker, always immaculately turned out for work with shirt and tie, highly polished shoes and his trade mark cap – peak down – reminding him of his days as a guardsman.

Conductors could be reported for what might appear relatively trivial matters, but these were taken very seriously by the company as they cost money! It might be a simple miss-fare, where, for example, a passenger on a busy bus escaped the attention of the conductor, or perhaps a passenger had over-ridden (gone past the place they had paid to go to). Back in the day, things were much more restrictive than today. When the conductor paid money in at the end of their daytime shift, they would often pay in to one of the garage traffic assistants (GTAs), and if the money was short of that necessary to match the ticket machine readings, the conductor would have the 'opportunity' to make up the difference from his own money. In the event that he couldn't pay or refused to pay, or (in later years) the paying-in had occurred at night (where the takings were placed in a night safe chute and there was no opportunity to correct matters), and this happened more than twice in a period, the conductor would receive a notice of impending disciplinary action and had to see the local garage traffic superintendent to discuss why this had happened. Failure to resolve the situation meant the conductor would have to see the disciplinary officer, who was divisionally allocated and would call periodically at each garage in his section.

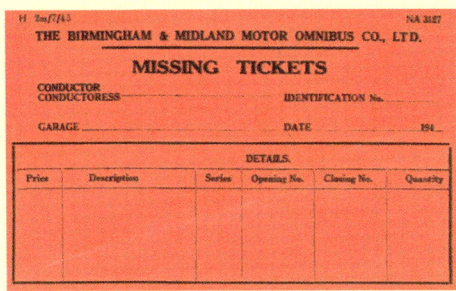

I remember when it was frowned upon to pay in using notes (ten shilling or pound notes back then) where the Queen's head was not facing all in the same direction, as this took the cash counting clerks time to correct when they were preparing the money ready for banking. If you were called up to the office too many times, you would risk a period of suspension! Of course putting notes into the bag in a uniform manner is neat and organised, and it is something you remember and practice in later life – all part of that subtle discipline that existed back then.

Drivers were the responsibility of the engineering department and were disciplined initially by their local garage engineering superintendent. In many cases, a chat with him would suffice, but in more serious cases, the divisional disciplinary officer would visit, and a time would be booked for an official interview. In most cases, the likely outcome was pretty well known before the culprit walked into the interview; the disciplinary officer would have chatted with the union official present, and a conclusion reached. During the 1970s, the unions were so strong that if it was a dismissible offence, and you were found guilty, then even if you did get the sack, you would likely be reinstated within days – sometimes hours – or there might be a strike! On reflection, these were interesting times.

Most employees, of course, escaped such troubles and just kept their noses clean – or, more likely, were lucky in getting away with minor unreported incidents. Most of us took the occasional risk and, fortunately, escaped any unwanted consequences. Time was generous, tea was flowing, vehicles were fun to drive, and enjoyment was had at work by most of us. I've come to that conclusion after speaking with newer drivers who work some of the routes that were once operated by Midland Red, and now by the newer entry companies who took over after privatisation. We must have had it good, as they say, because modern-day bus drivers don't have conductors to crew with, and schedules are so tight that there is hardly any time for them to get out of the cab for hours on end – let alone get a cuppa from a non-existent canteen!

The company's income was spent by all departments, but, compared to other bus companies, expenses were skewed towards the engineering departments such as design, experimental, development, and vehicle manufacturing – costs other bus companies did not have. But it is interesting to study Midland Red's 'What happens to the money?' pie chart for 1952: out of every £1 in income just 1/7d is spent on the provision of new buses and new equipment whilst double that is taken in government taxes, and just over half the income is spent paying wages.

FAR AND WIDE

Most of Midland Red's vehicles were very distinctive, and in post-war years were exclusively built for their own use. With their own make of engines and other units made to their own designs, spare parts were not readily available, which no doubt limited any use they may have had after their life with Midland Red. Even with the company's vehicle designs and reliability being held in high regard by many, it is understandable that life-expired vehicles were sent off to the scrapyard as newer designs were introduced. After all, it was a company policy that passengers should always see the latest Midland Red buses and coaches, and little attention or emotional interest was given to surplus old vehicles.

However, there was always outside interest in buying old and retired Midland Red buses. Travelling fairground folk knew they were long lasting; one of them told me that an SOS engine with good fresh oil and water will last a lifetime. They were always keen to buy old SOS and BMMO engines for use with their generators that provided power for the rides, saying they were equal in economy and reliability to a Gardner. They also bought the vehicles to provide living quarters. After WW2, building contractors were busy with a frenzy of new developments, and many Midland-based home builders bought withdrawn vehicles to use as staff buses, site offices, stores, and tea rooms. With wartime restrictions in the supply and availability of materials only slowly returning to normal, it is easy to see how old buses helped bridge the gap. Local authorities bought them for libraries, and private businesses used them as mobile grocery shops and mobile fish and chip shops. Some had their bodies removed, leaving just the cab and a flatbed to be used as lorries. All of these were used until they were no longer needed, and it would have been their *availability* rather than their ultimate reliability that was probably the consideration. Those who bought them for further use either knew that the SOS/BMMO brand of buses were highly reliable, or were perhaps just naive. As a company, Midland Red had always been helpful to those who had bought vehicles, and sold spares if they were available. That was fine if you were in or near the Midlands area.

We know that there were vehicles bought mainly by private individuals or small independent bodies, that operated well for their new owners for a few years. Some coaches, both pre- and post-war types, were taken far and wide across the globe and bought by dealers. But some vehicles were bought by local people and small groups for their own use. Indeed, a 1937 SLR-type coach ventured on a brave yet uneventful trip to Tehran and returned months later to Central Works in Birmingham, where the owners proudly showed the photo album of its exploits to the staff that had sold the bus to them just a couple of years before (the story is recounted in the earlier book *Midland Red Influence*).

Many 1939 ONC coaches were sold for further use, one by a company running 'The Indiaman', a service to Bombay! Another retired coach, this time a late 1940s C1, set off for Russia but sadly didn't make it back and was abandoned by its student owners in the Ukraine.

I was recently made aware of a pre-war ONC coach dating from 1939 that was taken *twice* to Sorrento in 1964 and 1965. After a good life with Midland Red, the coach was sold off in 1963 and collected from Central Works in Edgbaston by staff from Lyndon High School for Boys in Solihull. It was bought for the school youth club so that members could gain practical experience, the older boys with engineering, and the younger ones with interior work, cleaning windows, and making the cab area shine. The coach, still in company livery, looked a little in need of a repaint, but the youth club members, many of whom were interested in Midland Red, were keen to keep it in its red and black livery. So the colours were retained, and the Midland Red crests on the sides were replaced with a large L and a smaller H and S, for Lyndon High School. Over the following few years, it was used for many UK-based trips, but in 1964 a European camping tour was arranged, travelling down to Dover, over to France on the cross-channel ferry, then through Belgium, Luxembourg, Austria, Germany and on to Italy, with sightseeing trips around Zurich, Milan, Venice and Paris. Each evening, they set up camp at the side of the road for an overnight rest, ready for the next day's adventure. All for the cost of £25 all in!

It was on the Simplon Pass that the first and only sign of trouble occurred. There was a smell of burning brakes inside the coach, so they pulled in at the next safe place. It was found necessary to change the wheels around, and this seemed to cure the problem, and for the remainder of the journey, the coach just needed fuel, oil and water topping up. The happy campers arrived back in Solihull 14 days later, and the coach was none the worse for wear. In fact, it was so good that they did the whole thing again the following year. The driving was undertaken by Mr Ian Davies, who was the history master at the school, assisted by a navigator, Mr Alan Walters, who was the maths and sports master. The coach was well travelled and said to be well-liked by the students for making their lessons interesting. What an amazing opportunity for the students and a truly incredible feat for this pre-war coach!

Lyndon Hall School's ONC coach – destination Sorrento!

Right: Two D7s, 4110 and 4111, went to work in the film industry in the USA. They were overhauled and repainted at Central Works before embarking upon their long journey. One of the pair, fleet number 4111, is seen being hoisted aboard the ship. It has an interesting choice of advert: Rediffusion, a company owned by BET – just like BMMO.

Top: One of the wartime Leylands that was delivered to Midland Red is now a showman's storage truck, used for moving rides from site to site.

Bottom: Fleet Number 3744, a 1950 S10, that was acquired by Automotive Products of Leamington for a mobile brake testing unit. It passed to BaMMOT in 1981 and is now beautifully preserved at Transport Museum Wythall.

ENTHUSIASTS

Back in the days when steam trains ruled the rails and Midland Red buses served the towns and villages of the Midlands, the innocent occupation of the enthusiasts was chatting with fellow followers and recording vehicle numbers in Ian Allan or Midland Red-issued fleet list booklets.

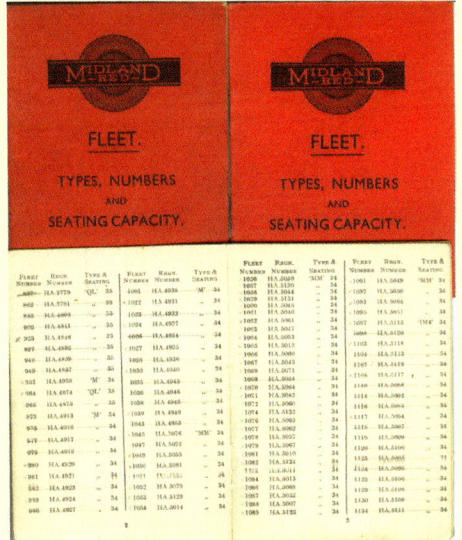

The Midland Red booklets became dual-purpose documents. At first they were intended for internal use, and then they were widely distributed by post, usually accompanied by a couple of postcards of buses, to anyone caring to write in and ask for one. If you were lucky you may have joined the official Midland Red Spotters Club and been rewarded with a pin badge to put on your anorak. Much like railway enthusiasts meeting up with friends at the railway station, spotters would meet up at bus stations where they would exchange the latest news of new arrivals of modern buses, discuss their sad recollections of the older buses being withdrawn or scrapped, and then take down the numbers of most vehicles that could be seen during their time there.

There were enthusiasts who built model buses from odd bits of card or metal. In later years, they were able to buy a model bus from the local model shop, but alas, there were precious few models representing Midland Red buses. This was largely due to their own designs of buses and coaches being local to the Midlands, and model manufacturers therefore assuming that they would be poor sellers. In the 1930s, there was a range of Chad Valley large scale model buses which featured a single-decker and a double-decker made from thin tin and loosely representing Midland Red prototypes, and these now sell for hundreds of pounds.

As the motorway express coaches became established, a large plastic model resembling the C5 type coach was introduced; it was made in Hong Kong and was even sold in the shop inside Digbeth coach station. In more modern times, there have been ranges of white metal kits (and later in resin) of many types of Midland Red vehicles, and these are popular and collectable when well-built and finished. But now we have everything in an instant, available online and at our fingertips – it's a long time since the days when we gathered at popular haunts to exchange fleet numbers and the latest news.

Besides bus models, some enthusiasts go to the next level of architectural bus modelling. In *Midland Red Influence* we were introduced to Andrew Dainty from Worcester who built a model of Ludlow garage, which was often displayed at Model Bus Federation events. Andrew has recently gone a step further and produced a splendid model of Midland Red's ancestral and spiritual home of Bearwood garage. This extensive model has taken months to produce with much delicate work done to provide the exceptional result. It is a model that brings many memories back to life for anyone fortunate enough to have visited the place prior to 1973.

In the 1960s, the bus preservation movement became active, no doubt spurred on by the increasing interest in railway preservation as operational steam trains drew to a close. There had for a long time been the rare and brave and often thought of as 'strange' individuals who had ventured into the world of bus ownership – 'who on earth would want to buy an old bus?'

This was an interesting period because showmen of the fairgrounds had bought old buses to provide accommodation and storage, and to use as generators for their rides, with many still around from the late 1920s and 1930s. But sadly most were lost to the scrap men because the enthusiast movement was not organised, and internal politics often caused rescue attempts to fail.

Fortunately, the odd group succeeded, mainly when the acquired vehicles had secure accommodation, in those days when farmyards, barns and backs of factories were plentiful and their owners less money-driven. Groups like the 1685 Group in Birmingham joined with BaMMOT at Wythall to become the Midland's premier bus museum – a safe haven for those important vehicles that make up our important transport heritage. Many vehicles have been lost along the way, but there are also many waiting for financial help which today is given by grants, donations, appeals, bequests, and often the support of enthusiastic members or supporters.

Midland Red as a company were supportive of staff wishing to purchase older vehicles, but always pointed out that it was not easy. And tyres would have to be purchased separately, once a price had been given by the tyre contractor based on their degree of tyre wear.

One very important vehicle, 4943, the first of the two D10s, was bought by excursions officer Alan Kelsall. Included in the purchase,

the company offered him some spares from the other D10 when it came off service later that year. Alan formed a D10 preservation society to take care of the vehicle. However, it was later decided to sell the vehicle, and after there were concerns that it may be sold abroad, an appeal by BaMMOT museum was successful and they became guardian of this very important vehicle. It can occasionally be seen out and about giving rides on special event days at Transport Museum Wythall.

The first owner of the preserved D10 4943 in 1972, Alan Kelsall, stands in front of his new acquisition.

Top Right: A group of enthusiasts back in the early days of bus preservation. Birmingham Omnibus Preservation Society members with Richard Grey on the left stand in front of a Midland Red C1 coach.

Middle Right: Enthusiasts from the Midland Red (Leamington) Preservation Society were instrumental in saving two BMMO vehicles: the CM6T 5656 and the last built S16 5545. They were later passed on to BaMMOT, now Transport Museum Wythall. The vehicle that the group originally wanted to own was D9 4851, and to raise funds various enthusiast excursions were operated with the vehicle being hired from the company. The photo here shows 4851 during a trip to the south coast, Brighton and the Bluebell Railway all in a day, and only months before the bus was withdrawn. Unbeknown to the group, the vehicle was sold to a dealer as part of a bigger purchase of withdrawn buses.

Bottom Right: Midland Red's own collection of handmade large scale model buses must also get a mention. These were constructed by professional bodybuilder Joe Faulkener at Central Works. These were available for use at special occasions, when each model was transported in its own wooden crate. This is the S1, one of the wartime prototypes converted/rebuilt from the pre-war REC rear-engined prototypes.

Probably the two most important and extremely valuable vehicles from the early days. They are best described as long term restoration projects from the 1920s and 1930s. On the left is the SOS Standard single-decker, one of the very first Midland Red-built buses. On the right is an REDD double-decker, the only surviving pre-war example of an SOS double-decker. They are exhibits and part of the collection at Transport Museum Wythall.

As this book was being prepared for print, the sad news arrived of the passing of Patrick Kingston. Patrick was a very well known transport photographer and author of the book *Royal Trains*, some years ago. He gave frequent slide shows of his many hundreds of images covering transport generally, but with particular attention given to Great Western Railway and Midland Red.

I have known Patrick personally since the very early 1970s when I joined the staff at Midland Red's Leamington garage, where we were both members of the Midland Red (Leamington) Preservation Society. At the time he worked for Warwickshire County Council in their public transport department and he had a free bus pass for Midland Red services as part of his council work. He was often seen surveying buses in the Leamington area. His mother was a regular passenger when I was a bus conductor, where she told me of Patrick's interest in O gauge model railways – something I took up in later years.

Almost twenty years after our first meeting, and after I finished work with Midland Red, I worked in the same public transport office in Warwick, doing a similar job. We had remained in touch and regularly met for coffee and bus chat in Leamington.

Patrick was born in 1937, and his earliest memories of Midland Red buses was seeing them turn around at the end of their service near his home, not far from The Oak Inn on Radford Road. Patrick kept detailed records of his photographs and slides and he was generous in allowing me to use a selection in my various books. Some of my earliest recollections of his Midland Red memories were of the LRR class of pre-war single-deckers, most of which were allocated to Leamington garage after the war. Patrick had travelled on many pre-war SOS buses and his descriptive stories were important in building my knowledge, as he was 18 or so years my senior.

Many of his pictures were taken around his home town of Leamington Spa and I have selected two below which were trademark Patrick Kingston. They both feature one of his favourite buses and his own Rover 2000 car, so often in his pictures like an anonymous piece of street furniture.

D9 4851 travelling towards the bottom of Leamington's famous Parade, just south of Debenham's store and approaching the junction with Dormer Place.

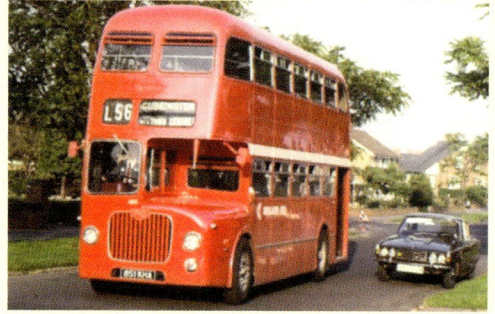

The same bus, catching the evening sunshine in September 1975. It is in St Margarets Road, Whitnash, approaching the junction with Brunswick Street, on its way to pass through the town centre en route to Cubbington via Campion Hill. 4851 was the third D9 to be built and it was hoped that the Midland Red (Leamington) Preservation Society would buy it for preservation, especially as the engineers at Leamington had kept this D9 in exceptionally good condition. It was withdrawn two months after this photograph was taken, but instead of being preserved it was already sold as part of a large batch of buses bought by a Yorkshire scrap dealer.

TALKING ABOUT BUS FIRES

Bus fires are certainly a 'hot' topic, with the dramatic rise in fires involving buses and coaches in recent years. Some explanation is offered here, but the bus industry of today has certainly forgotten the words that Midland Red emphasised when they led the industry in bus and coach design and technology.

Those words were: light, fast, economical and reliable. The reason Midland Red's own built vehicles were reliable is that their technology was kept *simple*. That included using the natural flow of air under the vehicle to cool the mechanical components, and only having the equipment fitted that was necessary to perform the job, without an endless increase in operational and in-bus entertainment electronics that wasn't essential for relatively short journeys. Do we really need charging points at every seat for mobile phones on a journey that takes perhaps 20 minutes? Do we really need enhanced Wi-Fi on the same journey? Is this more marketing than necessity? Perhaps a better way of making a journey by bus more attractive is to simply provide a clean vehicle running to time with clear destination blind information and a well trained driver!

Midland Red used big engines in their buses, which worked with ease and without the need to be overworked, so the parts lasted longer and economy was at its best. The engines were not racing at high revs like the smaller engines that are often used more in modern vehicles.

Midland Red vehicles were lightweight, yet well balanced. The auxiliary components and fittings were basic but well made. British parts were not the cheapest to buy but they lasted longer, meaning less downtime, fewer labour costs and longer life – and they could all be overhauled and used again. But even with the best engineering and care, with a fleet of almost 2,000 vehicles, things did sometimes go wrong.

There were many times on hot summer days with hard driving that the brake discs got hot – sometimes glowing red, sometimes smoking. But after a rest and a cup of tea, things were back to normal. Only on rare occasions did we see a fire engine arrive when flames came from (usually) the front wheel, but seldom did this cause anything but a delay and a change of bus. However, there were occasionally more serious incidents.

The worst UK bus fire

Possibly the worst of UK bus fires was in Nuneaton, Warwickshire – this was in Midland Red territory, but the incident did not immediately involve Midland Red. The fire had far-reaching effects. News reached Australia, and three weeks later an article appeared in the Melbourne Argus stating that an enquiry had been held following a recent fire in a motorbus full of people at Nuneaton, where several passengers were burned to death. The Construction and Use Regulations were later amended regarding the obstruction of emergency exits. In those early days it was permitted for a seat to be fitted across the rear emergency door, and in the panic of this incident it could not be removed in time, leaving the only exit at the front which was engulfed in fire.

The local operator, Tom Wilkinson from the Nuneaton suburb of Stockingford, had started a service between Nuneaton's Queens Road to Whittleford via Haunchwood Road. The incident occurred on Monday 30 August 1924 when his small bus stopped along the route, having run out petrol. It was dark and the driver started to fill the tank from a spare can he carried on the bus. The lights, which were run off the dynamo, went out or became very dim when the bus stopped. A passenger on the bus assisted the driver to see better by striking a match which ignited the petrol vapour and engulfed the bus in flames. It is reported that council workers were still on scene clearing debris some three days later.

Not long after this terrible incident, Midland Red put out a statement to reassure their passengers. The company pointed out that the circumstances of the Nuneaton fire could not possibly take place on one of their vehicles of the 'closed' type. The statement was reported in the press: "Not only is the emergency door extremely simple to operate should occasion to use it arise, but it is claimed that the presence of a driver and conductor on each vehicle adds materially to the factor of safety. Moreover, the petrol tank is entirely walled

S5 4617 at Central Works, just before it was cut up for scrap.

in by steel plates, rendering it impossible for petrol to drop upon the exhaust pipe, the tank is never filled up on service, and there are two stout partitions between the engine and the emergency exit. There are seats across the doors in these instances also, but it is claimed that the notifications are easy to follow, the doors are frequently opened, and kept in order, but perhaps the greatest point made was that all the bus windows are made to open."

Tom Wilkinson's business struggled on for a few more years, but its services were taken by Midland Red in May 1932.

Two S15 fires

On a cold January day in 1963, fleet number 4617, whilst on service at Bromsgrove garage, caught fire with terminal results. The vehicle was six years old and from the first batch of dual-purpose, black-topped S15 semi-coaches. After the fire brigade had put out the fire, the remaining shell was taken under-cover to Central Works for internal examination, and was eventually cut up for scrap. The response time in this era was longer, as the driver had to find a telephone to call for help, and this could vary considerably depending on whether the incident was in a built-up area or in the middle of the countryside.

In a similar incident, on Wednesday 29 March 1967, S15 fleet number 4624, allocated to Rugby garage, was on an early morning one-man operated rural service back to Rugby from the villages of Braunston, Willoughby and Grandborough. After leaving Grandborough, a passenger, Mr G. Goodhall, noticed steam or smoke rising from the floor just halfway along the gangway. He notified the driver Harry Kilden to stop. He pulled onto the side of the rural lane where the passengers and driver did their best to prevent further trouble by using the fire extinguisher, while Mr Goodall ran half a mile back to the village telephone box to summon the fire brigade. The rural location did not help, and by the time the firemen arrived the bus was beyond saving. Under cover of darkness, the remains of the bus were moved to Central Works for assessment and investigation, but it was withdrawn a month later, then cut up on site and scrapped.

A D9 fire in Nuneaton

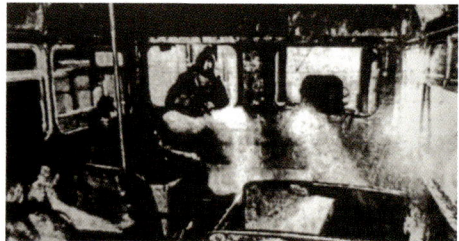

D9 fleet number 5298 was a victim of wiring becoming insecure in the engine compartment and causing an electrical fire. This very poor image shows the fireman dousing the remaining hot spots in the lower saloon. The white areas towards the centre of the image are the melted and distorted remains of the curved plastic light covers which were slotted in above the side windows.

An S17 victim

Despite its blackened top, this was not a dual-purpose liveried bus, but a heavily charred S17 bus, fleet number 5492. Whilst allocated to Stourbridge garage, it was involved in an incident in October 1973 where fire spread along almost the entire length of the vehicle. It was taken to Central Works for assessment, and officially withdrawn six months later after removal of some parts.

D9 fire – a Hinckley garage bus

It is alleged that on the late-night bus from Earl Shilton to Hinckley, driver Afsal, who had been with the company for over a year, thought he heard an unusual sound from the engine compartment of his D9 double-

decker (fleet number 5391), while still in Earl Shilton. He pulled up but it was difficult to see, as the street was not well-lit. He struck a match to help him see better, but it fell from his hand as the flame neared his fingertips. It dropped into the engine compartment and landed in the worst possible place: the fuel pump drip tray, which sat beneath the fuel pump. Diesel is not easy to ignite unless by contact with a naked flame – and this was a flame. The bus was well ablaze in a short time, and the engine oil and fuel all added to the inferno. The bus had many fibreglass components and panels, and by the time the fire brigade arrived from Hinckley the bus could not be saved. Some hours later it was brought back to Hinckley garage in the dead of night under a protective sheet and rested for some time, devoid of identity, at the back of the garage while investigations took place, after which its framework and remains were cut up for scrap.

S17 fire – a Bromsgrove bus

Languishing at Bromsgrove garage in the twilight hours of its life is S17 fleet number 5557. It had suffered an electrical fire in late 1969, when it was five years old. It was taken to Central Works, and within a few months it was back at Bromsgrove, hoping to fit in with other S17s. But it always stood out, as during the rebuild there were insufficient S17 parts. Rather than construct new fibreglass mouldings from the S17 stable, it was easier to use S23 parts, including the front and rear roof domes and interior panels. Midland Red were fortunate in making the fibreglass panels in-house at Central Works. These photographs were taken in mid-1976, when it was withdrawn and awaiting the scrap man, looking rather sorry for itself and still at Bromsgrove garage.

Fire in Stretton-on-Dunsmore

Things were much more relaxed 'back in the day', and it was a time when people were exceptionally public-spirited! Here's an incident that occurred on Friday 15 August 1969 which wasn't officially recorded.

A milkman who normally did his rounds local to his home in Stretton-on-Dunsmore found himself doing another job one lunchtime on his day off. He was assisting behind the bar of the local pub, The Oak and Black Dog, when a Midland Red bus pulled up outside and the driver, Singh Sandhu, asked to use the phone.

He called the engineers at Rugby garage and told them there was a burning smell under his bus. Mrs Armstrong, the landlady, was fearful of an explosion, exclaiming, "with all that fuel on board, it might break the pub windows!" So she called the fire brigade. As would be expected, several people went outside, including the barman who was Tom Nix, a local man of Fosse Way, and they found that the smell had developed into smouldering, with smoke coming from underneath. By this time, the passengers were safely off the vehicle.

Milkman, barman and now 'fireman' Tom, sprung into action and gathered five fire extinguishers. They found some worked better than others. The first extinguisher was from the bus; the second was from the drayman's lorry which was delivering to the pub; the third was from the village sub-postmaster George Hunter; the fourth from Borsley's Stores, and the fifth from Mr Bleach from nearby Carlton Cottage. Tom's work was done, and the fire was out when the fire brigade arrived, although they inspected the bus to check for a cause. They found that the air intake pipe had come adrift from the air filter box and had fallen across the hot exhaust pipe. With the offending air hose removed, Driver Sandhu transferred his passengers to the newly arrived replacement bus, and after their half hour of excitement they continued their journey. The engineer who brought out the replacement vehicle drove the unfortunate bus back to the garage, where a new air hose was fitted and secured, and the bus was out on service again within a few hours.

Small bus fire incidents

An incident that wasn't officially reported to the authorities occurred on Thursday 1 April 1955. Swadlincote firemen received a report of a bus fire at Stanton, and they promptly despatched two fire engines. However, on arrival they found that the fire had already been put out by the driver. There had been a short circuit on a wire to the engine, and the driver turned off the master switch and used the bus fire extinguisher. There was nothing for the firemen to do and the bus was back in service the following morning.

Another fire not officially reported occurred on Monday 3 July 1950 when a party of race goers were on their way to Nottingham racecourse. They had been delayed by taking a longer than planned breakfast stop, and the driver was making much needed progress until it was noticed that smoke was coming from the brakes. The driver stopped to investigate, but it was soon discovered that flames were now licking the brake drums, and so a 999 call was made. Firemen from Beeston were soon on the scene and the party was able to continue their journey when things had cooled down.

As far as more serious 'reported' bus fires are concerned, between the end of WW2 and 1980 (the end of BMMO vehicles widely running in service), there were 11 reported incidents. These are where investigations were carried out, and the incidents reported to The Ministry of Transport – the obligations that each operator has when holding appropriate licences to operate buses and coaches.

Buses used to be built with the bus company chief or senior engineers leading the specification and design. Today, it is mainly the vehicle manufacturing businesses that lead the specification and design of buses and coaches, which are then offered for sale 'off the peg'. Midland Red's approach was very different in that *they* were the designer, builder and operator of most of their vehicles, and their vehicles were built quite simply – necessary features were provided, and no more. There was lots of room under the bus for air to move freely, to keep mechanical units well ventilated in operation. In fact, their single-decker engines didn't even need a cooling fan!

We had to comply

A little background information may help to explain where we find ourselves today. In 1995, some 25 years after Midland Red's last home-made bus had left the factory, regulations were introduced by the EU across the motor industry requiring vehicles to have engine management systems (computerised control of fuel/air/ignition/exhaust etc). Coaches and buses had to be designed with their engines in enclosures (boxed in) to ensure that they reached optimum operating temperature in the shortest time. At the same time, ever more costly new engines were introduced in the quest to be cleaner. The first generation were known as Euro 1 compliant, and then more stringent emission controls led to Euro 2 and so on until we are currently (at the time of writing) at Euro 6. Along with modern engines, new common rail high pressure fuel lines became standard which added to both complication and risk, although we have now surpassed this with the drive toward electric vehicles.

New filtered exhaust systems became available with a built-in furnace that reduced smoke and noxious gas emissions by burning the exhaust gases at high temperatures. There were also similar retrofit systems, that could be purchased at great cost for fitting to older non-compliant vehicles. Not only were these a high risk option, but an expensive one. When these were introduced, I flirted briefly with the idea of adding a retrofit system to an already well-performing and MOT-compliant Leyland Royal Tiger Doyen – the kit had a price tag of well over £3k back in the day! This was a cost that could only be met by passengers. The only bonus at the time was that a new coach with its electronically controlled engine and exhaust systems (or an older coach with a modern retro-fit exhaust system) could go into London and be exempt from the London Low Emission Zone charge. Of course, that now affects some other areas of the country, too.

The 'traditional' bus and coach engines like Gardner, Leyland, AEC and indeed Midland Red's BMMO engines were in use at a time when the UK had a vibrant export market for passenger vehicles to all parts of the world – a market now sadly lost. But it is important to look at the pros and cons of these older engine designs. They were big and revved more slowly, so they didn't have to work so hard, resulting in them having exceptionally long lives – half a million miles was common, but some went on for far more. They were smoky when cold, but they were very efficient, giving miles per gallon figures that today's engines can only dream of – so a little dirtier, but using much less of a precious resource (i.e. fuel). They were also easy to work on, repair or rebuild, so although initially a costly product, their extended life and low upkeep costs made them very economical overall. At the end of their life in a bus, these engines would go on to have another life, such as being exported to Hong Kong for use in fishing boats, or nearer home to drive generators used by showmen etc.

Adding to the complications involved in the maintenance of modern vehicles are the costs of additional labour time to dismantle engine compartments and remove auxiliary items, which are now 'crammed in', just in order to reach the part that needs to be exchanged – yes, in this throw-away world, parts are *exchanged*, not repaired and refitted. The bus business is a much more costly industry than it was when things were more simple; when you lifted a panel or bonnet and the engine was there with all the regular parts much more accessible. An example of our throw-away culture is encountered in commonly used light clusters, perhaps holding headlight, side light and indicator; to repair a side light bulb (that used to cost a few pence) necessitates the replacement of the whole light cluster costing several hundreds of pounds! Surely this is not in the spirit of earning 'green' credentials.

The Midland Red bus was designed to be kept running with little work and little cost. Access to components for routine maintenance was simplicity itself!

Modern engines, at first, were mainly to be found on imported vehicles. Those like Scania, Volvo, Daf and Cummins tend to be smaller and higher revving, and so working harder than big engines like AEC, BMMO, Gardner and Leyland that run slower with less mechanical stress. Modern engines working hard in hot weather and boxed-in with restrictive airflow can easily result in a build up of excess heat. Add to this the highly complicated electronics and wiring, and the much greater power requirement of modern buses and coaches in service use, and bus fires happen much more often.

Vehicle construction is still of relatively lightweight materials – alloys, plastics, fibreglass etc – and most bus and coach fires leave just the remains of bent and twisted metal frames. Add lithium batteries, and the situation can be more volatile. The electric bus question will take more time in service to properly resolve.

The updated regulations governing bus and coach design stipulate that new vehicles must have built-in 'fire suppression' systems around the engine compartment (UNECE Regulation 107). However, judging by the examples we see on the sides of the roads and from discussions with fire officers, these fire suppression systems don't seem to be very effective in stopping fire development. With modern high pressure fuel lines and enclosed engines with exhaust systems that run at much higher temperatures, it would appear that many buses are designed in such a way that they are very likely to catch fire if any of a series of faults develop, and this is almost expected behaviour, as they have to have built in fire suppression systems! With buses being used so intensively, it only takes a tiny fracture in any one of the high pressure fuel lines and a resulting mist of fuel to spray over an extremely hot exhaust system, and it is in most cases a lost cause.

A closer look

There has been a dramatic increase in bus fires in the UK and worldwide in recent years. According to UK Government figures of bus fires recorded by DVSA, in the period 2019 to 2020 there were 25 incidents, yet in 2021 to 2022 there were 101.

Let's compare some astonishing statistics of bus fires affecting Midland Red and London Transport (now Transport for London).

Midland Red had a fleet of almost 2,000 vehicles, operating over 12,000 square miles of the Midlands during the period 1946 to 1976 (some 30 years).

Below are the reported bus fires causing severe damage or total loss of asset affecting Midland Red vehicles from 1946 to 1976:

1956	a six year old single-decker fire whilst allocated to Kidderminster garage.
1963	a six year old single-decker fire whilst allocated to Bromsgrove garage.
1967	an eleven year old single-decker fire whilst allocated to Rugby garage.
1968	an eleven year old single-decker fire whilst allocated to Sutton Coldfield garage.
1969	a six year old double-decker fire whilst allocated to Nuneaton garage.
1969	a five year old single-decker fire whilst allocated to Bromsgrove garage. †
1971	an eight year old double-decker fire whilst allocated to Sutton Coldfield garage.*
1971	an eight year old double-decker fire whilst allocated to Digbeth garage. *
1971	a seven year old double-decker fire whilst allocated to Hinckley garage.
1974	an eleven year old single-decker fire whilst allocated to Stourbridge garage.

*   This vehicle was a Daimler Fleetline and not of BMMO manufacture.

†   This vehicle was rebuilt at Central Works and worked for six more years.

DD11 Daimler Fleetline fleet number 5260, when nine years old in 1971 was operating a 159 service from Birmingham to Coventry. This was almost on the Coventry/Warwickshire border. The body was stripped and the chassis stored for a while at Hinckley garage.

Fires became much more of a cause for concern at Midland Red with the arrival of the Leyland National, from around 1973. Almost all of the earlier BMMO-made buses and those bought-in had 'insulated return' wiring, meaning that each electrical component was connected to a positive wire and a negative wire running from the batteries. This meant that the electrical system was isolated from the chassis, unlike the 'earth return' system which used the chassis (rather than a wire) as the return path for the electrical current.

An insulated return electrical system requires more wire, resulting in higher initial costs, but in fault conditions it would require both a positive *and* a negative to meet the chassis to cause a fire. In fact, Midland Red engineering service sheets that were used on mechanics' four-weekly vehicle checks had a corresponding section to complete, ensuring that the mechanic had checked to see if any voltage was recorded from the chassis/underframe. If there was a trace voltage the fault had to be rectified before the vehicle re-entered service.

Midland Red-built buses rarely had their electrical 'master switch' turned off. This might be done on vehicles returning to garage on Christmas Eve, where they might be parked up for a couple of days in the depot. However, with the arrival of the Leyland National onwards it was deemed necessary to turn off the vehicle's master switch each night. It is fortunate that the positioning of the Leyland vehicle's master switch was in the driver's cab, unlike the earlier

BMMO vehicles where it was positioned beneath or at the side of the battery box on single-deckers or under the stairs on the D9 double-deckers.

A Leyland National experienced an electrical fault whilst parked up in Nuneaton garage not long after its arrival as a new bus. Fortunately the smell and the smoke was noticed by the 'night driver' who extinguished the fire before it became a serious incident.

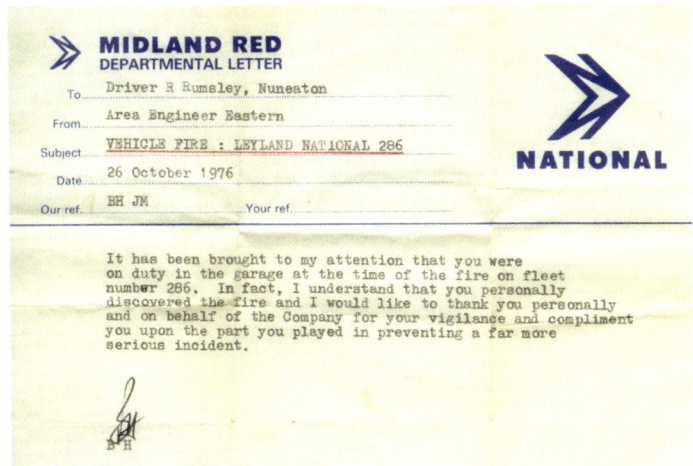

Letter of thanks from Area Engineer (Eastern) to Driver R. Rumsby for his actions in preventing what would have been a major fire.

The 'night driver' featured as a shift at each garage from the age of petrol buses. With cleaners and late shift mechanics finishing work at 0100 or 0200hrs and the early mechanics not starting until 0400hrs, the intervening period was a vulnerable time. It was usual for the night driver to do a short driving shift after his night duty role, and it was common for several drivers to share the night role as it was not liked by many, even though it was a financially lucrative duty.

Another fire involving a Leyland National occurred at Southgate Street garage in Leicester. Vehicle 830 was damaged to a more serious extent than the Nuneaton incident. The remains were taken to Central Works in Birmingham where, in its later days of providing such skills, the vehicle was rebuilt as a mobility vehicle featuring a wheelchair access lift and other wheelchair facilities.

Meanwhile, in London

Transport for London (TfL) has a roughly comparable area of operation and relevant fleet size to Midland Red. But in the period 2020 to 2022 (just 3 years), in London alone, in 2020 there were 37 reported fire incidents, in 2021 there were 46 reported fire incidents, and in 2022 there were 56 reported fire incidents.

The final figure shows that, on average, over one bus per week is lost to fire. Each bus is an asset worth an astronomical amount of money: just one London spec bus can cost more than a top-end Ferrari sports car. The data gathered from a number of sources, including Callum Marius, transport editor for MyLondon, fire officers, bus engineers and operating staff, all help to highlight the real costs in the drive towards the impossible to reach 'net zero'. Just one of these regular bus fires incurs huge costs: the emissions of toxic smoke, fire brigade costs, traffic management costs including police time, wreck recovery costs and clean up, scrappage and recycling costs. Then there is the actual asset value of the bus, approaching half a million pounds, and the cost of replacement. All of these costs undermine a lot of those net-zero ambitions.

On 22 May 2022, a fire in Potters Bar bus garage yard, involving an electric bus exploding, destroyed five other buses. Hertfordshire Fire and Rescue sent a total of eight fire engines and warned the public that the emergency could take a long time to conclude. This led to the temporary withdrawal from service of 92 electric buses.

There have been several other bus fire incidents in the streets of London. An experienced firefighter commented that it takes an average of four hours to extinguish an EV fire, and on average costs £1m an hour each time traffic is held up because of a burning vehicle.

The London incidents have not changed the priorities of the Mayor of London, who has told operators that only electric or hydrogen fuelled buses can be ordered for use in the TfL area. The operator of the buses is compelled to buy or lease only types of vehicle that are stipulated by TfL for use on contracted London services. This might be a type of bus that, given a free hand, the operator may not have wished to operate, yet they must incur the costs of changing garage operations and equipment, and must shoulder many of the risks when things go wrong.

Tube trains are under investigation for high levels of emissions from brake dust and from metal-to-metal rail-to-wheel contact, which are viewed as harmful to users of the London Underground. The pollution levels on the underground system are said to be higher than other forms of transport due to poor ventilation, with the Bakerloo Line emitting the highest levels of inhalable dust, sufficient to get into the bloodstream. Quartz and silica dust are associated with lung disease (silicosis) and kidney disease. Chrome, manganese and copper have also been detected in the tube network.

The authorities could not close down the underground system for any length of time without causing a major impact on the economies and well-being of London and, indeed, the country. They cannot afford to do the necessary work to reduce (not eliminate) pollution as the costs would be too high. Are buses perhaps an easier target?

Where are we heading?

Surely, more gradual and affordable improvements should be brought about by a considered approach to refurbishments and renewal, rather than, what many consider to be, harmful decisions to just ban diesel buses outright. The turmoil that vehicle manufacturers are going through, with indecisive and changing goalposts from governments and civil service, will soon have reached a tipping point where infrastructure, costs, and an experienced workforce can no longer be brought back into use, and we will be totally reliant upon imported Chinese electric buses – until perhaps the supply stops!

A hydrogen bus currently made in the UK has a price tag of £545k, and the production of hydrogen to supply it consumes a lot of electricity. An electric bus costs £400k and has imported raw materials within the batteries, notably lithium which is volatile and in certain conditions can be dangerous and temperature sensitive. There are ethical problems with cobalt mining in some countries (using child labour) and end-of-life disposal costs that are excessive and not yet fully understood. A modern clean diesel bus costs around £150-190k, with an optional addition of over £100k to have a hybrid power train (although order/supply can be an issue with the hybrid version).

It is interesting to note that the Boris Bus (officially known as the 'New Routemaster'), with a Euro 6 (clean diesel) engine and hybrid drive, costs circa £349k. However, it is said that some of these could be replaced four years ahead of their original planned lifespan by Chinese electric buses with a £400k price tag. They are being replaced as, according to TfL, they cannot afford the refurbishment of the whole fleet of Boris Buses, and the Chinese manufacturers have told them that the new electric buses have a much longer life. However there is some speculation as to exactly when the New Routemaster replacements will be made, and how many will be refurbished to give them up to another decade of life which would see them running in London well past 2030, the date by which the Mayor of London says London's transport will be 'zero emission'.

An electric bus involved in a breakdown or accident while in service can not be easily towed, and recovery costs, often by specialist low loaders, are extremely high. In these circumstances a replacement electric bus would be required to continue in service, but of course we are not always working in ideal conditions, and an expensive and fully charged electric bus may not be waiting on stand-by – resulting in unreliable services.

Can cascading continue?

To comply with new vehicle build requirements, we now have companies producing automatic fire fighting equipment, but judging by the many recent bus fires, they do not seem to work very effectively. Add over-complicated electronics and computerisation to the mix, and you wonder what has happened to the advances that Midland Red made to vehicle design. Lightweight vehicles that were economical, fast, safe and reliable were key words back then in a vibrant bus industry when Great Britain exported buses the world over. Now we see designs that are not of UK origin (often Chinese), and are over weight, over complicated, and overall are far less green and economic than we are led to believe. Whilst perhaps reliable when they are running under 'ideal' conditions, when there are hot summers and overworked vehicles we see regular reports of buses lost to fire. The electric bus is still in its infancy, and our industry will still have further changes to contend with. We will likely lose many, if not most, of our small, often local independent bus and coach companies the more we aspire to go green, as it is too costly. The age-old cascading of buses and coaches, passing from large operators to small operators in their later life, is likely to be no longer a viable option. The cascading of electric vehicles will be risky due to the high cost of replacement batteries in what is essentially an old vehicle.

The traditional London Routemaster, of which 2,800 have given great service to London residents and visitors for nearly 70 years, was certainly an iconic vehicle. Its appearance on the streets and on tourist merchandise simply shouted 'London'. It was, for sure, a revolution, and it was known and admired by almost everyone. It was so well designed, robustly engineered and reliable that it outlasted many different types of buses which were either running alongside them or were supposed to replace them! They have also been operated second hand by many bus operators all over the UK, and are still employed by many, operating heritage and tourist services. The British AEC Routemaster can also be seen operating in many foreign countries.

We don't learn from the past

I am sure that the Boris Bus has something of an individual look, but it will never be able to excel over its predecessor. Failures with air conditioning equipment meant that opening windows had to be retrofitted. Problems with having three doors and two staircases have led to extreme levels of fare evasion, resulting in the closing off of rear doors and other necessary adjustments. Now, at 13 years old (at the time or writing), the London examples are restricted to use in London only, and the costs of full refurbishment (what used to be called mid-life overhauls) cannot be met.

Historically, the longstanding arrangement for minor and major overhauls undertaken at London Transport central workshops at Aldenham and Chiswick was a continual process, undertaken thoroughly and swiftly. Many YouTube videos are available to view their remarkable work.

Public transport is a complex subject, and I have used the example of London Transport (now TfL) to reflect on how our desires for tomorrow go beyond the realities of today, and how other areas of Great Britain may find that operating costs escalate in the coming years, unless we adopt a more fundamental approach to reliable and experience-led public transport.

In the chapter about the Electrobus, you will read how London, Brighton and a few other towns benefited from a new battery electric bus over 100 years ago – described as a well engineered bus, the project failed due to corruption, fraud and its bosses living the 'high life'. But, its battery charging system was ahead of its time and a lesson for those trying to get it right now. The Electrobus had a removable battery tray that could be exchanged on a lift in the garage in just three minutes! This would certainly be a way forward to enable long-distance electric coaches to reach their destination.

Ask the users of public transport – the general public – what they require from buses and bus services and you are likely to hear: safe and well-trained drivers, and buses that are clean and turn up at their timetabled time. And more than a few older passengers said that the bus conductor should be brought back. Are we prepared to pay what is necessary to get people out of private cars and onto public transport?

ELECTROBUS: AN OPPORTUNITY MISSED   *Guest writer Colin Browell*

The early years of the motor omnibus

The early years of the twentieth century saw the introduction of an exciting new form of public conveyance – the motor bus. Between 1897 and 1904 there were several attempts to introduce a motor bus service in Birmingham.

The Motor Touring Co Ltd ran one of the earliest motor bus services, in Llandudno in 1898. The company's chairman, John James Horne, was a tyre manufacturer in Birmingham and, perhaps because of this, they established an office in Birmingham and secured a license to run a motor bus service there. However, the company ceased trading the following year so the service never materialised. Although it was short-lived, it may well have provided inspiration or experience to other companies seeking to establish a motor bus service in Birmingham. A couple of these also had one or more directors with family or business links to the Llandudno area, so were quite likely to have seen or experienced the early Motor Touring Company service operating there. However, the company that succeeded in running the first sustained motor bus service in Birmingham was the Birmingham Motor Express Co, headed by William Roberts.

William Roberts was born in Anglesey on 6 December 1862 and moved to Birmingham in 1877, where he grew up to become a well known public figure. He was a local councillor, a freemason, a treasurer of the local workhouse, a volunteer fireman and a philanthropist. He lived in Handsworth and built up a successful estate agency business, but he still maintained close ties with North Wales; his wife's family and even his servants came from the Llandudno area.

William Roberts.

In 1901 he developed an interest in the new public conveyance of the motor bus and was particularly impressed by the new Milnes Daimler 8.5 horsepower 16-seater. Two years later, he started a business called the Birmingham Motor Express Co with the help of a fellow councillor and businessman Edward Olivieri. A few months later he registered it as a limited company, persuading some of his other business contacts to be directors.

In order to generate more investment, the directors of Birmingham Motor Express created a new company in 1904 called Birmingham and Midland Motor Omnibus Co (BMMO), but it failed to attract sufficient investment. You can read more on the formation of BMMO in the author's earlier book *Midland Red Influence*. The Birmingham Motor Express and BMMO companies were sold in 1905 to the giant BET, and BMMO was used to operate buses in and around Birmingham. All of the directors were replaced during the takeover except Roberts, so he was clearly seen as the kingpin of the bus operation. But he also became involved in other bus companies outside the Midlands.

Reception to the early motor omnibuses could be described as mixed. They had many enthusiastic proponents in the transport industry who saw them as the future of passenger transport. But there were numerous problems with them that provoked opposition from residents in the roads where they operated: excessive noise and vibration was a common complaint, also smell, noxious fumes, dripping oil and frequent breakdowns, not to mention damage to the road surface.

There was particularly strong opposition in Birmingham. Most of the city's main thoroughfares were served by tramways except in Broad Street and the affluent Hagley Road where there was overwhelming opposition to their pleasant roads being ruined by metal rails and noisy tramcars. The Watch Committee (a council committee that controlled the police and had the power to grant or rescind bus licences) ruled that the new motor buses could not run over routes that competed against trams, so the only place that BMMO could run a motor bus service was along Broad Street and the Hagley Road. It seems at first the motor buses were welcomed by the residents there, perhaps being seen as an ally to fend off the threat of the tramcar, but opinion quickly turned against them. In October 1907, it was reported in the *Birmingham Gazette and Express,* "When there were prospects of trams on the Hagley Road, the motor omnibuses were welcomed by residents as an alternative, but, when the trams had been safely shelved, many of the residents turned round and commenced to abuse them." The Watch Committee were particularly responsive to complaints and applied additional rules and forced the operator to make design changes to the vehicles, which may have adversely affected their reliability. The restricted routes and the troublesome requests of the Watch Committee may well have played a part in BMMO's decision in October 1907 to cease all motor bus services and return to horse buses. This was a decision that shocked the industry and was seen as a retrograde step that was a great disservice to the poor passengers around Hagley Road that now had to use horse-drawn omnibuses. But with advances in technology, the motor bus eventually returned to the streets of Birmingham in 1912 with a much improved Tilling Stevens petrol electric vehicle.

After all the vociferous opposition to trams in Hagley Road, it is ironic that even with the availability of these new improved motor buses, the tramway men finally achieved a sufficient majority in the council to force through the installation of tramways in Hagley Road. At a meeting of the Birmingham Chamber of Commerce in September 1912, it was stated that 100% of the inhabitants in Broad Street, 96% of the residents in Hagley Road, and 80% of the residents in side streets had signed a petition protesting against the introduction of trams along the Hagley Road. It was also stated that no public authority contemplating a new traffic system would adopt the system that was now in general use. Nevertheless, the tram service began on 19 August 1913. *Commercial Motor* commented, "The much-debated Hagley Road tram route was opened on Friday of last week in Birmingham. In accordance with the terms upon which the Watch Committee had licensed motorbuses for this route, these latter vehicles were taken off on the same day. Thus is the destruction of one of the finest routes out of Birmingham finally encompassed."

William Roberts and the Electrobus scandal

This was a time before wireless and the main source of reliable information was newspapers, so the printed word held a lot of power and influence. Unfortunately, the business world was rife with con men, swindlers and fake company promoters, and there were very few prosecutions for fraud. There were also investment and industry journals that were set up specifically to blackmail companies under the threat of carrying fabricated articles that would alarm their investors and depress their share price. It was a minefield for the unwary investor and many lost their life savings to these fraudsters.

The first appearance of a motor bus on the streets of Birmingham was in 1897, apparently by a new company called the Birmingham Motor Omnibus Co. It ran briefly along Broad Street, but without a license it could not carry fare-paying passengers, so this was probably just to gain publicity. The company did not apply for a license and fell dormant for several years. Although not a named director at the time, it is likely that Henry J. Lawson was behind it. Harry Lawson (as he was known) was heavily involved in the developing motor car trade. To his credit, he was part-inventor of the safety bicycle in the 1870s, and established the Daimler Motor Company of Coventry having obtained the British rights to manufacture Daimler products. He also established the first London to Brighton run in 1897 to celebrate the passing of the Locomotives on Highways Act that kick-started the motor car industry by raising the speed limit to 14mph. Nevertheless, Lawson had many fraudulent businesses and schemes, and had close links to Ernest Terah Hooley, a renowned fraudster who for many years seemed to evade the long arm of the law due to his close involvement with many influential and powerful people. Lawson even bought up a large number of motor vehicle related patents with a view to receiving fees for every manufactured motor vehicle, but the plan failed under the weight of protests from disgruntled motorists.

Eventually Lawson was caught by his involvement in one of Hooley's schemes and sent to prison for 12 months in 1904. Unfortunately for him, this was just as the motor bus boom began. The motor car was still considered a plaything for the rich, and there was much more money to be made from motor buses, but Lawson's prison stretch came at just the wrong time.

In 1904, at a meeting arranged by Milnes Daimler at their London office, William Roberts met Clarence Freeland, the director of a Hastings bus company. Within a week of Roberts' formation of BMMO, he and Freeland set up another venture in London called the London Motor Omnibus Company (trading as Vanguard).

At some point, Roberts became involved with a notorious con man called Edward Ernest Lehwess. Mr Lehwess was born in Germany and made his way to this country in 1896. He was trained in international law and fluently spoke English, French and German. He inveigled himself into the world of the great and the good, and clearly enjoyed the attention and the high-life. He had an interest in the new world of motor cars and attracted backers for extravagant motor car expeditions across Asia and Russia that never materialised. But that was topped in April 1902 by a mammoth round the world drive in a huge and breathtakingly expensive car, named Passe-Partout after a character in Jules Verne's book *Around the World in Eighty Days*, complete with a 10 person entourage, including a chef. The car regularly broke down, and he spent several weeks at a time enjoying the fine food, wine and hospitality of enthusiastic aristocrats while it was repaired. Unsurprisingly, progress was slow. Road conditions were primitive and the car was extremely heavy. It was eventually abandoned in a snow drift near Nijni Novgorod in Russia.

At the time Lehwess arrived in England, Harry Lawson was a leading figure in motoring but his enforced term in prison left the way open for Lehwess to establish his own businesses along similar lines, which grew rapidly, assisted to some degree by deals he made with Lawson's businesses.

Lehwess was an eager self-publicist, but this was to change when he was convicted for trying to bribe a policeman over a false number plate on one of his cars. After that he continued his business dealings very much in the background, with other people named as company directors.

He set up a motor dealing agency called the Motor Car Emporium and supplied motor buses and vehicles to many of the new bus companies including the Edinburgh and District Motor Omnibus Company, of which William Roberts was a director. In fact, Lehwess and his associates had a considerable involvement in the Edinburgh company, and his emporium only delivered 5 fully working motor buses of the 30 that were ordered, and then forced the company into voluntary liquidation (a favourite trick of unscrupulous directors to avoid an awkward investigation).

In 1906-7 there was something of a motor bus frenzy. Apart from horse-drawn buses, the newer public transport vehicles were powered by electricity (trams and taxis), steam or petrol, and it was by no means clear which would win out. Even Frank Searle, the chief engineer of London's leading bus company, thought that steam power would be the winner.

The general public in London had very mixed views about the new petrol buses. Many welcomed the faster services, but residents on busy routes hated them for the noise, vibration and smoke. There were petitions for better regulation, and at a deputation of borough councillors at Scotland Yard in July 1907 there were tales of vehicles being too heavy and damaging the roads, being driven too fast, and sometimes running three abreast or late into the night. Tenants of flats in Maida Vale were said to be paying early termination penalties on their rental agreements in order to escape the intolerable nuisance.

In London buses were licensed by the Metropolitan Police, which in turn was responsible to the Home Office who treated the complaints dismissively and did not want to stifle this new industry. This approach gradually changed, particularly after the Handcross Hill disaster on 12 July 1906, when the brakes failed on a Vanguard petrol bus that was carrying a party of firemen on a trip to the sea-side and there were 10 fatalities. Regulation of motor buses in London then became much more strict, and bus companies found they were now incurring losses to such an extent that some reverted to horse buses. Their share price tumbled too. These developments may have been one of the factors that caused BMMO in Birmingham to return to horse buses in 1907.

At the beginning of 1906 there were only 230 motor buses in London, just a fraction of the number of horse buses, so clearly there was a window of opportunity for the cleaner, quieter technology of electrically propelled vehicles to win out.

In 1906, the London Electrobus Company was launched. It had several highly credible industry directors, including Philip Beachcroft, a director of the Electric Construction Company (the country's leading electrical firm), John Musgrave, a director of Wilkinson Sword and BMMO's William Roberts. It had developed a 34-seater double-deck electric bus powered by battery, and there were plans to purchase 300 of these 'electrobuses' at £700 each (equivalent to £72,000 in 2025).

An electrobus in traffic, outside the Bank of England. The building was largely demolished and rebuilt in the 1920s, so it looks rather different today.

These futuristic buses were silent, and their lead acid batteries, weighing in at one and a half tons, provided a range of 40 miles. However, they were ingeniously designed with a swappable battery crate, so in just a few minutes the depleted battery crate could be exchanged for a freshly charged crate and the bus could continue on service for a further 40 miles.

The electrobus was seen by many as a godsend – no noise, no noxious fumes, and much more reliable than the petrol bus, so fewer breakdowns. It was also claimed that it was cheaper to operate. It was apparently well engineered, and if it had been able to exploit that window of opportunity, it may have heralded a very different future of electric transport in the twentieth century. At the time, *Commercial Motor* journal commented, prophetically as it turned out, "If the pioneer company 'goes under,' it will not be because accumulator propulsion is devoid, for application in well-defined spheres, of inherent merits of the soundest nature."

A couple of days after the triumphant launch event of the electrobus on 18 April 1906, William Roberts resigned his directorship of Vanguard, so he must have seen the electrobus as the future; the Handcross Hill disaster was three months later, so couldn't have been a deciding factor.

There was certainly no shortage of enthusiasm for the new electrobus. In May 1908 there was a Franco-British exhibition to celebrate the signing of the Entente Cordiale four years earlier, and the Admiralty hired nine electrobuses to convey a party of 260 French sailors, who waved from the upper decks to onlookers as the convoy toured the streets of London. Special permission was given for them to travel through the royal parks, and they posed for photographs in front of Buckingham Palace.

But despite all of the positivity, the electrobus venture was scuppered by fraud and dodgy dealing – Mr Lehwess was involved behind the scenes! The launch of the company's prospectus on 23 April 1906 was nearly wrecked when it was discovered that an important patent that the company had paid £20,000 for was nothing to do with electric propulsion, and the mysterious Baron de Martigny, the supposed owner of the patent, was really a Canadian music-hall performer!

Such was the goodwill of the public who clamoured for the clean, quiet buses, that against the odds the company survived and at its peak, in autumn 1908, operated 20 electric buses on 2 routes from 6am to midnight. It also raised more money by four more share and debenture issues. Lehwess's Motor Car Emporium (later the Electric Vehicle Company) was to supply the finished vehicles, but at a price that most commentators thought was excessive. Moreover, it only supplied a fraction of the agreed number of buses, and the continual need for new buses was used to justify the next round of share issues, to squeeze even more money from the hapless investors. Most of this money was just being syphoned off by Lehwess for his own use.

While all of this was going on, William Roberts was still a director of the electrobus company. It is difficult to imagine that he was completely unaware of the fraud that was going on under his nose, and one wonders how much he personally profited from it. Witnesses in future court cases claimed that Lehwess was entirely in control of his associated businesses and the directors gave him carte blanche to do whatever he wished. Anyway, Roberts redeemed himself to some degree by resigning in 1909 and blowing the whistle on a new scam that was about to take over the, by then, struggling Electrobus company. An Italian con artist called Demetrius John Delyannis was mounting a rescue plan under the guise of the Reorganisation and Control Syndicate, which would help finance the purchase of new buses (heard that before?), and existing share holders would be asked to invest yet *more* money. In late 1909, Lehwess quietly sold the company's assets (including the remaining electrobuses) to the Reorganisation and Control Syndicate for a knock-down price. Roberts wrote to the shareholders warning them that they had been ripped-off and went to court to try to block the sale, but in the end the shareholders had no option but to vote for the voluntary liquidation of the electrobus company. On 3 January 1910 the electrobus finally disappeared from the streets of London.

In the end, the company was held back by a lack of real investment by the fraudsters, and it lost out to the petrol buses that started to make a come-back. If the electrobus company had been backed by genuine businessmen we may have seen electric passenger and goods vehicles become the preferred mode of road transport in the twentieth century, and perhaps earlier improvements in battery technology.

The remaining eight electrobuses were sold to Brighton and Hove where they ran until April 1917. Each electrobus ran more than 200,000 miles in a ten-year life. Brighton held the record for having the world's largest fleet of battery-powered buses until the 1990s.

Roberts remained a director of BMMO, eventually resigning in May 1913. In contrast to the other directors of Birmingham Motor Express, he appeared to have money problems in later years, and a bankruptcy petition was filed against him in 1922. He died in 1925 at the age of 63.

What of Mr Lehwess? Following the sinking of the Lusitania in 1915, the British government rounded up German citizens, Lehwess included, and interned them on the Isle of Man. After the war he left for Paris and continued to prosper, buying up inventions and patenting them. In 1928 he travelled to England for a meeting with Sir Herbert Austin, head of the Austin Motor Company to show him an invention that he thought he might be interested in – a sunshine roof. After a demonstration, Austin was very interested in it, but it was still patent-pending. Instead of buying it Austin patented his own sunshine roof. The ensuing court case, known as the 'sunshine roof case', became known as one of the most costly of the 1930s. After much tooing and froing it went to the House of Lords who finally awarded Lehwess £35,000. He died in 1941, aged 69.

More about the electrobus scandal can be found in *A Most Deliberate Swindle*, a fascinating book by Mick Hamer, that unravels the plot of the first electric bus, over a hundred years ago. *Edwardian Enterprise* by Brian Dicks and Andrew Gardner also has chapters devoted to many of the people who were involved.

I offer a final quote from Mick Hamer: "I should say that my reading of the evidence for the electrobus story is that William Roberts got mixed up with a crowd of dodgy characters, and seduced by a 'get rich quick' scheme. A bit of a chancer, maybe, but he did in the end come down on the right side of the fence".

REFLECTIONS

What is really noticeable when speaking with old, retired employees of any rank in the company is their initial assumption that they have very little to contribute worthy of inclusion in a book! But engage them in conversation on topics from their former employment, and it is quickly realised that they are talking, often affectionately, about important details of transport history as if it all happened only yesterday.

So much has changed in the working environment of today. Compared to 'the good old days', very few new and young employees in bus companies today have experienced a 'single company' career. It seems no longer of interest to work up the ranks of one organisation – that takes too long in today's 'instant' world. They don't get to know how the company really ticks. The employees often don't know who they are working for; the company's heritage, history and legacy are of little or no importance, having been overtaken by a new corporate identity promoted by the modern-day owners.

It is now common to see people in junior and middle management positions appear for a few months, or a couple of years at best, then move on to a new company to make their mark there. It's more to do with moving around within the industry rather than giving your service to a particular company and being rewarded with job satisfaction. I do realise that this is a common theme in most businesses in these modern times, but it does not provide stability in an industry where our customers need to feel secure in the dependability of reliable bus services.

Bus chief engineers of old would understand their company's requirements for vehicles, and manufacturers would build to meet their demands. The tables seemed to have turned. They no longer specify full details of the type of vehicle they are ordering – nowadays, they are off-the-peg choices.

Types and styles of buses fell in and out of fashion, and it was during a time when double-deckers were out of favour that a type of bus which had been relatively successful in Europe was thought to hold all of the answers: the Bendibus. Of course Midland Red were early investigators of anything new and were early to try out Bendibuses.

Been there, done that!

In the early 1980s, Redditch garage was chosen for the Bendibus trial. Redditch was one of the Government's designated 'new town' projects. It was to provide an overspill for growing Birmingham, and so was a good choice for Midland Red for its one year experiment on new town services. The population grew from 32,000 to around 70,000 by the mid-1980s, with vast estates being created to accommodate the new arrivals. The roads were developed with a network of highways. The town plan was designed by Hugh Wilson, who said its transport, which would be interlinked, might be buses, it could be monorail, or it could be something that has not yet been devised! Midland Red provided them with something very new – the Bendibus!

Vehicle reliability caused problems from the start, and spares were not easy to obtain, so one of the five Bendibuses on loan was a donor vehicle to help keep the remaining buses on the road. At the end of the trial, the manufacturer, MAN, wanted to offload them, and an arrangement was made with Midland Red North to take them on. In the end, *two* had been cannibalised for spares to keep the others on the road, but they were eventually put back together and ran for a further two years. One was scrapped and the others exported to Australia after around seven years use. Ironically, they were replaced at Midland Red with *mini* buses!

The Bendibuses were originally brought in to the UK as demonstrators, but after trials in Oxford, South Yorkshire, and with Midland Red, the experiment was over.

Although they could be registered in the UK, they had difficulty obtaining 'type approval' which prevented the collection of fares on board. However, once type approval had been given, Midland Red used Setright ticket machines on board and drivers earned a higher rate of pay for driving them. They were originally designed to have a capacity of 162 people, but after type approval in the UK their capacity was 120 (53 seated and 67 standing). The reasons given for not pursuing this type of vehicle were unreliability and passenger confusion caused by having three sets of doors.

Of course the UK has seen further trials in recent years, in expensive London experiments and in the West Midlands. But the idea began to fade and the vehicles were cascaded to more minor roles and then disposed of at knock down prices. It seems the Bendi is not for us!

Technicians replace engineers

Bus engineers, now called 'vehicle technicians', rely on computer diagnostics to determine a fault, and do little more than reset the computer, or replace (not repair) a faulty part that goes to scrap. Alternatively, they decide the job is for a main dealer to fix – especially if warranties are involved or if a risk analysis where the incident occurred determines that the fault is beyond what can be fixed at the roadside or at the bus garage.

Modern day bus operators no longer have the luxury of a 'central works' where qualified, experienced and able engineers can overhaul parts. Engineers of old would look and listen, diagnose and then repair a faulty item. Most major 'out of warranty' issues now result in the vehicle being taken from the bus garage to main dealer workshops, nearly always leading to many days of downtime and very large overall costs attached. Downtime, when the vehicle is not available, also requires 'spare' vehicles to be available to replace them.

In 2012, I was in conversation with a garage engineering manager whilst visiting his ex-Midland Red garage, now bought out by one of the big groups, and at the time they had been allocated a fleet of 10 brand new buses. That would once have been a time for celebration, but, after just two months (60 hard operating days) he was in a state of despair and had written a report to his senior engineering manager to request that the new buses were taken away and his old vehicles returned to his garage, as the new vehicles were completely unreliable for daily use. The faults included continually going into 'limp' mode when on a motorway service into Birmingham, which he considered dangerous, and breakdowns (which often needed a ten-minute fix involving shut down and a new set-up procedure) occurring so frequently it was causing delays and lost mileage. The new buses were under warranty, meaning that each breakdown had to be reported to the manufacturer's agent who should then send technicians to the bus. The agent was more accustomed to working with lorries rather than buses, and the urgency of timetables was hard for them to understand. Upon their eventual arrival on scene, they would investigate with their laptop and invariably declare in an almost scripted manner that the repair could not be safely carried out at the roadside. Much to the driver's and passengers' frustration (bus company engineers regularly worked on the roadside), they would have to recover the bus to their workshops for investigation and repair. The local bus garage would then have to provide a replacement vehicle, but with 10 unreliable new buses, the supply of replacement operational buses was soon exhausted, resulting in the garage losing mileage and getting a reputation for providing an unreliable service. The manager's request for the return of his old buses was, of course, refused. In the meantime, his own company-employed mechanics were sitting idle in their garage workshops for lengthy periods of time, as 20 percent of the garage fleet could not be worked on!

Garage administration staff have ongoing difficulties recruiting enough qualified drivers, complete with their up-to-date, yet often ill-respected, Driver CPC qualifications. Historically, our industry employed qualified and experienced managers or trained them either in-house or as part of the British Electric Traction training scheme. Manual workers were taught in-house (for example, drivers in the company's training school). The company was aware of the risks around employment, and planned accordingly. But in today's compliance-centric and risk-averse environment there is a continual need to prove compliance, with compulsory yet often unsuitable course subjects. When the Driver CPC was first introduced, it had much the same course modules as the corresponding scheme for HGV drivers, although some of them were inappropriate for bus drivers – for example, 'manual handling'. Drivers were also allowed to pick and mix the required number of modules to pass the qualification, even if it involved accumulating the required number of points just by repeatedly taking one of the easier modules, like first aid. This all led to the Driver CPC qualification being often treated with contempt. When this scheme was introduced, our industry lost many long-serving, well-respected and experienced drivers.

In times gone by, when the industry was less complicated, it ran well and prospered. Then came the EU era when new rules and regulations gradually dominated the industry, which had to be aware of the constant need to keep up with the new ways their operations were to be run.

In the 1930s, regulation was introduced by the Road Traffic Act that made operating fairer, and until 1973 things ran rather well and safely. Since then, continual changes and new regulations have made the industry a much more stressful place to work. One of our regulatory bodies changes its name frequently. It morphed from a managed advice, inspection and regulatory organisation called the Ministry of Transport into a money-raising organisation which operates one-step-removed from the government, called VOSA (Vehicle and Operator Standards Agency). It then merged with DSA (Driver Standards Agency) and formed DVSA (Driver and Vehicle Standards Agency), which is partly funded from fines and penalties. Somewhere in there is the Traffic Commissioner's role, which used to have separate areas of control (Scottish, North East, West Midlands, East Midlands, Metropolitan, South Eastern etc), but has now become more centralised, with admin at Leeds Harehills office.

I will always remember John Mervyn Pugh, the traffic commissioner for my own area of the West Midlands, who instilled the necessary fear in new operators to respect their Operators Licence, should they be granted it. He always said, "He who giveth can taketh away." And he often did!

The Operators Licence is the lifeline of any bus and coach operator's livelihood and that of its employees. It is a fragile thing and can be taken away if sufficient attention is not paid to operational practices and vehicle maintenance – and the proper record keeping to prove it.

The licence is to ensure that the entire operation, its people and its financial backing are of good standing, and to ensure that vehicles are well maintained and operated in a way which is safe. Remember that old phrase, 'The driver's prime consideration, as the holder of his own PSV driving licence, is the safety and comfort of his passengers.' So the Construction and Use regulations prevented overloading beyond the permitted number of passengers, and prevented passengers from carrying prohibited items on board. The employees would learn much more during their official training.

Vehicle inspectors used to call on operators sufficiently often to have checked all of their vehicles every year, but they could also arrive to spot-check any of the fleet at any time. Each vehicle would have a maintenance file which was updated each time the vehicle was worked on. The file would detail any repaired or new parts fitted, by which mechanic and on which exact date. Midland Red's vehicle files were comprehensive and moved with the vehicle during its life, should it be transferred to another garage.

This was part of the system of Certificates of Fitness, which were issued to each vehicle for periods of seven, five or as few as two years, depending upon the vehicle's age and condition. The Ministry of Transport officials were civil servants with good pensions and conditions. They tended to be around for many years and knew the operators and their staff. They knew who was good, and who needed a closer eye kept on them, and they gave helpful advice along the way where needed. Now, in fact since 1981, Certificates of Fitness are no longer issued and have been replaced by PSV (now PCV) MOT tests, which are now increasingly carried out in the premises of privately run commercial garages with the aim of lowering costs. A DVSA examiner (who could be based in any area of the country) visits these privately run premises to carry out pre-booked tests. The examiner is unlikely to know anything about the operator, apart from what shows up in a computer-printed vehicle identification sheet. In Midland Red days, standards were kept up for fear of the man from the ministry finding an issue of concern. Nowadays, bus companies fear the amount of the fine, if anything is found to be straying from the words in a manual.

Buses and commercial vehicles work under a preventative maintenance scheme, where MOTs are prepared for and the vehicle presented to pass, unlike a car MOT where often the vehicle is casually booked in to see what is wrong with it. Records of the pass rate of vehicles are maintained by the DVSA, and if the pass rate falls below a certain percentage it can trigger an unexpected visit from a vehicle examiner, or a vehicle being pulled up at the roadside. Faults from such a check can result in a court case or fines as deemed appropriate by the examiner.

I have worked with, and have experience of, both systems and firmly believe that the former Ministry of Transport examiner, with his helpful advice and support, was certainly more worthwhile than accruing fines in an industry which is not exactly flush with cash. If you have a maintenance problem, you ideally need help with it, not punitive fines, which may just exacerbate the issues.

Dealing with mechanical vehicles, human drivers and mechanics… what could go wrong?

How to dismantle an institution

Throughout the years of nationalisation and subsequent privatisation, there was an ongoing effort to rid the massive Midland Red company of its stubborn, entrenched spirit which had made it so unique in the industry. There was an inflow of new people, with many in management, needing to make their mark, effecting change and removing anything that was perceived to cost money. One could, of course, argue that new blood could help; indeed so, but these new junior and middle managers seemed to manage in a more remote style than we were used to. A new brush sweeps clean, so clean that it rubs off some of the good stuff too. This was all part of dismantling the structure of the Midland Red empire.

Of course, every company has areas where waste and duplication can be saved to improve the balance sheet – but every cut has implications. Middle management are only following instructions from above, so installing one new person at the top with different ideas could mean massive changes for the more menial workers. For example, closing the garage canteens has been disastrous for inter-staff relations.

The canteen was where everyone met up at the start of day or at break times half way through the shift for tea and toast, or for a tea time meal to help you through your late shift. It was where cards were played, dominoes shoved, darts were thrown and the sound of the pool cue was heard across the room. It was where the gossip was, where shifts were swapped, and where communication was easy for office staff to find drivers. It was also where drivers met the engineers – even though they sat at dedicated tables in their oily overalls. The canteen was a precious resource. All of that replaced by a soulless room with a basic drinks machine. That is not serving the staff well, especially on the occasions when the drinks machine wouldn't dispense your drink after you had paid for it! Yet it saves the wages of the serving staff and the provision of cooking equipment.

The Staff Bulletin informed us of humorous social events as well as those more serious business matters which all helped to foster that Midland Red family feeling.

When Midland Red was a 'whole' entity, it was all-encompassing. The *Staff Bulletin* helped us keep in touch with other garages and departments, and encouraged our sports teams to play together, all contributing to the 'one big family' ethos. When the *Staff Bulletin* came to an end in 1972, there was a permanent separation from the colleagues we had been with for so long. We all like gossip, and this was the way to find out what each garage and department was doing, in both work and pleasure.

After 1973 when Bearwood was closed, senior roles moved to Midland House, but inclusive tours and coach cruise bookings were centralised with National Bus Company, and standard white coaches used on the tours, taking away the special feeling that held Midland Red tour passengers together. Private hire also lost favour; its main office function had gone and was now a low priority. This was noticeable at garage level too. I worked in office roles throughout my time with Midland Red, even whilst being officially employed as a conductor or driver for periods of time. I remember at Leamington garage being lucky enough to work for the gentleman superintendent that was Mr Edwards, in the office, doing correspondence and small private hire quotations (the large party quotations were done by the private hire department), and as the years went by after the closure of Bearwood, the client list was reducing and business going to the competing operators.

Similarly, the major engineering functions, like the replacement of engines, gearboxes, axles and suspensions and the regular repaints, were carried out by Central Works. The vehicle was taken there or collected and then re-appeared again like new when work was completed. The accountancy involved in any work undertaken by Central Works for one of the company's own local garages was just a paper exercise, with no real money being paid by the garages. It just appeared on the balance sheet at the year end.

But when the company was split up, ready for selling off, Central Works became a separate company, and all work completed was accompanied by a real invoice – repaints and major works needed real money to pay for them.

Of course, it didn't work. Their old customers (the local garages) found that the purpose-built paint shop of Central Works (renamed Carlyle Engineering after it had left the family unit) was too expensive. Smaller businesses or one-man-bands would come and paint the bus in the garage at a lower cost, and eventually Carlyle Engineering could no longer function in its old ways. No longer were bus mid-life overhauls carried out (partly due to the 1981 changes where Certificates of Fitness were withdrawn in favour of annual MOTs), and more work was being handled in-house.

Carlyle Engineering was reorganised and began offering major vehicle conversions to any market. It had a further attempt at building vehicle bodywork with styles from the defunct Duple stable.

The catering department, based at Central Works, supplied equipment and staple dry supplies, with certain local buying powers being available at each garage for perishable and fresh foodstuffs. Perceived cost savings and the reduction of facilities offered from Central Works during its demise brought about the closing of the Central Catering Department, which in turn led to limited offerings, a gradual decline and eventual closure of the local garage canteens.

Midland Red was a respected and self-sufficient operation and it is often forgotten how well departments worked together to achieve the best result. An example is that Bearwood, besides being an engineering and bus garage, held the chief traffic office role which had very experienced and long serving officials. Departments like the coach cruise/inclusive tours department and private hire office could work together to achieve the best rates for clients, as longstanding arrangements with hotels and coffee stops often had preferential 'Midland Red' prices pre-arranged.

The Carlyle body had a characteristic asymmetrical front windscreen. It looks as though the destination blind box was something of an afterthought.

Initially, this looked promising: 140 for London Transport, others to Warrington Transport and Luton and District, and there were even exports to China Motor Bus and New World First Bus. But orders fizzled out, and the business eventually became Carlyle Parts, a PSV parts and glass provider for the bus industry. It even had an earlier dabble with an exciting coach design that was of modular construction, so the vehicle could be any length just by adding more sections, but like most things from the Carlyle stable, it was probably before its time. Certainly the biggest project that Carlyle carried out since the BMMO bus building days was during the minibus boom, where they produced hundreds of small bus bodies for Freight Rover chassis, and these sold well. They also offered body designs for Iveco and Mercedes light commercial chassis.

Sadly, Carlyle went out of business in 1991 and sold its Dartline body design to Marshall of Cambridge. Carlyle Bus and Coach Ltd was then reformed, through several companies and ownerships, and moved out to new, smaller premises, but eventually closed on 2 Oct 2019.

The gist of this story is that the once big and bold Midland Red as we knew it, along with its stubborn spirit, was being broken with each new decision made. Drivers no longer knew their bosses well (they didn't stay long enough), nor even their fellow bus drivers as they used to. This was very apparent when speaking to one or two colleagues who had bridged the gap, and seen life both during and after the reign of 'proper' Midland Red. Under the modern regimes they couldn't recall the names of many of their current workmates – or should we now say working colleagues!

The forces of change are, of course, not all down to these internal decisions, as Midland Red has slipped down the ranks from being at the top of its game in the industry; the bus industry itself has been affected by the economic and political forces at play in our country. It's been a cyclical journey, from private company to nationalisation to private company again, but with each cycle come new ideas that affect employees and passengers. I recall the phrase, "They'll be alright when they get used to it" bandied around when major changes to bus services were made. Of course, in reality, those changes might just drive down passenger numbers, or make staff shortages more acute which leads to service unreliability and the inevitable loss of passengers. Changes might be simply making timetable alterations or route diversions, or making more dramatic cuts to services that had previously run for many a year. This then causes passenger anxiety, so they find alternative means of getting about – and all at a time when we are told to use public transport more!

It is interesting to see how culture has changed bus companies which have now become so risk-adverse. We thought nothing of taking a shovel off the garage wall and driving off into the snow to get our passengers to work or home again. Yet now, in similar conditions, vehicles are taken off the road and parked up at the depot, leaving those passengers who need the bus high... and perhaps not so dry! Now, even the shovels have been taken away!

However hard we wish, we can't get back what we have lost. Now, with the passage of time, the new operators of bus routes on old Midland Red territory, with their new-era staff, have become much more fragmented, and back stage operations and budgets are compartmentalised – thus have they rid themselves of that Midland Red spirit.

LOOKING BEYOND THE GRAVE

The three most important men who steered Midland Red from small beginnings to the giant respected company it became would likely be mortified to see what happened to it in later years. They were all dead and gone before Midland Red had to relinquish its control and dominance, first to authorities that took away its Birmingham and West Midlands operations – its very heart – and then the National Bus Company that stole Midland Red's identity and sold it off in pieces that were eventually bought by the big bus groups.

L. G. Wyndham Shire was a demanding engineer. He was born in Lambeth in January 1885 and moved to Croydon in Surrey where he worked on trams, no doubt the place where he became acquainted with Sydney Garcke of the British Electric Traction Company (BET). He then moved to Deal, joining the BMMO subsidiary Deal and District, where he regularly encountered Emile Garcke, the son of Sydney, who regularly visited Deal to see his girlfriend.

When the motorbus returned to BMMO in 1912, Wyndham Shire was offered the position of chief engineer of the company in Birmingham. He soon made an impression by designing and producing improved parts for their Tilling Stevens buses, but he will always be associated with being the driving force behind their own-made bus production, starting with the SOS S type, The S type was the first complete production vehicle produced by BMMO, and the first to have pneumatic tyres. This started the trend of making outstanding vehicles for Midland Red and various associated operators up to WW2.

Sadly, his career with BMMO ended suddenly, a few months into WW2. I am convinced that he was pushed out of the company in 1940 (officially described as 'retirement', but he was only in his mid 50s) due to his perseverance with his rear-engined projects that were first produced in 1935. They needed further refinement to improve their reliability, but it was at such a difficult time for the company. As a distraction from his obsession with the rear engined vehicles, Shire was handed a written proposal for an alternative position within BET; it is thought that his failure to respond in good time was taken effectively as his resignation.

We need only look at almost every bus and coach produced in the current era and their engine layout to understand that Mr Loftus George Wyndham Shire was looking to the future and was ultimately right. It is hard to ascertain his 'real' personality. He was a strong and firm leader. His early work life was interspersed with periods in the army, rising to senior positions; he was successful and well liked by his seniors. Whilst at BMMO, he was often described as 'difficult and stubborn' by some. He gave several addresses on engineering matters to professional organisations, but his lectures were accessible, with the occasional humorous anecdote.

Here's an extract from one such address:

An amusing story of a bus, a burst tyre, and some terrified bookmakers.

"Some three years ago we were conveying a private party on an omnibus to a race meeting. The passengers mostly being connected with the pencil and satchel profession [bookmakers]. On the return journey when about half the distance had been completed, an eight-inch rear tyre, without any warning, suddenly burst, due to some long sharp instrument severing a length of the cover. The speed at which the vehicle was travelling allowed the portion of the tyre which was cut to travel round so that the force of the expanding air struck the underside of the wheel arch, forcing the inside of the wheel arch inside the bus, which was filled with a dense atmosphere of dust, mud and fumes. Whether the passengers thought that the 'Old Man' was after them or not is not known, but the next thing the driver knew was that the back door which was of the emergency type, was lying on the road, having been forced off its hinges by the 'wind-up' attitude of the passengers. The vehicle which had been stopped almost at once was empty in a flash."

When Wyndham Shire moved from Deal up to Birmingham, he lodged at 331 Hagley Road, the home of Ethel and George Granville Clarke. The couple were married in London and moved to Birmingham and it is thought that George was known to Wyndham Shire as he was a fellow mechanical engineer. For a while he then lived at 1959a Bristol Road South in Rubery. Following the sad death of George in 1926, Wyndham Shire formed a relationship with Ethel and they married on 10 May 1928. It is thought that after the marriage he joined Ethel living at the same Hagley Road address, which was mid-way between Bearwood and Central Works and therefore ideal for unannounced site visits at all hours of the day or night.

He died on 29 January 1963, aged 78, leaving an estate valued at just £24,687, which is around £517,000 in 2025. His ashes were placed in his wife's grave on Great Orme, Llandudno.

Orlando Cecil Power, the compassionate and well-liked traffic manager at Midland Red, was from Irish stock but born a Brummie in 1879. He attended King Edward VI Camp Hill School for Boys and always claimed that as a young lad he wanted to be a bus conductor. However, he trained as a journalist and became secretary to George Parker, the American editor of New York World, who was working at the consulate in Birmingham. Parker remained in Birmingham and in 1898 became chairman of Birmingham General Omnibus Company (BGO), then in September 1899 he recommended O. C. Power for the post of local secretary when he was just twenty years old. BGO by this time had become a subsidiary of BET.

OCP, as he was often known, was certainly of entrepreneurial spirit. He became BMMO's first traffic manager, a full time position, yet he soon had a growing portfolio of directorships. He was a very busy man, but always made time for his employees. Besides his BMMO role he was director of many bus company subsidiaries such as Stratford Blue Motors, Leamington and Warwick Transport Company, North Warwickshire Motor Traction, Trent Motor Traction, Potteries Motor Traction, Worcester Motor Transport, Black and White Motorways and Majestic Motor Services. He was chairman of Birmingham Horse and Motor Owners Association from 1907, a Birmingham justice of the peace, and for ten years was the chairman of the Birmingham and Midland section of the Institute of Transport.

However, things could have been very different. He had been on holiday in Germany in mid 1914 and left just in time before war started. On his return he made significant contributions to the war effort and assisted the military in obtaining horses from around the Midlands. Recreation was important to him too: he was a keen rugby player, boxer and swimmer, and was said to be the first one on the dance floor at social gatherings!

Sadly, Mr Power died in service, whilst representing Midland Red at a passenger transport meeting in London in 1943, and so did not reach retirement. His body was returned to Birmingham and his funeral service was held at St Martin's Parish Church; the day became quite a spectacle with hundreds lining the streets. His circle of business was vast and representation was sent from all. But, amid the sombre black attire of everyone present there was a striking contrast: a bright and polished Midland Red single-decker bus filled to the top with wreaths. A guard of honour was mounted by the Midland Red Home Guard and several bus inspectors, and the service was conducted by the Rector of Birmingham Canon Guy Rogers, assisted by the Archdeacon of Aston and the Rector of St Mary's Church in Bearwood.

OCP lived at 34 Vernon Road, Edgbaston, Birmingham 16, just a few doors away from what would become Midland House just nine years later. He left an estate of £14,406, equivalent to £552,000 in 2025. The large headstone on his family grave describes him as "Organiser of Midland Red."

It is well recorded that there was friction between Mr Shire and Mr Power throughout their joint control of BMMO, which created an unmistakable divide between the company's engineering and traffic operations. But it could be that some of the rivalry that existed between them may just have originated from their wives! Both ladies were dog breeders of some distinction, with many high level prizes to their credit. But it is likely that we will never know all of the reasons for their disagreements that made others in their joint company feel so uncomfortable.

Donald MacIntyre Sinclair was born in Glasgow on 18 December 1901. He assumed control of engineering as chief engineer upon the sudden departure of Mr Wyndham Shire in 1940. Upon the death of O. C. Power in 1943, he embraced the role of traffic manager and became Midland Red's first ever general manager. To help him concentrate on managerial matters, he appointed S. C. Vince as chief engineer in 1946; but, always a true engineer, he kept his eye on all engineering developments, especially those involving the motorway express coaches, of which he was justifiably very proud. His hobbies included shooting, golf, cruising and holidays, especially in the USA. He lost an eye in a childhood accident but he did not let that get in the way of his work or his hobbies.

He retired in 1966 to spend time with his sick wife. They lived in Viceroy Close, Birmingham. He died on 17 June 1971, leaving an estate of £26,238, the equivalent of around £322,000 in 2025.

These three men were of very differing character, but all were career transport managers and steered Midland Red from its chaotic beginnings through its many triumphs to the start of its decline and downfall – Wyndham Shire and Power until 1940 and Sinclair from 1940 until 1966. You can see from the above valuations of their estates (which would include any property they owned), as top executives of a major Midlands employer they were clearly career driven rather than get-rich-quick men.

Delving into "what if" theories is only to dream, but as the 'real' Midland Red only survives today in our fond memories, then why not?

Imagine if WW2 had not wiped out a decade of progress, there would not have been the urgency to curtail Wyndham Shire's relentless but dedicated work of improving the designs of the rear-engined REC class; a pursuit many at the time thought misguided. Add to this the development of the diesel engine around the same time, and it is likely that design improvements, including the use of diesel rather than petrol power, would have brought far-reaching improvements in the reliability and performance of Shire's stylish prototypes.

Outside sales of vehicles may have continued to provide associated companies with these new vehicles, and, with higher production numbers, we may have seen the introduction of lower-floor vehicles earlier than we did; their design and engine placing making this a more natural development. Wyndham Shire's design approach of keeping everything dirty behind the back wheels would have spread more quickly to the UK bus industry.

The move away from the traditional front-engined designs had been affected by Sinclair, following his experience with the Northern General Sentinel vehicles of the same period, in which a half-way measure was adopted where the engine was placed underfloor in the mid-vehicle position. From an engineer's perspective, this provided better all-round access for maintenance and repair. However, the underfloor engine came with step access and higher floor layout, though this was much less of a social issue at the time.

Once wartime shortages had eased and restrictions of the Ministry of Supply had been lifted, great advances were made in modernising and renewing the fleet, as well as giving some TLC to the vehicles that had carried on working continually without regular maintenance and overhauls during wartime.

Midland Red's longstanding approach in demanding 'fast, simple, light, and reliable' design features ensured their reliability in service, and among the many evolutionary designs were some truly stunning revolutionary vehicles that introduced the latest leading-edge technical advances that always gave Midland Red the ability to outrun their many competitors over the years.

So now it's time to remove those rose-tinted spectacles and return to the modern world. I do hope you've enjoyed this excursion into the nostalgia and magnificence of the friendly Midland Red, once the biggest provincial UK bus and coach operator - it certainly was a very proud company.

Great Bookshelf Companions

by the same author

"Splendid, nicely designed books. Fascinating and engaging stories. Superb!" - *Classic Bus magazine*

"Attractive layout with plenty of interesting pictures." - *Ray Stenning*

"A wonderfully written book. I can heartily recommend it." - *Buses magazine*

"Every Midland Red enthusiast and omnibus historian needs this book on the shelf!" - *Bus and Coach Preservation*

"Beautifully presented, solidly bound, printed on glossy paper with well-rendered photography and great value."

"This beautifully designed and realised book is both well-written and a triumph of design quality." - *Kenilworth Books*

"Well done with 'Midland Red and its People'. It is like no other book on transport and is a great companion to the two previous books." - *S.K. Media*

"A very, very good read, and lots of anecdotes by a guy who was there at the centre of things." - *P.K., Leamington*

See more reviews and recommendations at midlandred.co.uk/reviews

ACKNOWLEDGEMENTS

Contained in this book are many previously unpublished images, some taken by me. I am also grateful to the following for their images used therein. If any have been used from others whom I have not credited, then this is not intentional, and I wish to thank you for taking such evocative and story provoking pictures that help to illustrate my words. Where possible, efforts have been made to contact owners of images contained herein.

Images reproduced with thanks given to Steven Knight / SK Media / and jointly owned images from The Midland Red Collection, R. E. S. Richards Collection, Bernard Warr Collection (Midland Red Collection / Ashley Wakelin), Roger Harman / BMMO / Midland Red Omnibus Co for the use of company images and slides including from the Davenport Collection, Mick Hamer, Patrick Kingston, Andy Dainty, Gordon Smith, Michael Holloway, Christian O'Flaherty, Chris Martin, Mike Street, Geoff Edmunds, Warwickshire County Record Office, The Bus Archive, LTHT Archive, R. R. Paramor and Mike Lambden.

Also images purchased or acquired with copyright from Kevin Lane collection, Robert Edworthy, Diane Turner, S. G. Jinks, Les Simpson, Tony Hoskins, Clifford Essex, Brian Ambrey, D. J. Hayward, P. A. Fozard, Robert 'Bob' Rumsby, S. Brown, M. C. Mugridge, Dave Pritchard, Mineralcraft North Limited, MPT Archive, Rod Allen, R. Emsworth collection, Peter Mitchell collection, Ken Draper, Geoff Edmunds, Phil Sposito, Ian Chanceller, W. Rawlings, Robin Fell, Andy Dixon, Martin Baulf and John Carroll.

Also illustrations from commissioned artworks and illustrations by Derek Roberts, Patrick Moore and Transport Museum Wythall. The Institute of Mechanical Engineers for references made in their paper *Design and Operation of Motorway Coaches*. Thanks to Brian Dicks of Isle of Wight Bus and Coach Museum and co-author of *Edwardian Enterprise* for specific background information. Mike Greenwood, Leicester Transport Heritage Trust.

It should be pointed out that this book contains some images that were found as old photographs, slides and plates that were left lying in a desk drawer at Central Works for many years, then inherited and retained by an official of the company for a further 40 years, and then given to me. I have had them professionally restored, retouched and some colourised to benefit from better definition; even so, they are not of a quality normally worthy of printing, but they do allow us to see images from the important progressive years of Midland Red and so surely better seen than remaining hidden away and unrestored. In this regard, special acknowledgements go to Grant Kemp for superb image enhancements and photographic restorations that help bring images of dubious quality from the past to life in my books.

Special thanks to Colin Webster, Alan Eatwell, R. E. S. Richards, Len Edwards, Mick French, John Henry, Jean Frew, Mick Gilbert, Timothy G. O'Connor, Nick Hiley, Dave Haughton, William 'Bill' Eldridge, Harry Roake, Malcolm Dyke, John Dancocks, Rod Allen, Paul Icke and many other former friends and colleagues from BMMO/Midland Red. Also Colin Browell for detail checking and many hours of proof reading. Stephen Duxbury (Prestset) has once again turned my pages of words into an attractive and easy to read book; his typesetting and layout skills have enabled the aspirations of quality, image and presentation of my Midland Red books to become a reality.